Bicycling FOR *Women*

Gale Bernhardt

BOULDER, COLORADO

Printed on acid-free paper
Distributed in the United States and Canada by Publishers Group West

VeloPress®
1830 North 55th Street
Boulder, Colorado 80301-2700 USA
303/440-0601 • Fax 303/444-6788 • E-mail velopress@competitorgroup.com

Library of Congress Cataloging-in-Publication Data

Bernhardt, Gale, 1958-
  Bicycling for women / Gale Bernhardt.
     p. cm.
Includes index.
ISBN 978-1-934030-28-8 (alk. paper)
1. Cycling for women. I. Title.
GV1057.B45 2008
796.6082—dc22
                          2008019029

Cover design by Stephanie Goralnick
Interior design by Anita Koury
Illustrations by Tom Ward
Cover photo by Tim De Frisco

Set in Prensa and Archer display

For information on purchasing VeloPress books, please call 800/234-8356 or visit www.velopress.com.

08 09 10 / 10 9 8 7 6 5 4 3 2 1

To my mother, Margie:
the strongest woman I know.

Contents

Preface

My love affair with cycling began when I received a cherry-red tricycle for Christmas at age two and a half. My parents tell me I spent hours on that tricycle, riding up and down the same flagstone sidewalk, in and out of driveways. Surely the tricycle offered freedom, adventure, and transportation that was faster than walking, easier than running.

Cycling became more exciting when my parents moved to a new section of town. There were new roads to explore, and a blue Schwinn replaced the red tricycle. The Schwinn was a trusty steed, sometimes merely a bicycle and occasionally an imaginary horse. Although it wasn't designed for dirt, my Schwinn often ventured off-road.

My next trusty bike had to be earned. At age nine or ten, I saved my allowance, and with my parents' help I bought a lime-green three-speed Stingray, complete with banana seat and big, slick back tire. It had a nifty stick shift, like a car's, on the top tube. That bike was cool.

The Stingray spent hot summer days at the cyclocross course (before the kids on my block knew anything about cyclocross) that was a dream come true for 10-year-olds, the infamous Rumper-Bumper. Mounds of fill dirt dumped in an empty lot by construction workers made a perfect place to play. The neighborhood kids wore several trails around and over the mounds of dirt. The route with "Dead Man's Curve" was particularly difficult. One instant of poor judgment would send bicycle, pigtails, and bare arms and legs airborne before the final landing into a patch of Canadian thistle. It always made for an exciting racecourse, where the rewards were simply bragging rights for the week.

Through my early teen and college years, the bicycle remained a viable mode of transportation, even though a car was also an option. My bicycle was refreshing to ride in the cool morning air, it was easy to find parking, and it was cheap transportation.

A few years after college graduation, I grew interested in cycling longer distances. I remember my first long-distance goal was to ride home from my job, 18 miles. Next, riding to and from work in the same day. I recall being tired, yet exhilarated, for a week after completing that ride.

In those years, I rode for fitness, only in perfect weather. This meant riding in the summer, two to three days per week, and doing other sports during the winter. It was riding with other people and occasionally experiencing a brief moment of speed that ultimately gave me a desire to go faster for longer periods. In my late twenties, I sought to improve speed and endurance.

As I gained knowledge about cycling-specific training and endurance athletics, more people began to ask for my advice. Having sought opportunities to teach or coach sports since the age of 16, I channeled my energy into coaching endurance athletes, including cyclists.

Today I coach a wide variety of cyclists. One of my female athletes, Nicole Freedman, competed on the USA Olympic Cycling Team in 2000. I was honored when Nicole said in an interview with

ProCycling News that I was her "dream coach": "Gale is knowledgeable, supportive, and truly cares about all her athletes. Before some of my largest races, she tracks me down at host families across the country to chat, give me confidence, and wish me good luck. She has been instrumental in my success."

I am occasionally asked to write about my experience coaching female athletes such as Nicole. Over the years, my response hasn't changed. The truth is, I see no blanket differences between training women and men. Each person I coach has different goals, strengths, performance limiters, personal life challenges, and personalities. Given these differences alone, I've never written two plans exactly alike—even if I have two athletes of the same sex with similar racing schedules.

I wrote this book (and others) because not everyone is able to hire a coach, but there is no lack of athletes looking for a training plan that will help them get faster or go farther. I've included five training plans in this book to fill that need. From a 12-week plan in preparation for a century ride to a 6-month plan to improve hill climbing, my training plans bridge the gap between cycling for recreation and cycling for increased distance or speed.

You might be wondering why I would write a book specifically for women. Both women and men can make use of the training regimen detailed in this book, but there are anatomical and physiological differences between women and men that influence the peripheral aspects of athletic training. I want women to have a better understanding of these differences so they can train more deliberately to reach their goals.

It's my hope that this book will encourage more women to ride. All women should have the opportunity to join a weekend group ride, cultivate their own appetite for speed, or even race. Regardless of what your goal is, I hope cycling brings to your life the joy and fulfillment it has brought to mine.

Acknowledgments

I want to thank Delbert, my husband, for being my number-one fan and supporter. He provided encouragement through a risky career change several years ago that allowed me to coach and write for athletes as a full-time profession.

In the late 1980s, my interest in cycling gravitated from satisfaction with participation to an interest in racing. I hired a coach, Joe Friel. I learned a great deal by being an athlete under his guidance. Following our coach-athlete relationship, we worked as business partners, which also helped to shape my coaching philosophies.

The most difficult chapter for me to write was Chapter 1 on anatomy and bike fit. When I wrote my first book in 1998, all the information—and really, I mean all—available to the public told women they had "short torsos." When I began searching for examples to illustrate the widely accepted notion, I was surprised to find that the data didn't support this idea about female dimensions and bicycle fit. I'm grateful to Dr. Andy Pruitt, Lennard Zinn, and Dr. Patrick Allen for taking time out of their busy schedules to answer questions and further increase my confidence in my interpretation of the data. There are still some bike manufacturers that insist women have short torsos, but those are now few and far between.

Dr. Betsy Cairo provided input for the original chapters concerning the female body, the reproductive system, and menopause. Lisa Ryckman provided a good deal of research and information on the female-specific chapters. She was a big help in the reorganization of the book as well. Dr. Pauline Entin reviewed the chapter on pregnancy and exercise and provided good feedback.

Chris Book, a registered dietitian, was a tremendous help in the transformation of my own diet years ago and furnished a good deal of information for the nutrition chapter. Athletes and nonathletes alike value her expertise. Dr. Deborah Shulman, registered dietitian, exercise physiologist, and elite distance runner, reviewed the nutrition chapter and supplied useful information based on firsthand experience and her work with endurance athletes.

Certainly this project wouldn't have been possible without encouragement and support from the ace team at VeloPress: Renee Jardine, Iris Llewellyn, and Liza Campbell.

Finally I want to thank all of my family and close friends, a long list, for understanding the huge amount of effort it takes to write a book. They patiently listened in the tough times, understood when I was staring at the computer instead of having fun with them, and told me, "You can do it"—as they always have.

Introduction

If you are looking to improve your cycling fitness or simply get started in the sport, then this is the book for you. At your fingertips you'll find all of the essential information on effective training, good equipment choices, and smart nutrition. As a woman, an experienced coach, and a cyclist, I've long been aware of the limited attention given to concerns unique to female athletes. I am convinced that any woman with a good understanding of her physiology and the basics of training can enjoy a lifetime of cycling success—so let's get started!

Part I begins with useful information for both women and men. Chapter 1 gives tips for proper bike fit, which is critical to your cycling comfort and success. Although women and men have some obvious anatomical differences, it is the not-so-obvious differences and common misconceptions (for example, the misconception that women have shorter torsos than men) that can make bike fit a frustrating experience.

Chapter 2 begins the discussion on training. I'll explain how to improve athletic performance with periodization, gauge intensity, determine your personal target heart rate exercise zones, and evaluate your progress. Chapter 2 also includes tips on goal setting to help you avoid common mistakes. If you learn how to set reasonable goals, progress will follow. Your fitness and health can be undermined by unreasonable goals because you'll eventually become discouraged and all progress will come to a halt.

With your personal goals in mind, you can get down to the details in Chapter 3 with training plans for five different cycling objectives. There is a 12-week plan to prepare for a 50-mile ride, a 12-week plan to prepare for a 100-mile ride, a 13-week plan to prepare for a 3-day tour, a 25-week plan to prepare for a 40-kilometer time trial or faster group rides, and a 25-week plan to improve climbing.

Although cardiovascular conditioning is critical for achieving cycling goals, strength training and stretching are also significant components of fitness, especially for women. Strength training can help prevent and repair damage from osteoporosis. Stretching can improve strength and range of motion; it also aids in the prevention of injury. Strength training and stretching recommendations are included in Chapter 4.

Physical training is not all you need for optimal athletic performance, and certainly not for optimal health. Proper nutrition is also crucial. Chapter 5 covers macro- and micronutrients, phytochemicals, caloric intake, and other nutritional guidelines essential to athletic training and recovery. Nutrition is always a hot topic; however, I do not prescribe a particular "diet." Your diet should be customized to meet your particular daily nutritional needs, and this chapter will help you identify what your body needs for optimal performance and health.

Chapter 6 offers mental tools that can prove useful in daily life and athletics. Two athletes can begin an event with comparable genetic abilities, physical strength and conditioning, and solid nutrition, and the race will go to the one with the strongest mental skills. The mind is a powerful ally.

Part II of this book is dedicated to women. It wasn't that long ago that women's participation in many events was prohibited because of traditional beliefs. In the August 1998 issue of *Runner's World*, a columnist noted that Danelle Ballengee, a world-class endurance athlete, had not been allowed to run the 1996 Ixta 18-mile mountain run because officials claimed it was too difficult for women. *Runner's World* quoted Ballengee as saying, "I guess they were afraid my ovaries would fall out or something." We are making progress in eliminating such barriers, but the job is not complete. I prefer to celebrate the ways in which women are unique rather than considering these qualities as limiters.

How different are we, really? Chapter 7 is an overview of some of the current research being conducted with female test subjects and female athletes. Although these research projects are valuable for both sexes, I'll pay particular attention to how a woman's physiology differs from a man's. As the data continue to amass, we can look forward to further progress in this arena.

Chapter 8 covers female hormones, the menstrual cycle, and how both affect athletic performance. Although the physical components of the system can be surgically altered, the hormones are critical to good health for women. This chapter also addresses some important issues such as prevention of osteoporosis through better hormonal balance.

Many women wonder if they can remain active throughout pregnancy. You'll learn more about the experiences of women who have already made the journey and review the current medical recommendations in Chapter 9.

As you age, you may be wondering if you should trade in your bicycle for a recliner or should boldly forge ahead as if you were still sweet 16. Our bodies inevitably change as we age. In Chapter 10, I'll help you anticipate those changes and give you plenty of recommendations to minimize some of the inconveniences associated with aging.

Finally, Chapter 11 is a collection of information about things that make cycling more comfortable or safer. It includes tips on such matters as saddle sores, travel, and hot- and cold-weather riding. This chapter answers some of the questions most frequently asked by athletes.

I hope you find the information in the book helpful. It is intended to give you a good understanding of the vast knowledge available to today's athletes, and more specifically, women athletes. I hope that men may find this book enlightening too—perhaps the female-specific wisdom will help some men understand what is going on with the women in their life. But first and foremost, this book is intended to answer the concerns specific to women like you, provide you with a practical plan for improved fitness, and challenge you to reach your next great accomplishment as a cyclist.

Enjoy!

Part I
Make the Most of Your Training

Part I of this book focuses on anatomy and bike fit, training concepts (periodization, intensity, testing, progress, and goal setting), training plans, strength training and stretching, nutrition, and mental tools. With the exception of the female anatomy and how it affects bike fit, and some nutrition information as it applies to women's health, all of the information in this section could be between the covers of a gender-blind book for cyclists. I believe there are no blanket differences between assembling training plans for men and for women. Based on research and my experience as a coach, how an athlete responds to a training stimulus is less about gender and more about genetics, anatomy, and lifestyle. I've trained women who could handle very high training loads and high levels of intensity work, and I've trained men who couldn't. Individual response to a training load is covered in Chapter 7.

But I'm certain you already know there are indeed differences between men and women. Women cope with a number of issues that men do not. When you dive into Part II, you will learn more about these issues and how they may impact your training and successful completion of an event. What I will tell you now is that you can do most anything you want to. All you need is know-how, patience, and perseverance. Let this book be your inspiration and guide.

chapter one

Anatomy and Bike Fit

Everybody wants to be treated like an individual and not as a statistic, and this is particularly critical when it comes to something as intimate as the fit of your bicycle. —LENNARD ZINN

Riding your bicycle shouldn't hurt. The only discomfort you should ever feel is the self-induced muscle ache or fatigue that comes from riding fast or riding far. If you do experience bad pain, chances are the trouble can be understood through your anatomy or your bike fit.

Cycling equipment, from the bicycle and all of its components to the proper clothing, can make a big difference in your comfort and performance. While the best equipment cannot make up for poor conditioning, poor equipment choices can cause short-term and chronic pain.

Choosing the correct bicycle is determined not just by your height and weight but also by the length of your legs, arms, and torso, and more specifically by other measurements, such as the distance between your shoulder and hand grip. When all of these aspects are taken into consideration in choosing cycling equipment, much of the pain and discomfort that cyclists experience can be avoided. Throughout this chapter, you'll be learning how to take your individual body dimensions into consideration when choosing a bike and whether you fall into the "average" range or outside it.

DOES GENDER MATTER?

The simple answer is no. Despite studies proving the contrary, the misconception that women are proportionately different from men endures. But in fact, while we are all individuals and have individual

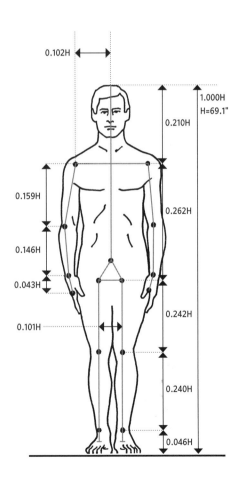

FIGURE 1.1 Body Segment Length in Proportion to Stature—Men
This illustrates the major body segments for men. The equations to predict the length of arm and leg segments from height (H) for U.S. men appear next to each segment.

(Data adapted from "The Measure of Man & Woman.")

4

dimensions, in the critical dimensions for cycling, the difference between the average U.S. male and female is surprisingly small. Proportional to height, the male and female dimensions of leg length, hand length, and arm length are nearly identical.

Figures 1.1 and 1.2 display the average dimensions from current anthropometric data. The average female measures 64 inches in height, while the average male measures 69.1 inches. The rest of the dimensions in the figures are expressed as a proportion of height. For example, in Figure 1.2, the female's femur (thigh) length is 0.241 × height (H). This average female's femur measures 0.241 × 64, or 15.42 inches.

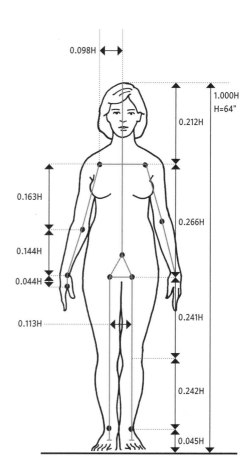

FIGURE 1.2 Body Segment Length in Proportion to Stature—Women
This illustrates the major body segments for women. The equations to predict the length of arm and leg segments from height (H) for U.S. women appear next to each segment.

(Data adapted from "The Measure of Man & Woman.")

0.098H

1.000H
H=64"

0.212H

0.163H

0.266H

0.144H

0.044H

0.113H

0.241H

0.242H

0.045H

Table 1.1 shows the differences in body dimensions for a male and a female of equal height. You can see that the female's key dimensions for bike fit are slightly shorter than those of the male except for grip area to shoulder length and shoulder width.

Because bicycles are not fitted by overall height, Table 1.2 shows the differences in key body dimensions affecting bike fit for a male and a female of equal leg lengths. For people within this data set, there is very little difference in the leg-length dimensions. There is less than a half-inch difference in torso length and hand-grip point to shoulder length.

It's important that you learn about your body dimensions so you can optimize your bike fit. We are not all carbon copies of the data set, with proportions exactly equal and to scale. While it's quite possible that your proportions fall within the average range, it is also possible that you have measurements that fall outside the average measurements on one or more dimensions.

One female cyclist I know is 64 inches tall, which puts her in the average range, but her arm, leg, and femur lengths are longer than average; her shoulders are wider than average; her torso length is

TABLE 1.1 Comparative Body Measurements
for a Male and a Female of Equal Height

	MALE 64 in		FEMALE 64 in		DIFF* 0
Femur Length	.242H	15.49 in	.241H	15.40 in	-0.09 in
Tibia Length	.240H	15.36 in	.242H	15.10 in	-0.26 in
Leg Length	.528H	33.80 in	.522H	33.40 in	-0.04 in
Torso Length	.262H	16.77 in	.266H	17.00 in	-0.23 in
Grip-to-Shoulder Length	.348H	22.27 in	.351H	22.43 in	0.16 in
Total Arm Length	.414H	26.50 in	.414H	26.50 in	0 in
Shoulder Width	.102H	6.528 in	0.98H	6.272 in	-0.26 in

*H = height in decimal inches. Difference between female and male data, in inches. Positive numbers indicate the female dimension is greater than the male dimension. Negative numbers indicate the female dimension is lower than the male dimension.

shorter than average; and her hands are smaller than average. This knowledge helps her find and modify bicycles and clothing to fit her individual proportions, thus ensuring her comfort and ultimately enhancing her performance.

Similar Proportions

One of the tasks of Dr. Patrick Allen, coroner and forensic pathologist for Larimer County, Colorado, is to determine gender from skeletal remains. While this is easiest when he has the entire skeleton, if only the pelvic bone is available, he can accurately determine gender 95 percent of the time. If there's only a skull, accuracy is about 90 percent.

"In forensic pathology, we do not determine the sex of skeletons based on ratios of leg lengths to torsos," Allen says. "That type of data varies with the particular population sampled, including nationality."

If some things are of equal leg length, for example, men and women have very similar anthropometric proportions.

TABLE 1.2 Comparative Body Measurements for a Male and a Female Having Equal Leg Lengths of 35 Inches

	MALE 63.26 in		FEMALE 64 in		DIFF* 0.74 IN
Femur Length	.242H	15.31 in	.241H	15.40 in	-0.09 in
Tibia Length	.240H	15.18 in	.242H	15.10 in	-0.08 in
Leg Length	.528H	33.40 in	.522H	33.40 in	0 in
Torso Length	.262H	16.57 in	.266H	17.00 in	0.43 in
Grip-to-Shoulder Length	.348H	22.01 in	.351H	22.43 in	0.42 in
Total Arm Length	.414H	26.20 in	.414H	26.50 in	0.30 in
Grip Length	.043H	2.72 in	.044H	2.80 in	0.08 in

*H = height in decimal inches. Difference between female and male data, in inches. Positive numbers indicate the female dimension is greater than the male dimension. Negative numbers indicate the female dimension is lower than the male dimension.

FINDING A BIKE THAT FITS

Knowing the facts about men and women and proportionality will help you when searching for the appropriate bike frame. Finding the right bike and a good fit is more than just standing over the top tube and looking for clearance. Let's look at the important considerations for determining whether a bike fits you.

Figure 1.3 shows the anatomy and geometry of a road bicycle. Learning the proper terms is helpful in purchasing a bicycle. The rest of this chapter is focused on selecting a road bike.

One rule of thumb for selecting a standard road bike frame, not a compact frame, is to begin by standing over the bicycle in stocking feet. Lift the bicycle until the top tube is snug in your crotch. There should be one or two inches of clearance between the tires and the floor. Riding a frame that is either too large or too small compromises performance and handling and can put you at risk for injury.

Bicycle size is typically given in centimeters and refers to the length of the seat tube. A 54 cm bike will have a 54 cm seat tube. Frames are measured in two ways: center to top and center to center. Center to top measures the distance from the center of the bottom bracket to the top of the top tube or seat lug. Center to center measures from the center of the bottom bracket to the center of the top tube at the seat lug. The center-to-center measurement is 1 cm to 1.5 cm smaller than the center-to-top measurement. Be aware of this when you compare frames. Some time trial bikes have curved seat tubes. In this case, the "functional" length of the seat tube is used, which is the straight-line distance measured center to center or center to top. This is similar for compact frames. The functional top tube length is the distance from the center of the top tube, where it attaches to the head tube, to the center of the seat tube measured parallel to the ground.

Frame sizes in the 49−60 cm range are fairly easy to find. Some manufacturers make 48 cm, 47 cm, and even smaller frames, down to 43 cm. Small frames will often have 650 cc wheels that keep your foot and the front tire from interfering with each other on turns,

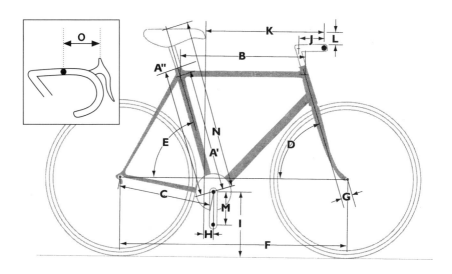

FIGURE 1.3 Road Bike Measurements

A'–Seat tube length, measured center to center

A"–Seat tube length, measured center to top

B–Top tube length

C–Chainstay length

D–Head tube angle

E–Seat tube angle

F–Wheelbase

G–Fork offset

H–Seat setback

I–Bottom bracket height

J–Stem length

K–Saddle to transverse centerline of handlebar

L–Seat to handlebar drop

M–Crank

N'–Seat height, measured from bottom bracket centerline (also shown in Figure 1.5a)

N"–Seat height, measured from pedal spindle (shown in Figure 1.5b)

O–Transverse centerline of handlebar to brake hood

and the overall length is shortened for better handling. Different frames may have different seat tube angles, the most common being in the range of 73 to 75 degrees, which allows the "average" cyclist to position her knees over the pedal axles with minor adjustments in the fore and aft position of the saddle.

A cyclist with a proportionately short femur wants a steeper seat tube angle to position her knees correctly over the pedals. A cyclist with a long femur wants a shallower seat tube angle. A cyclist who is planning to purchase a time trial—only bike may choose a seat angle greater than 75 degrees. A steeper seat angle shortens the wheelbase, putting the rider in a more powerful and aerodynamic position. The ride of the bike, however, can be uncomfortable and not as responsive as a regular frame.

The next consideration when selecting a frame size is the length of the top tube. Top tubes are typically within 2 cm of the seat tube length. A guideline is to divide your height by your inseam length, as measured in Figure 1.4. If that value is between 2.0 and 2.2, you are considered average, and a frame that has a top tube equal to the seat tube will fit you.

If your value is greater than 2.2, you have a long torso, and a longer top tube may be what you need. Less than 2.0 indicates that your torso is short in comparison to your legs, and you will be better off with a top tube that is shorter than the seat tube.

For example, if your inseam is 32.5 inches and your height is 64.5 inches, your ratio is 64.5 divided by 32.5, equaling 1.98. You would

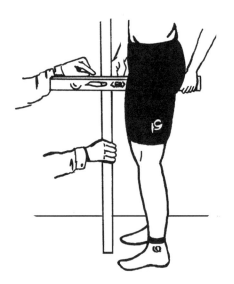

FIGURE 1.4 Inseam Measurement with a Level
Using a carpenter's level that is 2 to 3 feet long, stand in stocking feet on a flat, hard surface and snug the level into your crotch. The pressure between the level and your crotch (how much force you apply upward) should be similar to the pressure between a bicycle seat and your crotch. Have an assistant tell you when the level is parallel to the floor and have him or her measure the distance from the floor to the top of the level. This value is inseam length.

be just under the 2.0 guideline. You may be able to ride an average frame, depending on the length of your arms. If your arms are not considered long, you may be more comfortable on a frame in which the top tube is shorter than the seat tube.

Top tube and seat tube lengths vary between manufacturers and within the product line of a single manufacturer. Catalog sales will typically list frame dimensions, and bike shops will have brochures that list the frame dimensions of each bike they sell.

Seat Height

There are several ways to estimate seat height. If you already have a bike and know the seat height is correct, take the measurement with you to the bike shop (as shown in Figure 1.5a or 1.5b). If you aren't sure what your correct seat height is, you can estimate it by taking an inseam measurement and multiplying by 0.883. The product of those two numbers is the distance from the center of the bottom bracket to the top of the saddle, as in Figure 1.5a.

The type of pedal and shoe used influences seat height. If you use toe clips, the seat height method mentioned in the previous paragraph will be close to what you need. If you use clipless pedals, you may have to adjust the seat height measurement by about 3 mm.

How much you adjust the value will depend on your shoe, cleat, and pedal combination and how far that combination puts your foot from the pedal axle. Seat height is also affected by muscle flexibility. If you decide to change your current seat height, make changes slowly, about one-quarter inch per week.

Another easy way to estimate seat height is to sit on the bike while it is mounted in a stationary trainer. A quality bicycle shop will put the bicycle in a trainer to help you get it set up correctly. On the trainer, pedal the bike at a seat height that seems comfortable. Unclip your cleats from the pedal system, put your heels on the top of the pedals, and pedal backward. The height of the seat should be at a location that allows you to keep your heels on the pedals while pedaling backward and doesn't allow your hips to rock from side to side. When you are clipped into the pedals and begin to pedal forward again, you should have a slight bend in your knee, about 25 to 30 degrees.

Some visual cues to indicate the correct height are "quiet hips" and knees that align with your feet and hips. With the bicycle in the trainer, pedal for a few moments until you are somewhat settled and comfortable with your riding position. Then continue to pedal and have someone look at your hips from the rear. Your hips should have a slight rocking motion, but it should not be excessive. Excessive rocking, as if you are straining to reach the bottom of every pedal stroke, indicates your seat is too high.

While still pedaling, a view from the front should reveal your knees tracking in a straight line from your hips to the pedal. There is minimal side-to-side motion of your knees. This is normal. Knees that travel too far outside a straight line from the hip to the pedal may indicate the seat is too low. If you are bowlegged, as some cyclists are, this should be taken into consideration when watching knee tracking.

Keep in mind that your anatomy may require that you make special adjustments. If you have very wide hips, for example, you may need spacers added to the pedal spindles in order to move your feet more in line with your hips. Others may have a pedaling motion that, when viewed from the rear, seems uneven. It may appear as though they are "limping" on the bike. This may indicate a leg-length discrepancy. Modifications can be made to the bike to accommodate leg-length discrepancies, such as including spacers in the shoe or on the cleat and fore-aft positioning of the cleat on the pedals.

If you suspect you have some anatomy issues that cause problems on the bike, it is best to seek the help of a qualified professional. A good start is a sports medicine physician. He or she can take X-rays and measurements and conduct a physical examination to determine whether you have anatomical abnormalities.

FIGURE 1.5A Seat Height Measured from
the Center of the Bottom Bracket

The distance from the center of the bottom bracket to the top of the saddle,
measured along a line that would connect the bottom bracket to the point where
the rider's crotch would rest on the bicycle saddle, is one way to measure seat
height.

FIGURE 1.5B Seat Height Measured from
the Top of the Pedal Spindle

The distance from the top of the pedal spindle to the top of the saddle, measured along a line that would connect the spindle to the point where the rider's
crotch would rest on the bicycle saddle, is a second way to measure seat height.
This particular method is helpful when changing crank lengths or saddles. The
distance from the saddle rails to the top of the saddle varies from saddle to
saddle. When changing saddles or cranks, be certain the saddle height remains
the same, otherwise discomfort or injury may result.

13

Pedals

Clipless pedals are the pedals of choice for most competitive road cyclists. Pedals that allow some rotation may prevent injury by allowing your foot to "float" instead of being "fixed." It is commonly thought that a pedal that allows for some knee and foot travel minimizes the risk of injury.

No matter which type of pedal you choose, a guideline is to position the ball of your foot over the pedal axle. When the ball of your foot is ahead of the pedal axle, the lever arm from your ankle to the pedal axle is shortened and puts less stress on your Achilles tendon and calf muscles.

If you have tight Achilles tendons or problems with calf tightness, you can consider moving the ball of your foot ahead of the axle. This position also requires less force to stabilize your foot. Time trialists use this position because it allows the cyclist to produce more force while using larger gears.

If the ball of your foot is behind the pedal axle, it lengthens the ankle to the pedal axle lever arm. Some track cyclists prefer this position because it allows a higher cadence during fixed-gear events.

Saddle Position

While on the stationary trainer, pedal the bicycle until you feel settled. Once settled, stop pedaling and put the crank arms horizontal to the ground, in the three and nine o'clock positions, as shown in Figures 1.6a and 1.6b.

Your feet should be horizontal, or as close to horizontal as your flexibility allows. A neutral foot position will have your knee in line with the front of the crank arm. The position can be measured with a common yardstick, a plumb line, a wooden dowel, a sturdy piece of one-by-one-inch lumber, or a carpenter's level. Whatever you use, make sure the measuring tool remains perpendicular to the ground and doesn't bend beneath the measuring pressure.

Some time trial specialists prefer to have their knees slightly forward of the neutral position. Remember that if you slide the seat

FIGURE 1.6A Knee
in Relation to the
Crank Arm
The yardstick should
touch the knee and align
with the end of the crank
arm. The assistant can
make certain the yardstick
is perpendicular to the
ground.

FIGURE 1.6B Knee
in Relation to the
Crank Arm
When a plumb line is
looped around the leg and
dropped from the front of
the knee, the line should
touch the end of the crank
arm. A plumb line can be
constructed with light-
weight nylon string and a
nut, available at hardware
stores.

forward on its rails, you are, in effect, lowering seat height. So if you
adjust the seat forward, you may have to fine-tune your seat height.
A rule of thumb is for every centimeter forward you move your seat,
you need to raise the seat post a half centimeter.

Most bike fit experts recommend beginning with the saddle level
or parallel to the ground for general riding purposes. If the saddle
nose is pointed downward, you will tend to put more pressure on your
upper body because you are trying to keep from sliding forward.

If you need your saddle pointed down, you probably have your seat too high or your handlebars too low. If you decide to tilt your seat downward a degree or two, be certain you aren't constantly pushing yourself back on the seat. Some people prefer to tilt the nose of the seat up a bit; be certain it doesn't put pressure on your genital area and cause pain or numbing.

You can use a carpenter's level to get your seat level. Have someone hold your bike while you check seat tilt. If you check seat tilt while your bike is on a stationary trainer, be certain it is level and both tires are equally raised off the ground.

Stem

The position of your knee over the pedal is important. Don't compromise this position in an attempt to reach the handlebars. If your arm reach is short, the stem on the bicycle can be changed. Along the same line, don't use a longer stem to compensate for a bike frame that is too small. If you need a stem length beyond about 14 cm or shorter than 6 cm, it is an indication your top tube length is incorrect. The sizes most often used are 11 to 13 cm.

To determine if the stem length is correct, pedal the bicycle while it is in a stationary trainer. Again, pedal until you feel settled. With your hands on the drop bars, in your comfortable cycling position, your stem length is correct if the front wheel axle is blocked from view by the top, transverse part of the handlebars. This method will be affected by fork rake, so it may not always be reliable.

A second way to measure the correct position is to have a friend drop a plumb line from your nose toward the ground while you are looking forward, settled in your comfortable riding position. The plumb line should intersect the center of your stem, as shown in Figure 1.7.

The amount of stem post visible affects the height of your handlebars. Stem height can be measured by using the same tool you used to measure your knee position over the crank arm. Lay the straightedge across the saddle and have someone measure the distance from the straightedge to the top of the handlebars, as shown in Figure 1.8. Typically, handlebars are about 1 to 2 inches below the top of the saddle. Some tall people or those with long arms will go as much as 4 inches below the top of the saddle.

A lower stem puts your body in a more aerodynamic position. To be comfortable in a lower position, you need flexible hamstrings and an ability to rotate your pelvis. Signs that the stem may be too

FIGURE 1.7 Stem
Length Measurement
To determine if the stem length is correct, position the hands in the drops, in a comfortable riding position, with bent elbows. With the proper stem length, a plumb line dropped from the nose, while looking down at approximately 45 degrees, will bisect the stem.

FIGURE 1.8 Stem
Height
Using one straightedge like a yardstick, touch the saddle and hold the yardstick parallel to the ground, to the handlebars. Using a second straightedge, measure the distance from the bottom of the first straightedge to the stem.

low include pain or numbness in the genital area; your quadriceps hitting your torso on each pedal stroke; neck, shoulder, or arm pain; and hand numbness.

Raising the stem puts you in a more upright riding position and can take some of the pressure off those areas. There is a mark on the stem post that warns you not to raise the stem beyond that line. Raising the stem beyond the line risks damage to the head tube or breaking the stem post off in the head tube.

There are adjustable stems on the market that allow you to make changes as your fitness or cycling needs change.

Handlebars and Brake Levers

The width of the handlebars is roughly the same width as your shoulders. This is an important aspect of bike fit that affects handling and comfort. Handlebar widths are different and can easily be changed to suit your anatomy. Many female-specific bike manufacturers put narrower handlebars on the bikes designed for women compared with the same frame size in a bike designed for men. If you are purchasing a bike designed for men or a gender-blind design, be sure the handlebar width is appropriate for your anatomy.

If you happen to have small hands, you might consider shorter brake levers, which can be found through several manufacturers. Some female-specific designs already have these short-reach brakes on the bike. Also, there are shim kits that can be used to modify the reach of some braking systems. Check with your bike shop about the options for shortening the reach to your brakes.

Crank Length

Crank length is a much-debated topic when it comes to optimizing performance. In general, crank length should be proportional to leg length, which is the dimension that originally determined frame size. Generally speaking, new bicycles come with crank arms that are proportional to frame size. If you are building a custom frame, see the data in Table 1.3 as a starting point for crank length.

TABLE 1.3 Crank Length Beginning Measure Estimates

FRAME SIZE (cm)	CRANK LENGTH (mm)
45–48	160–165
47–52	167.5
50–58	170
55–61	172.5
59–65	175
62–67	177.5
64–70	180

Cyclists with disproportionately long legs or those who will focus on time trialing can consider using longer cranks. Longer cranks have a mechanical advantage and are good for pushing larger gears, such as in time trialing.

Keep in mind, however, that the crank arm length influences cadence. This can cause extra stress on the knees, typically in the form of patellar tendinitis, and will affect saddle height compared with a shorter crank. A switch to longer cranks typically means you need to lower your seat in order to keep your hips from rocking at the bottom of the pedal stroke.

Once the seat height is properly adjusted, these new, longer cranks may cause interference between the quadriceps and your torso. If you find interference or pain in your knees after switching to longer cranks, you may need to return to the shorter cranks.

Saddles

Saddle style is probably the most intimate and frustrating part of bike fit. No saddle is going to make up for an ill-fitting bicycle, and no one wants to ride any distance if his or her private parts are in pain or have gone numb.

Saddles come in various styles, lengths, and widths. As shown earlier in Figures 1.1 and 1.2 that, on average, women tend to have wider pelvic bones than men do when expressed in proportion to height. As we've already learned, individual anatomy varies. Whether your anatomy prefers a wide or narrow seat, minimal padding or a gel insert, and a solid seat or a seat with a cutout depends on your riding style, the length of time you will spend in the saddle, and personal preferences.

The saddles touted as "women's models" tend to be wider because they are designed for a typically wider female pelvis. Many men find that these wider saddles can eliminate genital numbness, which is a concern for some because of recent information about a possible link between bicycling and erectile dysfunction, by providing a wider platform for pelvic bones. A few manufacturers have begun producing wider saddles designed for men for just this reason.

> ## Shopping Etiquette
>
> Out of courtesy, do not request component changes from a bike shop unless you are serious about purchasing the bike. Do not expect friendly service on your purchase if you use a bike shop to find your perfect fit and then order the bike by mail.

It's important that a saddle be padded for comfort; however, too much padding can cause numbness too. If the saddle is overpadded, it can conform to the perineum, which is the area between the vaginal opening and the anus. Compressing the arteries and nerves in this area can cause pain.

Some shops will change a saddle and let you try it out while riding the stationary trainer. If you ask around, you're likely to find that saddle choice is a bit like ice cream flavors—everyone has a favorite for different reasons.

Some saddle discomfort is due to fitness and riding style. Novice cyclists do not have the leg and glute muscles of an experienced cyclist. Strong leg muscles will help support a cyclist, so the saddle doesn't become a chair. Novice cyclists who haven't developed strong leg muscles tend to "sit" on the saddle and move their legs, while experienced cyclists are somewhat suspended by their legs. If you are a novice cyclist, slowly build cycling miles to increase leg strength and saddle time—even experienced cyclists need to build saddle time after being off the bike for a while.

Custom Frames

Unfortunately, there is no easy way to determine if you need a custom frame or not. That formula, yet undeveloped, is a function of overall height in addition to the ratio of leg length, torso length, and arm length to height.

Custom-frame maker Lennard Zinn says people who are on the low and high ends of the spectrum might consider a custom frame. In general, you're a good candidate for a custom frame if you're under 5 feet 3 inches or over 6 feet 4 inches with an inseam of more than 36 inches, or if you have trouble getting a normal frame to fit due to an abnormally short or long torso.

Time Trial Positions

If you decide to do a time trial, aerodynamics is a big concern. To reduce the effect of wind drag, you want to be as compact as possible. Being compact means getting a lower body position and minimizing anything that may cause wind turbulence and drag. Opinions on what constitutes a good aero position have changed over the years and have gotten more technical support with the use of wind-tunnel testing.

Three pieces of cycling equipment that have a major influence on improved aerodynamics are aerobars (aerodynamic handlebars that lower the body position), truncated teardrop-shaped aero helmets, and an aerodynamic wheelset.

People used to believe that getting your arms as close together as possible was the way to go for position in the aerobars, but this is no longer true. Arms are best placed far enough apart to allow the wind to travel between them and around the body. It is still important to ride with a flat back, if possible; however, it is far more important to maintain a smooth line from the front of your helmet to your lower back.

For aerodynamics, it is best if your knees are close to the bike frame while cycling, but don't compromise power output, biomechanics, safety, or comfort. Riding in an aerodynamic position may take some time to accomplish, and the best aero position for you may not work for someone else.

For example, arm position affects steering responsiveness and balance, and riding with a flat back requires a flexible back and hamstring muscles as well as forward rotation of the pelvis. This forward rotation and new position may put added pressure on the genitals. A seat that has gel padding on the nose or a portion of the nose relieved (a cutout area that relieves soft tissue pressure) may help.

When lowering your head to become more aerodynamic, be certain it's possible to comfortably see where you are going. Also know that if you are wearing one of the aero teardrop helmets and you look too far down, lifting the tail of the helmet into the air, you negate some of its aerodynamic effect. Eyeglasses or sunglasses with thick frames may cause forward-vision problems. If seeing the road ahead is an issue, you may have to sacrifice some aerodynamics for safety. Also, craning your neck to see the road may be a prescription for a stiff neck; adjust your position to get comfortable.

There are several considerations when purchasing an aerodynamic wheelset, but these are not covered in this book. Before investing in new wheels, do some research and decide how you'll use the wheelset—for everyday riding or only for racing?

CLOTHING

One of the best investments you can make for a comfortable cycling experience is padded cycling shorts. These shorts are designed to be worn without underwear and protect your genital area from pressure and friction. Wearing underwear with cycling shorts is likely to cause chafing and pressure-point problems, so don't do it.

Cycling Shorts by Riding Level

NOVICE Some riders are more comfortable in baggy-style shorts. Other riders like the compressive feeling of tight-fitting Lycra shorts. In either case, it is possible to find good-fitting and inexpensive cycling shorts. All the seams should be free of raised areas and thread knots.

INTERMEDIATE The midrange cycling shorts are typically made of more expensive materials than the get-rolling version. They also tend to have a longer life span.

HARD-CORE The high-priced shorts and bib shorts are made from fabrics boasting the current technology for wicking, comfort, and style. Some styles boast aerodynamic qualities, while others boast the latest "in" fashion. The seams are flat or hidden.

There are three basic designs for cycling shorts: the baggy style, the skirt or skort style, and the tight-fitting Lycra style. Which style you choose depends on your personal preferences, riding style, and cycling goals.

The padded portion of a cycling short is called a chamois. In the early days of cycling, the chamois was made from animal hide. Now most cycling shorts have synthetic chamois manufactured from performance-oriented materials intended to wick moisture away and reduce pressure and friction.

The major variables for chamois include the material, size, shape, thickness, and placement within the short. These items vary among styles and manufacturers. A pair of shorts and chamois that is comfortable for one rider may not be comfortable for the next rider. It is best to try on a few different pairs of shorts. When you try shorts on, wear underwear for hygiene purposes. Always wash shorts before wearing them for the first time.

After you finish a ride, get out of your cycling shorts and get showered as soon as possible. If it isn't possible to shower at the end of your ride due to a commute, at least get out of your cycling

Gearing Up for the Cold

Moving from toe to head, here are some cold-weather gear suggestions to get you started:

- Make sure your socks give your toes enough room to move. Cramped toes are cold toes. Be sure your socks are made out of moisture-wicking material.
- Wear booties to keep the wind off your toes. For cool temperatures, try the wind-stopper booties. For colder temperatures, neoprene is great.
- For your legs, wear tights or leg warmers, with or without wind protection on the front.
- Wrap your torso with a base layer that wicks moisture away from your body, a second layer to insulate, and a third layer that provides wind protection, yet allows moisture to escape.
- Wear gloves or lobster-claw mittens with wind-stopper material on the outside and moisture-wicking material next to your hands.
- Use an oil-based moisturizer for your face. Water-based lotions wet the skin, increasing the likelihood of frostnip or frostbite. Or consider a balaclava to cover your face. For athletes with asthma, a balaclava can slow moisture loss and help preheat cold air before you suck it into your lungs.
- For head protection, a helmet cover and ear warmers are a favorite combination. If it gets too hot, you can easily peel off the helmet cover or pull down the ear warmers. Some cyclists prefer a skullcap that fits under a cycling helmet.
- Fill your insulated water bottles or a backpack hydration bladder with hot energy drink. A good apple flavor mimics hot apple cider.
- In your pocket, carry small chemical heat packs. These are little packages that produce heat once the outer wrapping is opened. Carry a package of these to warm fingers and hands that have changed a flat tire in cold conditions.
- Carry a cell phone in case you need to call for help. While you are waiting for your ride, keep warm by putting the chemical packs in your shoes or gloves.

shorts. You can use disposable towelettes or carry a damp washcloth in a baggie for a quick cleanup. This helps reduce the likelihood of saddle sores caused by bacteria.

Next to cycling shorts, padded gloves are the best clothing invest-ment. Besides preventing numbness and soreness, they keep your hands protected in the unfortunate event of a crash.

Cycling jerseys have pockets in the rear panel to carry food, ex-tra clothing, or flat-repair materials. While cycling jerseys are not mandatory for comfortable cycling as cycling shorts are, a jersey gives a cyclist added storage.

Cold-Weather Clothing

Most of the time, beginning cyclists head indoors when the temper-ature drops below a certain mark on the thermometer. Intermediate riders have a slightly higher threshold, and the hard-core people are found cycling in all kinds of weather and temperatures.

When the weather is cold—say 20° or 30°F—you prepare for it. Problems can occur when the temperature is in the 40- or 50-degree range and you are unprepared for sudden weather changes, such as an approaching storm that makes conditions wet and/or windy.

For example, a 40°F ambient temperature changes to 34° on your skin with the addition of a 10 mph headwind. Add a cycling speed of 20 mph into that headwind, and the windchill takes the temperature to a brr-cold 28°F.

You can increase the fun factor on these long rides by protect-ing yourself from the outside elements, such as wind and rain, and keeping sweat off your skin. Find buddies who are willing to ride in the cooler conditions. Riding with a group is much easier than facing chilly temperatures on your own.

• • •

WE ARE ALL INDIVIDUALS AND HAVE INDIVIDUAL DIMENSIONS. JUST because you might be of "average" height does not mean your legs are of average proportion. In any regard, a bicycle should be reason-ably comfortable to ride, given a gentle buildup of mileage.

When you shop for a new bicycle, be informed. Know bicycle geometry and the rules of thumb for bike setup so you can be a smart shopper. Go to a reputable bicycle shop where the personnel are willing to help you and spend time answering questions. A shop with good mechanics who are willing to teach you about a bicycle is a place worthy of your business.

chapter two

Training and Fitness

Individualization in training is one of the main requirements of contemporary training and it refers to the idea of each athlete, regardless of level of performance, being treated individually according to his or her abilities, potential, learning characteristics, and specificity of the sport.... Quite often coaches apply a completely unscientific approach in training by literally following training programs of successful athletes, completely disregarding their athlete's personality, experience, and abilities.
—TUDOR BOMPA, THEORY AND METHODOLOGY OF TRAINING

Maybe it's your first century, a weeklong tour, or just a need for speed. Whatever your motivation for trying to go faster or farther, the roads to both goals have similarities. Unfortunately, athletes often take a wrong turn and end up disappointed with their performance. For endurance athletes, one of the most common mistakes is training at the same speed all the time. This chapter will help you avoid this pitfall. We'll cover riding intensities, self-tests to estimate training zones, and ways to determine whether you're actually making progress.

RIDING FAST ALL THE TIME

Have you ever been on a group ride where the speeds were sizzling from the start? For a few moments, you were right there, hanging with the pack—then you dropped like a rock. Your heart was pounding, your legs were burning, and you gave it all you had. The group speed was obviously too fast for you to sustain. But other people were going that fast, so what were they doing that you weren't?

It seems to make sense that if you want to be fast in a race, you have to train that way. This is true to a point, but you can't train at that rate all the time and make progress. Athletes who train at a consistently fast rate end up going one mediocre speed—not too fast, not too slow. They're too tired for their arms and legs to turn over a fast pace, but they've got enough energy to go at a decent pace. How do you avoid that rut?

Building and improving fitness are like building a house. The first part, the foundation, must be constructed properly or the rest of the house won't last—at least not for very long. After the foundation is laid, a strong frame and roof can be built. The best results come from an orderly process in the initial stages of the construction. When it comes to the finishing details, the order of some tasks can be adjusted somewhat to accommodate the construction schedule. Once constructed, the house must be maintained. If the house is properly maintained, improvements can be made a few at a time to meet the owner's needs.

It's the same with fitness. You need a solid base before you add long duration or long bouts of speed. If long duration is attempted prior to a gradual increase in training volume, you risk injury and limited success. Once you achieve a certain level of fitness, it needs to be maintained. Each season, further improvements can be made, but it can often take years to build a world-class athlete.

RACING

In this book the words "race" and "event" are used interchangeably. The fact that you're reading this means that you're likely preparing for an event and want to deliver the best possible performance. For some people, this means aiming for a podium performance in a sponsored event, while for others, it means a self-designed goal event.

While you might not be entering a race, you still want to optimize your performance in a goal event. I have coached many cyclists to achieve top race-day performances. I have also trained several cyclists who had goal events such as:

- Improve speed to ride with the "A" group on Sunday rides.
- Beat Fast Fran on at least three group rides this year. (Yes, there are people who treat group rides as a race, and we have planned for optimal performance at selected group rides.)
- Improve average speed for tough century ride from last year's average of 14 mph.

If you're not interested in optimizing your performance with a plan, put the book down and just ride when you feel like it at any speed you please on any given day. There are no guarantees, but I believe a structured plan increases your chances of improved performance. If you want to improve your performance at a sponsored event or a self-designed event, read on.

PERIODIZATION

You may or may not be striving to be world-class. Either way, periodization will help to guide your training for faster or longer races. Briefly, a periodized plan manipulates exercise volumes and intensities over the course of weeks, months, and years.

A periodization plan for an Olympic athlete will span the course of several years. This type of plan is designed so that the athlete will be at peak fitness and speed for the Olympic Games. No athlete, even an Olympic-caliber athlete, can maintain peak fitness year-round. True peak performances are planned and can occur only about two or three times a year. Even if you're not aspiring to the time or distance of top professionals, your training process shares the same basic training principles:

1. Individual and progressive **overload** must be applied to achieve physiological improvement and bring about a training change. A widely accepted rule of thumb is to increase annual training hours, or annual volume, by 10 percent or less.

2. Training **volume** can be defined as the combination of frequency and duration. When looking at your training plan, annual training volume is one piece of the puzzle. Broken down, the monthly, weekly, and daily training volumes are as important as annual volume. Establishing your personal training volume based on what "the pros do" is faulty logic. Your personal training volume, in order to bring about physiological improvement, should be based on your personal profile, past training volume, current lifestyle, goals, number of weeks you have to train before your key event, and response to training.

3. The **duration** of your longest workout may or may not be the length of your goal race. Generally, the shorter the event and the more time you have to train before the event, the greater likelihood that you will complete the event distance sometime within your training.

4. Depending on your current fitness, race goals, the sport, and available training time, the **frequency** of your workouts will vary. Some athletes will work out only once a day, while others will work out two or more times a day. Frequency also encompasses the number of weekly workouts and recovery periods.

5. **Individual response** to training does vary. Given the same goal and training plan, athletes can make improvements at different rates and achieve varying gains in overall fitness.

6. The duration and frequency of workouts should vary with each particular training block, and within those workouts, the ***intensity*** varies depending on the goal of the workout. Intensity can be measured as heart rate, pace, miles per hour, power output, and rating of perceived exertion, to name a few methods. The appropriate training intensity minimizes the risk of injury while stressing the body enough to achieve the goal on race day.

7. The ***mode*** of training becomes more important as race day approaches. For athletes utilizing a year-round approach to training, aerobic crosstraining in the early training blocks is appropriate. For example, northern latitude triathletes often use cross-country skiing and running workouts to bolster

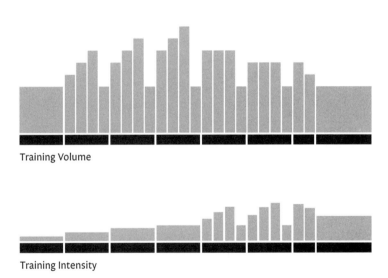

Training Volume

Training Intensity

FIGURE 2.1 Typical Interrelationship of Volume and Intensity

In many textbook models, training volume increases during early training periods and training intensity increases at modest rates. As training volume decreases or remains constant, training intensity increases. These graphs display how training volume and intensity might interrelate on the same training plan for the same periods of training.

endurance for cycling. As the athletes approach their key event training, which is specific to the sport, generalized training will take a backseat. In other words, the **specificity** of training becomes more important.

8. Goal-oriented athletes must consider **rest and recovery** as two critical training components. Performance gains are made when the body has a chance to repair and absorb the effects of the training workload.

Figure 2.1 shows a textbook model displaying the interrelationship between training volume and training intensity. Training volume begins at a steady rate, then increases in three-week blocks. After each three-week build of training volume, one week of reduced volume is included for recovery. After three blocks of increasing volume, training volume is reduced and intensity begins to increase. Near the end of the plan, volume and intensity decrease before a

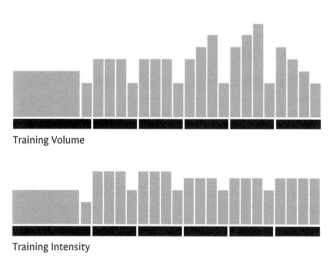

Training Volume

Training Intensity

FIGURE 2.2 Interrelationship of Volume and Intensity
for Long-Distance Training
For some training circumstances, such as training for long-distance racing, training volume may increase while training intensity decreases.

race or a block of races. This is one example of a training strategy covering 30 weeks of training for key races that are within a six-week block.

A different approach to training is shown in Figure 2.2. Notice how training volume builds near the end of the training plan. This is a training strategy that might be used by an athlete racing long-distance events. She might keep volume steady while including some higher-intensity training early in the plan. As the athlete gets closer to race day, volume builds to accommodate an event that will take 10-plus hours to accomplish. As shown in the figure, this particular athlete decreases intensity when volume starts to build and holds the intensity level steady.

These figures are just two examples of the endless training strategies that are available to accomplish a particular racing goal. The most important thing is that your training plan is appropriate for your fitness, lifestyle, and race goals. Figure 2.3 shows the

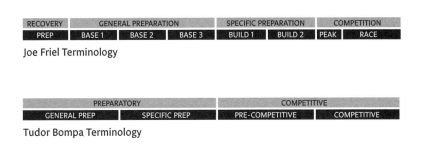

FIGURE 2.3 Training Terminology
The terminology used in this book most closely resembles Tudor Bompa's and is utilized across multiple sports worldwide.

training phase terminology used by a few notable authors. The terms used in this book are closest to those used in multiple sports worldwide.

RECOVERY

This phase is specifically intended to help you recover from the rigors of training and racing. It is often one to four weeks in length for the competitive athlete. There are no specific parameters, usually just basic guidelines to help maintain fitness. The most common guidelines I use are:

- Take at least one to two days off from "training" each week.
- All training intensity is aerobic in nature.
- All training sessions are two hours or less.

GENERAL PREPARATION

Some cyclists crosstrain during this phase of training, with the goal of building or maintaining cardiovascular fitness. There can be several blocks within this phase, such as General Preparation 1, 2, and 3. Intensity (discussed below) tends to be mostly aerobic during this phase. Both General Preparation and Specific Preparation are often referred to as base training.

SPECIFIC PREPARATION

The goal of this phase is to move toward sport-specific training, reducing or eliminating crosstraining. Race-paced training is introduced in this phase, but the race-paced work segments tend to be short with ample recovery at the beginning of the phase. The intention is to build neuromuscular movement patterns. As this phase continues, a greater percentage of the training resembles race pace. There can be several blocks within this phase, such as Specific Preparation 1, 2, and 3.

PRE-COMPETITIVE PREPARATION

The goal of this phase is to prepare the athlete for her specific race requirements. These requirements—race time and intensity—differ for a 30-mile event, a century ride, and a multiday tour, and they also vary among individual athletes. An athlete who has minimal conditioning has different requirements than a highly conditioned one. There can be several blocks within this phase, such as Pre-competitive 1, 2, and 3. This phase can also include low-priority races, used as training events.

COMPETITIVE

This phase may include a series of races over the course of six to eight weeks, or it might be a period of tapering volume in the lead-up to a single race, such as an ultradistance event.

The outline of training phases shown in Figure 2.3 is perfect if you have several weeks to prepare for an event. If you have only six to twelve weeks to prepare for an event, you will obviously have a shallow level of fitness and your training phases will be quite truncated compared with someone who has maintained a training routine for several years.

All plans intentionally stress the body with increasing volume or intensity, then allow it to rest, so your fitness level after the rest will be greater than before the stressful workout. This concept is called "overcompensation" or "supercompensation."

Supercompensation, however, is a fine line. Too much stress and your body will break down, resulting in illness or injury. Too little stress and no progress is made. Getting yourself into peak condition will require both science and art. Science provides data from laboratory studies, while art is knowing when to follow a plan exactly and when to make deviations. Each training plan in this book will help you blend science and art and provide more tips on the art of training.

INTENSITY

So how do you know how fast to ride? Table 2.1 lists seven heart rate training zones and the training purpose of each zone. You can also reference the percentage of lactate threshold heart rate (LTHR) for each zone, or if you have yet to purchase a heart rate monitor, you can use the Borg Scale of Perceived Exertion and the description of breathing and exertion.

TABLE 2.1 Training and Racing Intensities
Based on Lacate Threshold Heart Rate

ZONE	% LACTATE THRESHOLD HEART RATE (Bike)	% LACTATE THRESHOLD (Power)	RATE OF PERCEIVED EXERTION (RPE)	
			Original Borg Scale	New Borg Scale
1	≤80	≤55	6-9	1-2
2	81-88	56-75	10-12	3-4
3	89-83	76-90	13-14	4-5
4	94-99	91-99	15-16	6
5a	100-102	100-105	17	7
5b	103-105	106-120	18-19	8-9
5c	106+	121+	20	10

ENERGY PRODUCTION

Before we discuss each training zone (see sidebar, "Training Zones"), it's important to understand more about energy production within the body. Our bodies need to have a continuous supply of energy—even to sleep. Energy is supplied by complex chemical reactions. The end result of these chemical reactions is a rich compound called adenosine triphosphate, or ATP. The potential energy within the

BREATHING AND EXERTION USING CYCLING AS THE EXAMPLE	X-REFERENCE OF TERMS COMMONLY USED TO DESCRIBE EACH ZONE
Gentle rhythmic breathing. Pace is easy with legs feeling relaxed, minimal pressure on the pedals.	Easy, Aerobic, Recovery
Breathing rate and pace increase slightly. Many notice a change with slightly deeper breathing, although still comfortable. Legs remain comfortable and conversation is possible.	Aerobic, Extensive Endurance, Aerobic Threshold Endurance
Aware of breathing a little harder, pace is moderate. Legs begin to feel some stress and it is more difficult to hold conversation.	Tempo, Intensive, Endurance
Starting to breathe hard, pace is fast and beginning to get uncomfortable, approaching all-out one-hour ride pace.	Subthreshold, Muscular Endurance, Anaerobic Threshold Endurance
Breathing deep and forceful, many notice a second significant change in breathing pattern. Pace is all-out sustainable for one- to one-and-a-half hours. Mental focus required, legs are moderately uncomfortable, and conversation is undesirable.	Lactate Threshold Endurance, Anaerobic Threshold Endurance, Superthreshold Muscular Endurance
Heavy, labored breathing. Pace is noticeably challenging but sustainable for 15 to 30 minutes. Leg discomfort is high but manageable.	Aerobic Capacity, Speed Endurance, Anaerobic Endurance
Maximal exertion in breathing, pace is sprinting effort, and legs experience high discomfort that is unsustainable for over one minute.	Anaerobic Capacity, Power

ATP molecule is utilized for all processes requiring energy in the cells of your body.

There are two basic methods your body uses to produce ATP. One method is *aerobic* (meaning with the presence of oxygen), and the other is *anaerobic* (meaning without the presence of oxygen). The method of energy production your body uses depends on the rate of demand for energy (intensity) and the length of demand for energy (duration). Short bursts of high speed utilize the anaerobic system of energy production to fuel the muscles. For longer efforts, fat and glycogen are burned in the presence of oxygen to create ATP.

A small amount of energy is available to be utilized "on demand." For example, when you sprint to make it through an intersection before the light changes, a small amount of energy is needed instantly. The majority of the energy necessary for this sprint is created anaerobically. After you have made it through the intersection and a slower speed is resumed, energy is created mostly through aerobic means.

For short sprints, energy is primarily created anaerobically and uses ATP stored in the muscle cells in limited quantities to complete the work. It is readily available but used up quickly. Aerobically produced ATP, on the other hand, takes more time for the body to produce but is available in huge quantities. These large quantities of energy allow an athlete to exercise for several hours at easy to moderate speeds.

Even at a moderate pace, however, some of the energy is produced anaerobically. In other words, both systems are working at the same time. As the intensity or speed increases, energy production and utilization need to happen more rapidly. Remember, the aerobic system needs time to produce energy; it is not as quick as the anaerobic system. So the body relies more on anaerobic energy production as the pace increases.

A by-product of the anaerobic energy production system is lactic acid. Lactic acid is often viewed negatively, but in fact, it is a good energy source for the body. When given enough time, the body can process and use lactic acid to produce ATP. Lactate (a salt of lactic acid) is always present in the blood at rest. Even while you read this book, low levels of lactate are circulating in your bloodstream.

At low levels, lactic acid is not a problem. However, as you continue to increase your workout intensity, your body increases energy production, relying more heavily on anaerobic metabolism. More reliance on anaerobic metabolism means the lactate level in your blood begins to increase. When your body can no longer process lactic acid fast enough, lactate begins to accumulate at an increasing rate in the blood. This condition is called "onset of blood lactate accumulation" or "lactate threshold" (LT). This accumulation has a close correlation with heart rate and ventilatory rate. Athletes can often tell when they have reached LT because their breathing becomes labored and they begin to feel a burning sensation in their muscles.

If you exceed LT pace, you can sustain the increased pace only for a few minutes before the discomfort forces you to slow down. The margin by which LT is exceeded is inversely proportional to the time you are able to sustain that pace. In other words, if your LT heart rate is 162 and heart rate is pushed to 172, you will be able to hold that pace for a shorter period of time than if working at a heart rate of 164.

Lactate threshold can be understood as the pace and correlating average heart rate that you can sustain for approxima tely one hour while participating in a single sport. For example, the LT for a highly fit cyclist is approximately the pace and average heart rate that that athlete can hold for a 40 km time trial on a bicycle. Research has found that LT heart rate varies depending on the particular sport. Generally speaking, running LT heart rates tend to be 5 to 10 beats higher than cycling LT heart rates.

Lactate threshold typically occurs at 55 to 65 percent of VO_2max (the maximum amount of oxygen the body can utilize during a specified period of usually intense exercise) in healthy, untrained people. In highly trained endurance athletes, LT is often greater than 80 percent of VO_2max. Lactate threshold is trainable, and that's good news. In other words, you can train your body to process lactate at higher percentages of VO_2max, which means increased levels of speed before discomfort forces an end to the effort.

Studies have shown LT to be a reliable predictor of endurance race performance. VO_2max is not nearly as reliable. So, if you've been tested for VO_2max and your numbers weren't stellar, don't panic.

It's important to know that the training zones are approximations. If you were to test blood lactate levels daily for a period of time, you would find that a heart rate of 162 would produce some variation in the levels of lactate. The more experience you gain as an athlete, the more attuned you will become to your personal exercise intensity levels.

TESTING

There are various ways to estimate your LT and the corresponding heart rate. One way is to go to a laboratory for a graded exercise test. In this test, the exercise workload is incrementally increased and blood samples are taken at specific intervals to measure the level of lactate in the blood. During a graded exercise test at a laboratory, the ratio of oxygen to carbon dioxide being expelled from your respiratory system can also be measured and used to estimate LT.

There are also ways to estimate LT heart rate in the field (see Appendix A). For all of the tests, you'll need a wireless heart rate monitor. In order to get the best estimate, you need to be rested and highly motivated. If you do the test when you're tired, the results may be inaccurate. These tests, however, are not intended to find maximum heart rate because all the training and racing zones are based on a very trainable LT heart rate. To use this book and the training plans, determining your maximum heart rate is unnecessary. If you have any concerns about any of the tests, seek the advice of a physician first. It is not wise to conduct the tests during the first couple of workouts after a long period of inactivity.

Before beginning the tests to estimate LT heart rate, you can get a sense of the different racing and training zones by reviewing the rate of perceived exertion (RPE) and the corresponding description of breathing and exertion levels in Table 2.1. RPE uses the Borg scale, which was originally designed to correlate with heart rate for young athletes and derived by dividing the heart rate by 10. For example, easy exercise at a perceived exertion value of 6 was intended to correlate to a heart rate of 60. Although the numbers do not always correlate exactly to heart rate, the perceived exertion scale can be very valuable and is still widely used. (See Tables A.1 and A.2 in Appendix A for correlations between the Borg rate of perceived exertion [RPE] scale and the heart rate training zones.)

Training Zones

The preceding comments for each of the seven training zones are not all-inclusive, but they do give an idea of the uses for each particular training zone. We will use the seven training zones to measure speed and help you avoid mediocre workouts. Remember that anyone can train and race "hard," but not everyone is fast.

ZONE 1 Zone 1 is used to build fitness in beginning athletes and for recovery purposes by more experienced athletes. The energy production is primarily aerobic. Zone 1 is also used in conjunction with Zone 2 to build exercise endurance for long-distance racing.

ZONE 2 Zone 2 is used to build fitness and maintain current levels of fitness. Lactate begins to increase, but the accumulation tends to be linear and manageable by the body for very long periods of time, such as for long-distance training and racing lasting over eight hours. Within this intensity zone is what many coaches call "aerobic threshold." Some scientists and coaches define the lactate measurement of 2 millimoles per liter (mmol/L) and the associated heart rate as aerobic threshold. There is disagreement about this value. (See Zone 5a for further discussion.)

Often Zones 1 and 2 are used in conjunction with drills to improve athletic skills. Good form improves athletic economy, which translates to less oxygen needed for a given pace.

CONTINUES

CONTINUED

ZONE 3 Zone 3 intensity is used for early-season tempo work and to begin LT improvement. Zones 1 through 3 are used by experienced athletes training and racing in events lasting longer than about three hours.

ZONE 4 This zone is used in conjunction with intervals, hill work, and steady-state work to improve LT speed and muscular endurance. It is common for the intervals in this zone to have work-to-rest ratios of 3:1 and 4:1 in cycling and running, respectively.

ZONE 5a The lowest heart rate value in Zone 5a (100 percent of LT heart rate in Table 2.1) is called LT in this book. Some coaches and scientists call this value "anaerobic threshold." Laboratories often associate a blood lactate value of 4 mmol/L with LT. Be aware that the 4 mmol/L value is common for many athletes, but there are wide variations. Lactate threshold can be as low as 2 mmol/L or as high as 8 mmol/L for individual athletes. This is why the statement that "anaerobic threshold is 4 mmol/L" may be incorrect for some athletes. Good laboratories typically provide lactate curves and interpret the data for you, eliminating a "one size fits all" value for both thresholds.

This zone is used in conjunction with intervals, hill riding, and tempo rides to improve LT speed and muscular endurance. It is often used in conjunction with Zone 4.

ZONE 5b The major use for this zone is to improve anaerobic endurance. The cycling and running intervals in this zone often have a work-to-rest ratio of 1:1. This zone is also used in hill workouts.

ZONE 5c Zone 5c is fast–really fast. Sprinting to grab a competitor's wheel in a draft-legal race and climbing hills out of the saddle both elicit heart rates in Zone 5c. Exercise in Zone 5c cannot be maintained for extended periods of time. It is common for the intervals in this zone to have a work-to-rest ratio of 1:2 or more.

Using a Heart Rate Monitor to Estimate Intensity

The heart rate monitor is one tool available to estimate exercise intensity. Monitors come in a variety of models and price ranges. The least expensive model simply reads heart rate, while the more expensive models have the capability of storing several hours of data that can then be downloaded for analysis.

The heart rate monitor consists of a transmitter belt worn strapped around the chest, just below the breasts, and a receiver worn on the wrist or mounted on the handlebar of a bike. The transmitter belt picks up electrical impulses from the heart and relays the information to the receiver via an electromagnetic field. The receiver then displays the heart rate. It's like having a tachometer for the body, similar to the one on a car.

Know that your heart rate is affected by your conditioning, current level of rest, the amount of stress you're experiencing, heat, humidity, and fatigue. If you have a heart rate monitor, you should wear it for most workouts. Whether you wear it during a race depends on your experience level as well as the type and distance of the event. In an event where others dictate your speed, such as a road race, controlling intensity is irrelevant. In events where controlling intensity is left to the individual athlete, a heart rate monitor is more valuable.

Experienced athletes are typically more skilled at judging intensity and pace; whether they wear a heart rate monitor during a race tends to be personal preference and depends on the type of race. Inexperienced athletes can use a heart rate monitor during races such as individual time trials to help them keep from going out too fast and "blowing up" before the end of an event. In general I suggest all athletes wear a heart rate monitor for events longer than three hours. At minimum, the data collection can help you learn more about how your body reacts to race situations.

While heart rate is a valuable tool, the subjective measure RPE is also very useful and no less important than heart rate. Many athletes using one of the training plans for the first time may be new to endurance sports and may not own a heart rate monitor. For them, homing in on RPE intensity is critical. RPE is also preferable to a monitor if you are taking any medication that keeps your heart rate artificially low, such as a beta-blocker for hypertension.

If you have a heart rate monitor and know your LT heart rate, you can use Table A.2 in Appendix A to calculate the training zones yourself. If you don't have a heart rate monitor, or are new to it, use breathing and RPE to estimate the appropriate training zone. For example, if one of the training plans instructs you to ride in Zone 1, use RPE and your breathing to estimate intensity and speed. Note your heart rate, RPE, and speed in comparable conditions whenever possible so you can begin to correlate the relationship among the three measures.

The methods outlined in Appendix A are ways to estimate LT and LTHR. There are other methods, but these work well. Once you've determined your threshold heart rate for cycling, you can use that heart rate to estimate a second sport, such as running. As mentioned previously, for multisport athletes, running LT is often 5 to 10 beats higher than cycling LT. Hence, if you did the cycling test and found your LT heart rate to be around 168, your running LTHR would probably be around 173 to 178.

Power Meters

Training with power is becoming more popular, and that's good news. There are several power meter companies competing for your business, which means they'll be cheaper.

You can blend the use of a power meter with the heart rate intervals given in this book, using the following guidelines. When you test for LT heart rate using the time trial outlined in Appendix A, use the 30-minute time frame. Using your power meter, collect the average power you produced during the 30-minute period, along with the average heart rate you produced. To estimate lactate threshold power (LTP), take the average power produced during the 30-minute time trial and subtract 5 percent. For example, if the average power of your 30-minute time trial was 250 watts, your LTP is approximately 250 minus (250 × 0.05), or 238 watts.

To use power-based intervals in the training plans, utilize the range of power in that zone. Begin with power in the low end of the zone and progress to power in the high end. For example, if lactate threshold power is 238 watts, the interval power range for Zone 4 is 259 to 282 watts. Therefore, if a workout calls for 4 × 6 minutes at Zone 4 intensity, instead of shooting for a heart rate, aim for 259 to 282 watts. It's best to begin on the low end of the wattage on the first interval and plan to finish strong on the last interval, producing average wattage at the high end of the zone.

When training with power, notice how your heart rate responds to the power-based intervals. Combining heart rate, power, and RPE is the best of all worlds. You'll notice that the three numbers might not match past performances for a given situation. If this happens, evaluate the cause. Know that your fitness, life stresses, weather, course profile, and current fatigue levels all affect the numbers.

For athletes with access to multiple power systems, note that power output on System 1 is relative to System 1, and power output on System 2 is relative to System 2. Power output values from the two systems might not match.

Why Use Power and Not Heart Rate?

I've found that using heart rate as a tachometer for high-end speed training (Zones 4 to 5) can be inaccurate and difficult to monitor. In fact, for short sprints, a heart rate monitor is useless. For longer intervals, many athletes ride the first couple of intervals too fast and end up with fading speed at the end of the set. A power meter allows you to be more consistent with energy and speed, aiming for a strong finish.

Tests to Check for Progress

How do you know if your training plan is working? Race or tour conditions, group tactics, and sometimes event courses can change from season to season, so your event results can be a misleading measure of fitness and training. That's why I suggest you measure training progress at regular intervals, such as every four, six, or eight weeks, with each test preceded by reduced volume and rest.

Chapter 3 has more information on periodization plan construction and the use of rest weeks. You should take a rest week every three to four weeks. During the rest week, volume is reduced and intensity is kept in some of the workouts. Some of the intense or fast workouts can be fitness testing. I like to use standard tests that can be repeated each rest week. It's best if the tests are done under circumstances that can be repeated; the easiest way is on an indoor trainer.

AEROBIC TIME TRIALS

Early in the fitness-building plan, do aerobic time trials. As mentioned previously, these are done during the rest week. An aerobic time trial is done at a particular heart rate. In this case, it is LTHR minus 9 to 11 beats. For example, if your cycling LTHR is 163, your aerobic time trial is done at a heart rate between 152 and 154. If you have access to a CompuTrainer or a similar indoor wattage meter with the calibration mode, you can ride a 5-mile time trial and be reasonably sure the resistance against your tire will be the same for the next time trial. Be sure you calibrate the trainer each time you test.

Select a gear in which you can turn the cranks at 85 to 120 revolutions per minute (rpm) for the entire time trial. You won't change gears during the test. Before the time trial, warm up in heart rate Zones 1 and 2 for 20 to 30 minutes. Toward the end of the warm-up, elevate your heart rate into the aerobic time trial zone. Go right into the time trial, not stopping to rest or stretch out. Ride 5 miles steadily in the designated heart rate zone.

If you don't have an indoor trainer with a wattage readout, a regular cyclometer with a rear wheel pickup works, although the test won't be as accurate as one on equipment that can be calibrated. Do your best to set up the trainer and bicycle exactly the same way each time you do the test.

In your workout journal, record the date, the gear used, the time for the 5-mile time trial, any special bike setup notes, and comments. When you did the test in subsequent sessions, did the test seem easier, but your time didn't improve? Did the test seem too easy? Did you have trouble getting your bike set up on the trainer? Did you just change tires? Did you have trouble getting your heart rate into the aerobic zone? Comments like these may tell you if your setup contributed to poor results. Keep all your cycling time trial data in a single location so the information can be referenced at a later date.

You can also use the CompuTrainer LT test as another indicator of fitness. In this case, you compare your heart rates at the various power levels. Riding at the same wattage increments with a lower heart rate marks progress. You can also use the data to compare your fitness levels, year after year.

Figures A.1 and A.3 in Appendix A show Betsy Guist's fitness improvements. Betsy measured fitness in September of one year and compared it with results a year later. She was able to produce higher wattages for the given heart rates the second year compared with a year earlier. In other words, Betsy was able to ride any particular wattage at less cost—a lower heart rate. The improvements also allowed the achievement of a higher maximum wattage.

Another marker of improvement using the CompuTrainer lactate threshold test is the ability to achieve a higher wattage at lactate threshold in relation to body weight. Some people lose weight, only to lose muscle mass and power. If your lactate threshold power (LTP) is 300 watts and your body weight (BW) is 128 pounds, your LTP as a function of body weight (LTP/BW) is 2.34.

If you maintained 300 watts as your LTP but lost 10 pounds, your LTP/BW would equal 2.54. If you lost that 10 pounds and your LTP also decreased to 250 watts, your LTP/BW would be 2.12. So if you lost weight to go faster and also lost power, the weight reduction did not improve your speed.

BAD TEST RESULTS

Through time trials and data collection, you can chart your progress during the season and from one year to the next. You can use the data to make changes in your training or as reinforcement that your training is going well. This information can be more accurate and timely than a race situation, which will help you shape your training for the season.

But what if your test data show no improvement, or worse yet, show that fitness or speed is degrading? Does that mean your season is heading down the tubes? Is your training completely off? Sometimes test data show no improvement, even when you know you're getting stronger. The data may show slow numbers because you were on the edge of becoming ill, tired from a restless night, or unmotivated. You may do poorly in one of your tests and within a week have a personal best performance in a race.

Pay close attention to subjective test and training comments in addition to raw test results. If one test came up slower but other workouts show you are making significant progress, don't make drastic changes to your training just yet.

GOAL SETTING

Multitasking has become a worldwide way of life. Go, go, go! Do, do, do! Faster, faster, faster! Cyclists of every fitness level know the challenge of trying to fit another group ride, or a longer ride, into their week. But most cyclists are riding with a major objective in mind that necessitates scrutiny of their schedule. Whether it is a short- or long-term goal, it's worth assessing how to make the most of your time in order to reach it. Identifying a goal allows you to work backward and design a plan for success. If you set a goal that is weeks or months away, creating subgoals helps you track your progress and provides opportunities to feel good about your efforts.

You may think setting goals will only add to your busy life, but it actually provides you with an opportunity to stop and recognize your accomplishments. It's important to pause long enough to appreciate

and celebrate what you've done. These moments reinforce your re-
solve to press forward or to shoot for a new goal. Goal setting may
seem simple, but well-crafted goals have certain characteristics.

Be Positive

A goal should explain what you want to achieve, as opposed to what
you don't want to happen. State your goals in positive terms. For
example, "I don't want to be dropped on Sunday group rides" is a
negative statement—something you don't want to happen. Instead,
make "Stay with the group on the Sunday ride" your major goal. This
means that even if you have to draft someone the entire time, you
want to stay with the pack.

Challenge Yourself

Don't make your goals too easy. You shouldn't be 100 percent certain you can achieve them. If you already stay with the group on
Sunday rides, that's no longer a challenge. Instead, a goal might be
"Go to the front and lead for part of a group ride." This goal is stated
in positive terms, and it's going to make you work harder.

Set Achievable Goals

A common mistake involves making goals *too* challenging. If your
goals are so challenging that they become impossible, you will be
easily discouraged. Goals need to be within reach. It's easy to get
discouraged and quit if a goal seems impossible to achieve. An eager
rider might make a goal to ride every day for the next six months,
but it's too restrictive; missing one day the second week of the plan
makes achieving the goal impossible.

A goal that's achievable and still provides health benefits might
be "Ride bike and strength train between five and seven times a week
for the next six months." You may even add an illness disclaimer:
"Being sick will not count against me." This kind of goal statement
encourages the healthy behavior of consistency and exercise with
enough flexibility for unforeseeable interruptions.

Healthy goals also consider your lifestyle. The best athletes have strong career and family ties. Athletic goals that put your job and relationships at risk are not balanced and need close examination.

Base Your Goals on You

Your goals should be based on your performance and within your control, not someone else's. Trying to measure up to someone else can be disappointing. Say you achieve a goal of riding faster than Gale on next Sunday's ride, only to learn that Gale is just getting over the flu. Will you feel success or a shallow victory?

You can use other people as benchmarks for your fitness goals, but there's no way for you to control their training or how they ride. Have other ways to measure your success, such as "Improve my 5-mile time trial speed from 16 mph." Achieve that goal, and you might end up outpedaling Gale. Measure success against yourself as often as possible.

If you set a goal to race and place within a certain percentage of the field or to make it to the podium, your achievement of the goal will be based on how other people ride and place. While that ultimate goal is based on other people, establishing subgoals based on improving your own performance will increase the odds that you will place well in a race.

Be Specific

This can be tough. Instead of saying, "I want to ride fast," say, "I want to improve my speed for a 5-mile time trial from 15 mph." In this case, any time improvement is acceptable.

I always ask riders who want my coaching help this question: "At the end of our first season together, how will we know if we were successful?" A common response is "If I'm a better rider." But how will we know when you've become a better rider? What does a better rider look like? Below is a list of more specific goals describing a better rider:

- Improve my average speed on the dump loop from the current 17 mph.
- Ride 50 miles in a single day .
- Improve my hill riding so that I can ride Carter Lake Hill without walking.
- Complete a 40 km time trial.
- Ride 100 miles in a single day.
- Complete a three-day tour, averaging three hours of riding each day.
- Feel strong on the group rides.

Notice that some of the goals are number-specific, while others are more subjective. Anyone could look at your performance and see that your average speed changed from 17 mph to 18 mph on the dump loop, but only you will know if you're feeling strong on group rides. Although the measurement is subjective, you can still measure your success. For example, on a scale of one to seven—one being the best—how would you rate your hill climbing today? Ask yourself that question every couple of weeks. Can you see progress?

Another example of a behavioral goal is "I will begin hills conservatively and plan to finish each one stronger than I started." You can subjectively judge the difference between blasting up the bottom half of the hill and fading at the top, and beginning with a smooth, relaxed cadence and finishing the hill strong. Although the goal seems subjective, you may also measure success by looking at average speed for the last quarter of the hill climb.

Subgoals

Chapter 3 gives specific training plans to complete specific goals, such as "Ride 100K or 50 miles, averaging 14.3 mph, at the end of 12 weeks." Since it will be three months before you complete the goal, I suggest you look at the training plan and shoot for three subgoals each week.

Your subgoals can come from the training plan; they can be nutritional in nature, recovery-oriented, or in another area you need to work on. For example, your goals for one week might be:

• Complete the Saturday two-hour ride.
• Drink enough fluids daily so my urine is light straw-colored .
• Get between seven and eight hours of rest each night.

So each week, jot down three things you want to accomplish. As you complete each one, give it a check mark and celebrate. Accomplish three subgoals each week for thirteen weeks, and you have thirty-nine reasons why you achieved your ultimate goal.

Celebrations

Kids really know how to celebrate: They jump up and down, victory dance, and shout with joy. Then they run to tell their parents and relive the moment again and again. The best part is that they celebrate even the smallest accomplishments.

Unfortunately, many adults have lost that childlike ability to celebrate. Find it again! It's the celebration of each small success that will help propel you toward a larger goal. Whether others are told of your accomplishments or they are kept private, take a moment to recognize your success—and maybe do a victory dance.

• • •

THE UTILIZATION OF TRAINING INTENSITY ZONES IS IMPORTANT TO fitness improvement. A heart rate monitor is a valuable tool that can give immediate feedback on exercise intensity. Exercising heart rate in conjunction with regular time trials can measure training progress. Time trials, exercise journal information, and subjective feelings are all tools to evaluate training progress.

Goals and subgoals are handy tools for achieving success. Improve your chances for accomplishing your goals by writing them down instead of allowing them to float in your head. Take time to celebrate success before pressing on to the next goal.

chapter three

Training Plans

Unless you try to do something beyond what you have already mastered, you will never grow. —RALPH WALDO EMERSON

Books on training can frustrate busy athletes because many give guidelines for plan preparation rather than including ready-to-use plans. If you don't have time to sit down and write a plan for yourself, this chapter is for you.

The five training plans included here each have a specific goal, so you'll know what you should be able to do when you complete them. All the plans have an athlete profile, a description of who would benefit most from the plan, and some typical questions and answers. If you find the training plans offered here to be appetizers and you want to take a stab at designing your own training plan, check out Joe Friel's *The Cyclist's Training Bible* (VeloPress).

All of the plans follow a periodization format to introduce your body to training stresses in a planned and controlled manner. At the same time, rest periods allow your body to repair, recover, and achieve a higher level of fitness.

A written plan helps you see the future and be patient. Those without plans often train like maniacs for two weeks and then become ill, injured, or burned-out—and give up. Sometimes you have a plan, but it's poorly designed. A good example is the ever-increasing riding plan, using the common rule of thumb, 10 percent. Three months before a group tour, you begin with what seems to be a reasonable idea: Increase volume each week to prepare for the event. And so it goes; the riding volume increases slightly each week so that by the time the tour comes, you are fried and have no desire to ride. You need to schedule some rest weeks within your plan.

The twelve- to thirteen-week plans are pared down to provide minimal amounts of training necessary to complete the goal, while the six-month plans offer more variety and more dramatic results.

SPECIFIC WORKOUTS

All of the workouts are based on the training heart rates you determined for yourself by doing one of the tests in Appendix A. If you aren't fit, you shouldn't do the lactate threshold test, and you should consult a physician before beginning an exercise program. If you have any special health conditions, it would be wise to consult a physician about any special restrictions he or she may place on your exercise intensities.

WARM-UP AND COOL-DOWN

Always warm up before beginning intervals, tempo rides, or races. A warm-up needs to be 10 to 30 minutes, depending on the particular workout and how much time you have assigned. This means beginning in Zone 1 and slowly increasing speed so that your heart rate is close to the zone in which you will be doing the work intervals. If you can't get your heart rate into the specified zone by the third interval, quit trying, slow down, and head home; it wasn't your day.

After each workout and race, spin easily to cool down. By the end of your cool-down, your heart rate should be Zone 1 or less. Stretch your muscles shortly after a cool-down.

CYCLING WORKOUT CODES
Endurance Workouts

E1 (z1). Ride in the small chainring on a flat course, keeping your heart rate in Zone 1. Some of the plans allow for E1 crosstraining. Keep in mind the target heart rate zones will be different for each sport. If you do aerobics or cross-country ski as crosstraining, you can use perceived exertion to gauge your intensity level.

E2 (z1–2). This level is used for aerobic maintenance and endurance training. Your heart rate should stay primarily in Zones 1 and 2. How much time is spent in each zone depends on how you feel that day. Ride on a rolling course if possible, with grades up to 4 percent. For reference, most highway off-ramps are 4 percent grade. Remain in the saddle on the hills. If you ride with a group and have an E2 ride to do, you must have the discipline to let the group go if the other riders want to hammer.

E3 (z1–3). This workout is used for endurance training and the beginning of lactate threshold training. Ride a rolling course in Zones 1 to 3. Stay seated on the hills to build and maintain hip power. Ride a course and use gearing that allows you to work intensity into Zone 3, but not so hard that you break into Zones 4 and 5.

E4 (z1–4). This is a multifaceted workout to build endurance, speed, and strength. The first time you do an E4 workout, keep your heart rate in Zones 1 to 4. As you continue to do more E4 workouts, you can spend some time in Zone 5. The final progression is to spend more time in Zones 4 and 5. This progression is not detailed in the plans and is left to the individual athlete. If hills are available, ride a hilly course for this workout.

Speed Workouts

S1—Spin Step-ups. This workout helps improve pedaling form and neuromuscular coordination. On an indoor trainer: Warm up with low resistance and a pedaling cadence of 90 revolutions per minute. After 15 to 20 minutes, increase the cadence to 100 rpm for 3 minutes, 110 rpm for 2 minutes, and more than 120 rpm for

1 minute. If time allows, spin easy for 5 minutes to recover, and repeat.

If you are just beginning to increase pedaling speed, you may have to cut all of the times in half to maintain the recommended speeds. It is important that the resistance be low to allow you to focus on the speed of your feet and not force on the pedals.

This workout can be done on the road if it is flat or slightly downhill.

S2—Isolated Leg. This workout helps work the dead spot out of your pedal stroke. After warming up with light resistance on an indoor trainer, do 100 percent of the work with one leg while the other leg is resting on a stool. You can do this on the road outdoors by relaxing one leg while the other leg does 90 percent of the work.

Change legs when fatigue sets in or set an interval to prevent excess fatigue. Work up to a work interval of 30 to 60 seconds per leg. After doing a work segment with each leg, spin easily with both legs for a minute, and then go back to single-leg work.

Stop pedaling with one leg if you become sloppy. Don't worry about achieving any particular heart rate; smooth pedaling form is most important. Begin with a total of 3 to 5 minutes on each leg and build time as you become stronger. The plans included in this chapter suggest times of work for each leg.

S3—Accelerations. This workout is for leg speed and the neuromuscular pathways. Warm up well, then do the specified number of 30-second accelerations, spinning an easy 2 minutes and 30 seconds between accelerations. The end of the 30 seconds should be faster than the beginning. On the plans, it looks something like 4–6 × 30" (2' 30" RI), which means do four to six repeats of 30-second accelerations, with 2.5-minute rest intervals between accelerations.

Muscular Endurance Workouts

M1 (z3)—Tempo. This workout begins lactate threshold speed work. After a warm-up on a mostly flat course, ride in Zone 3 for the time indicated on the plan.

M2 (z3)—Cruise Intervals. These intervals will also begin work on lactate threshold speed in the early season. On a mostly flat course or an indoor trainer, complete the number of intervals given on the plan, allowing your heart rate to rise into Zone 3 over the course of the interval.

For example, 4–5 × 4" (1" RI) means after your warm-up, ride four or five repeats of 4 minutes, allowing your pulse to rise into Zone 3 and no higher. After your heart rate is in Zone 3, try to hold it there until the end of the interval. Begin timing the interval as soon as you begin an increased effort—do not wait to begin the clock when your heart rate is in Zone 3. (All work intervals begin when effort is increased, and rest intervals begin when effort is decreased.) Spin easily and recover for 1 minute between efforts.

M2 (z4–5a)—Cruise Intervals. These intervals are for lactate threshold speed as the season and your fitness progress. On a mostly flat course or indoor trainer, complete the number of intervals given on the plan, allowing your heart rate to rise into Zones 4 to 5a over the course of the interval. For example, 4–5 × 4" (1" RI) means after your warm-up, ride four or five repeats of 4 minutes, allowing your pulse to rise into Zones 4 to 5a and no higher. After your heart rate is in Zones 4 to 5a, try to hold it there until the end of the interval. Take 1 minute to spin your legs and recover between work intervals.

M3 (z3)—Hill Cruise Intervals. Same as M2 (z3) except on a long 2 to 4 percent grade.

M3 (z4)—Hill Cruise Intervals. Same as M2 (z4–5a) except on a long 2 to 4 percent grade.

M6 (z4–5a)—Tempo. This workout is for lactate threshold speed. After a warm-up on a mostly flat course, ride in Zones 4 to 5a for the time indicated on the plan.

Speed Endurance (Anaerobic) and Taper Workouts

Some of the workouts specify a rolling course or a hilly course, which is relative to where you live. In general, a rolling course has grades up to about 4 percent, and a hilly course has steeper grades. If you live in Flat City, simulate hills by shifting up a gear or two to make the pedaling seem like a hill ride.

A1a (z1–3)—Easy Group Ride. This particular workout is not anaerobic but is part of a series of group rides. Ride with a group, and stay mostly in Zones 1 to 3.

A1b (z1–4)—Faster-Paced Group Ride. Ride with a group, and stay mostly in Zones 1 to 4. Some time can be spent in Zone 5, but keep it minimal.

A1c (all zones)—Fast, Aggressive Group Ride. Ride with a group, and ride in all zones. Be aggressive and power up the hills, chase riders who might have been faster than you in the past, and most important—have fun!

A1d—Ride as You Feel. If you're feeling great, ride aggressively with some time in all zones; if you're tired, take it easy.

A2 (z5b)—Speed Endurance Intervals. After a good warm-up on a mostly flat course, do the specified number of intervals, allowing your heart rate to climb into Zone 5b. The intervals may be done on a flat course or slightly uphill. For example, 4–5 × 3" (3" RI) means do four or five repeats of 3 minutes getting your heart rate into Zone 5b and keep it there until the end of the interval. Take 3 minutes between intervals.

A6 (z5b–c)—Hill Repetitions. After a good warm-up, go to a 6 to 8 percent grade hill and complete the specified number of 90-second hill repetitions. Stay seated for the first 60 seconds as you build to Zone 5b, then shift to a higher gear, stand, and drive the bike to the top, allowing your heart rate to climb into Zone 5c. Recover completely for 3 to 4 minutes between repetitions.

A7 (z4–5a)—Taper Intervals. After a good warm-up, do the specified number of 90-second accelerations, getting your heart rate into Zones 4 to 5a. Take 3 full minutes to recover and get your heart rate back to Zone 1 before going to the next interval. On the plans, the intervals will look like 4–5 × 1' 30" (3" RI). These intervals help keep your legs feeling fresh and speedy while volume is tapering prior to a race or important ride.

TESTING

T1—Aerobic Time Trial (ATT). This workout is best done on a CompuTrainer or similar trainer with a rear-wheel computer pickup. Power readings are optional, but change in wattage output over the course of time is a good indicator of fitness improvements. The ATT can also be done on a flat section of road, but weather conditions, such as wind and heat, will affect the results. After a warm-up, ride 5 miles with your heart rate 9 to 11 beats below your lactate threshold heart rate. Use a single gear, and don't shift during the test. Record the gear you used, your time, and how you felt in your training journal. Each time you repeat the test, try to make your testing conditions the same. As aerobic fitness improves, the time should decrease.

T2—As-Fast-as-You-Can-Go Time Trial (TT). After a 15- to 30-minute warm-up, complete a 5- to 8-mile time trial as fast as you can possibly ride. If you are a novice, use 5 miles. You may find that you need to use a distance somewhere between 5 and 8 miles because your course dictates the exact distance. Your course needs to be free of stop signs and heavy traffic. You can use a course with a turnaround point. Use any gear you wish, and shift anytime. Each time you repeat the test, try to make testing conditions—wind, temperature, subjective feelings, outside stressors—as similar as possible.

CROSSTRAINING

XT. Some of the plans show an option of crosstraining, such as aerobics, cross-country skiing, and in-line skating. Keep in mind your crosstraining sport heart rates will not match your cycling heart rate. Use RPE to estimate correct training zones. These workouts should be mostly easy.

PLANS

All of the plans assume you have some level of current fitness. They are not written for someone just beginning an exercise program. Most of the plans have at least an aerobic time trial and perhaps an all-out time trial somewhere within them. As one measure of your fitness gains, you can do a baseline time trial before beginning one of the plans. Use the 5-mile aerobic time trial for this. Before beginning any of the plans, determine your lactate threshold heart rate from one of the tests in Appendix A and then do an aerobic time trial (T1) before beginning the plan. Use the Q&A section at the end of the chapter to help with common questions.

Note that for all of the plans, the cycling workout codes can be found on pages 57–61. Strength workout codes are detailed on pages 93–98.

PLAN 1 Ride 100K or 50 Miles

WEEK		MONDAY	TUESDAY	WEDNESDAY	
1	Time	1:00		1:00	
	Workout	Strength	Day off	Strength	
	Specifics	AA		AA	
2	Time	1:00		1:00	
	Workout	Strength	Day off	Strength	
	Specifics	AA		AA	
3	Time	1:00		0:30	
	Workout	Strength	Day off	E2	
	Specifics	AA			
4	Time	1:00		1:00	
	Workout	Strength	Day off	Strength	
	Specifics	AA		AA	
5	Time	1:00		1:00	
	Workout	Strength	Day off	Strength	
	Specifics	AA		AA	
6	Time	1:00		1:00	
	Workout	Strength	Day of	Strength	
	Specifics	SM		SM	

Plan 1

Goal: Ride 100K or 50 miles, averaging 14.3 mph at the end of 12 weeks.

Profile: If you're currently riding about four hours per week and looking for a new challenge, and you have between three and seven hours available to train each week, this plan is for you.

Plan 2

Goal: Ride 100 miles, averaging 16 mph at the end of 12 weeks.

Profile: If you're currently riding at least four hours per week and doing some strength training, and don't have a lot of time to train but would like to complete a century, this plan is for you.

THURSDAY	FRIDAY	SATURDAY	SUNDAY	WEEKLY TOTAL
0:30		0:30	1:00	4:00
S3	Day off	E1 (z1)	E2 (z1–2)	
4 x 30" (2' 30" RI)				
0:30		0:45	1:00	4:15
S2	Day off	E1 (z1)	E2 (z1–2)	
3–5 min ea. leg				
0:30			1:00	3:00
S3	Day off	Day off	E2 (z1–2)	
4 x 30" (2' 30" RI)				
0:30		0:45	1:15	4:30
S2	Day off	E1 (z1)	E2 (z1–2)	
3–5 min ea. leg				
0:30		1:00	1:30	5:00
S3	Day off	E1 (z1)	E2 (z1–2)	
4–5 x 30" (2' 30" RI)				
0:45		1:00	1:30	5:15
S3	Day off	E1 (z1)	E2 (z1–2)	
5–6 x 30" (2' 30" RI)				

CONTINUES

PLAN 1 Ride 100K or 50 Miles (continued)

WEEK		MONDAY	TUESDAY	WEDNESDAY	
7	Time	1:00	Day off	0:45	
	Workout	Strength		T1	
	Specifics	SM		5-mile ATT	
8	Time	1:00	Day off	1:00	
	Workout	Strength		Strength	
	Specifics	SM		SM	
9	Time	1:00	Day off	1:00	
	Workout	Strength		Strength	
	Specifics	SM		SM	
10	Time	1:00	Day off	1:00	
	Workout	Strength		Strength	
	Specifics	SM		SM	
11	Time	1:00	Day off	0:45	
	Workout	Strength		T1	
	Specifics	SM		5-mile ATT	
12	Time	1:00	Day off	0:45	
	Workout	Strength		E2 (z1-2)	
	Specifics	SM (lighten weights)			

PLAN 2 Ride 100 Miles

WEEK		MONDAY	TUESDAY	WEDNESDAY	
1	Time	1:00	1:00	1:00	
	Workout	Strength	E2 (z1-2)	Strength	
	Specifics	AA		AA	
2	Time	1:00	1:00	1:00	
	Workout	Strength	E2 (z1-2)	Strength	
	Specifics	AA		AA	
3	Time	1:00	Day off	1:00	
	Workout	Strength		Strength	
	Specifics	AA		PE	

THURSDAY	FRIDAY	SATURDAY	SUNDAY	WEEKLY TOTAL
0:30		0:30	1:00	3:45
S2	Day off	E1 (z1)	E2 (z1-2)	
5-6 min ea. leg				
0:45		1:00	2:00	5:45
E2	Day off	E1 (z1)	E3 (z1-3)	
0:45		1:00	2:15	6:00
E2	Day off	E1 (z1)	E3 (z1-3)	
0:45		1:15	2:30	6:30
E2	Day off	E2 (z1-2)	E3 (z1-3)	
		1:00	1:15	4:00
Day off	Day off	E2 (z1-2)	E1 (z1)	
0:30			3:30	5:45
S3	Day off	Day off	Ride 50 miles	
4 x 30" (2' 30" RI)				

THURSDAY	FRIDAY	SATURDAY	SUNDAY	WEEKLY TOTAL
1:00		1:00	1:30	6:30
S3	Day off	E1 (z1)	E2 (z1-2)	
4 x 30" (2' 30" RI)				
1:00		1:00	2:00	7:00
S3	Day off	E1 (z1)	E2 (z1-2)	
6-8 x 30" (2' 30" RI)				
		0:45	1:30	4:15
		S3	E2 (z1-2)	
Day off	Day off	4-6 x 30" (2' 30" RI)		

CONTINUES

PLAN 2 Ride 100 Miles (continued)

WEEK		MONDAY	TUESDAY	WEDNESDAY	
4	Time	1:00	1:00	1:00	
	Workout	Strength	E2 (z1–2)	Strength	
	Specifics	PE		PE	
5	Time	1:00		1:00	
	Workout	Strength	Day off	Strength	
	Specifics	PE		PE	
6	Time	1:00	0:30	1:00	
	Workout	Strength	S2	Strength	
	Specifics	PE	3–5 min ea. leg	PE	
7	Time	1:00		0:45	
	Workout	Strength	Day off	E2	
	Specifics	PE			
8	Time	0:45		1:00	
	Workout	Strength	Day off	M1 (z3)	
	Specifics	SM		4–5 x 4' (1' RI)	
9	Time	0:45		1:00	
	Workout	Strength	Day off	M1 (z3)	
	Specifics	SM		3–5 x 5' (1' 30" RI)	
10	Time	0:45		1:15	
	Workout	Strength	Day off	M1 (z3)	
	Specifics	SM		3–4 x 6' (2' RI)	
11	Time	0:45		0:45	
	Workout	Strength	Day off	E2 (z1–2)	
	Specifics	SM			
12	Time	1:00		0:45	
	Workout	E2 (z1–2)	Day off	S3	
	Specifics			4–5 x 30" (2' 30" RI)	

THURSDAY	FRIDAY	SATURDAY	SUNDAY	WEEKLY TOTAL
		0:45	2:30	6:15
Day off	Day off	S2	E3 (z1-3)	
		3-5 min ea. leg		
1:00		1:30	3:00	7:30
M1 (z3)	Day off	E1 (z1)	E3 (z1-3)	
4-5 x 3' (1' RI)				
1:00		1:30	3:30	8:30
M1 (z3)	Day off	E2 (z1-2)	E3 (z1-3)	
5-6 x 3' (1' RI)				
		1:00	1:30	4:15
Day off	Day off	T1	E3 (z1-3)	
		5-mile ATT	(mostly z1-2)	
	1:00	Day off	4:00	6:45
Day off	E2		E3 (z1-3)	
0:30		1:15	4:30	8:00
E1 (z1)	Day off	E2 (z1-2)	E3 (z1-3)	
0:45		1:00	5:00	8:45
E1	Day off	S3	E3 (z1-3)	
		4-8 x 30" (2' 30" RI)		
		0:45	2:00	4:15
Day off	Day off	T1	E2 (z1-2)	
		5-mile ATT		
	0:30	Day off	6:00	8:15
Day off	S3		Ride 100 miles	
	2 x 30" (2' 30" RI)		16 mph	

Plan 3

Goal: Ride a three-day tour at the end of 13 weeks, averaging approximately three hours of riding each day.

Profile: This plan will suit you if you need to keep Tuesdays and

PLAN 3 Ride 3 Days, Average 3 Hours of Riding Each Day

WEEK		MONDAY	TUESDAY	WEDNESDAY
1	Time	1:00		1:00
	Workout	Strength	Day off	S2
	Specifics	AA		3–5 min ea. leg
2	Time	1:00		1:00
	Workout	Strength	Day off	S1
	Specifics	AA		
3	Time	1:00		1:00
	Workout	Strength	Day off	S2
	Specifics	AA		4–6 min ea. leg
4	Time	0:45		1:00
	Workout	Strength	Day off	T1
	Specifics	SM		5-mile ATT
5	Time	1:00		1:00
	Workout	Strength	Day off	S1
	Specifics	SM		
6	Time	1:00		1:00
	Workout	Strength	Day off	S1
	Specifics	SM		
7	Time	1:00		1:00
	Workout	Strength	Day off	T1
	Specifics	SM		5-mile ATT
8	Time	1:00		1:00
	Workout	Strength	Day off	M3 (z3)
	Specifics	SM		4–5 x 3' (1' RI)
9	Time	1:00		1:00
	Workout	Strength	Day off	S3
	Specifics	SM		6–8 x 30" (2' 30" RI)

Thursdays free for other commitments. Fridays need to be easy, and weekends need to be open to exercise hours. You currently do five to seven hours of exercise each week, at least three hours of which is cycling. The weekday workouts are structured so they can be done on an indoor trainer or at a gym.

THURSDAY	FRIDAY	SATURDAY	SUNDAY	WEEKLY TOTAL
	1:15	1:15	1:15	5:45
Day off	E1 (z1)	E2 (z1–2)	E1 (z1)	
	1:15	1:45	1:30	6:30
Day off	E1 (z1)	E2 (z1–2)	E1 (z1)	
	1:15	2:00	1:30	6:45
Day off	E1 (z1)	E2 (z1–2)	E1 (z1)	
		1:30	1:00	4:15
Day off	Day off	E2 (z1–2)	E2 (z1–2)	
	1:15	2:30	1:30	7:15
Day off	E1 (z1)	E2 (z1–2)	E2 (z1–2)	
	1:15	3:00	1:30	7:45
Day off	E1 (z1)	E2 (z1–2)	E2 (z1–2)	
	1:15	3:00	2:00	8:15
Day off	E1 (z1)	E3 (z1–3)	E1 (z1)	
		1:30	1:00	4:30
Day off	Day off	E2 (z1–2)	E2 (z1–2)	
	1:15	3:00	2:30	8:45
Day off	E1 (z1)	E3 (z1–3)	E2 (z1–2)	

CONTINUES

PLAN 3 Ride 3 Days, Average 3 Hours of Riding Each Day (continued)

WEEK		MONDAY	TUESDAY	WEDNESDAY
10	Time	1:00		1:00
	Workout	Strength	Day off	M3 (z3)
	Specifics	SM		4-5 x 3-4' (1' RI)
11	Time	1:00		1:00
	Workout	Strength	Day off	S3
	Specifics	SM		6-8 x 30" (2' 30"RI)
12	Time	0:45		1:00
	Workout	Strength	Day off	S3
	Specifics	SM		6-8 x 30" (2' 30" RI)
13	Time	0:45		0:30
	Workout	S3	Day off	S3
	Specifics	4-6 x 30" (2' 30" RI)		3-4 x 30" (2' 30" RI)

Plan 4

Goal: Ride a 40 km time trial, or ride faster on the weekend group rides.

Profile No. 1: This plan will work for you if you've been cycling for a few years, mostly in the summertime, but want to try a race, and a time trial seems like a good way to start. You may be doing the 40 km cycling leg for a triathlon team or doing a USA Cycling–sponsored time trial. Either way, you want to be fast on race day. You already cycle about three hours each week and strength train one or two times per week.

Profile No. 2: This plan will also work for you if you've been riding for years, mostly in the summertime, and have been frustrated when joining group rides. It seems like just when you are getting in shape in August or September, the group rides are dwindling. You already ride about three hours each week and strength train one or two times per week.

THURSDAY	FRIDAY	SATURDAY	SUNDAY	WEEKLY TOTAL
	1:30	3:30	2:30	9:30
Day off	E1 (z1)	E3 (z1-3)	E2 (z1-2)	
	1:30	4:00	2:30	10:00
Day off	E1 (z1)	E3 (z1-3)	E2 (z1-2)	
		1:30	1:00	4:15
Day off	Day off	E2 (z1-2)	T2	
			5-mile TT	
	3:00	3:00	3:00	10:15
Day off	Bike tour	Bike tour	Bike tour	

If you are looking to increase your cycling speed beyond a recreational level, it will require more than the three months summer can offer. More than likely, the faster cyclists in your club or group ride are those who maintain some type of cycling fitness year-round. If you want to be in reasonable shape for spring group rides and progressively get faster as summer approaches, this plan is for you.

Plan 5
Goal: Ride hills faster or improve speed on hilly weekend group rides.

Profile: This plan is written for those who already have several years of cycling experience. If you ride mostly in the summertime and are often frustrated when trying to climb hills and join group rides—particularly when the course is hilly—and you already cycle three hours each week and strength train one or two times per week, Plan 5 will help you improve.

To measure progress on hills, you can make your 5-mile time trial—not the aerobic time trial—on a section of road that includes a climb. You also could measure progress on this plan simply by noting how you feel climbing hills compared with years past.

The group rides are specified as hilly or rolling. The plan tapers and keys on a group ride at the end of 24 weeks of training. Your group rides will be getting progressively stronger from weeks 17 to

PLAN 4 40 km Time Trial or Faster Group Riding

WEEK		MONDAY	TUESDAY	WEDNESDAY
1	Time	1:00	0:45	1:00
	Workout	Strength	S2	Strength
	Specifics	AA	5-7 min ea. leg	AA
2	Time	1:00	0:45	1:00
	Workout	Strength	S1	Strength
	Specifics	AA		AA
3	Time	1:00	0:45	1:00
	Workout	Strength	S2	Strength
	Specifics	AA	6-8 min ea. leg	AA
4	Time	1:00	0:45	1:00
	Workout	Strength	S1	Strength
	Specifics	AA		AA
5	Time	1:15	1:00	1:15
	Workout	Strength	S2	Strength
	Specifics	MS	7-9 min ea. leg	MS
6	Time	1:15	1:00	1:15
	Workout	Strength	S1	Strength
	Specifics	MS		MS
7	Time	1:15	1:00	1:15
	Workout	Strength	S2	Strength
	Specifics	MS	8-10 min ea. leg	MS
8	Time	1:00		1:00
	Workout	Strength	Day off	Strength
	Specifics	MS		MS

24; however, the group ride at the end of the plan should be a humdinger. You'll be rested and ready to climb like a goat.

It is important to note that hill climbing requires technique as well as aerobic stamina and strength. If you begin a hill too fast, you will fizzle and fade by the end. Try to begin the hill repeats and hilly group rides a bit conservatively. Plan to finish each hill stronger than you began it.

THURSDAY	FRIDAY	SATURDAY	SUNDAY	WEEKLY TOTAL
1:00		1:00	1:00	5:45
E1 (z1)	Day off	E2 (z1-2)	E1 (z1)	
(or XT)			(or XT)	
1:00		1:00	1:00	5:45
E1 (z1)	Day off	E2 (z1-2)	E1 (z1)	
(or XT)			(or XT)	
1:00		1:00	1:00	5:45
E1 (z1)	Day off	E2 (z1-2)	E1 (z1)	
(or XT)			(or XT)	
1:00		1:00	1:00	5:45
E1 (z1)	Day off	T1	E1 (z1)	
(or XT)		5-mile ATT	(or XT)	
0:45		1:00	1:00	6:15
E2 (z1-2)	Day off	E2 (z1-2)	E1 (z1)	
(or XT)			(or XT)	
1:00	1:00	1:30	1:15	8:15
E1 (z1)	E1 (z1)	E2 (z1-2)	E1 (z1)	
(or XT)			(or XT)	
1:00	1:00	2:00	1:30	9:00
E1 (z1)	E1 (z1)	E2 (z1-2)	E1 (z1)	
(or XT)			(or XT)	
1:00		1:00	1:00	5:00
S1	Day off	T1	E2 (z1-2)	
		5-mile ATT		

CONTINUES

PLAN 4 40 km Time Trial or Faster Group Riding (continued)

WEEK		MONDAY	TUESDAY	WEDNESDAY	
9	Time	1:00	1:00	1:00	
	Workout	Strength	E2 (z1–2)	Strength	
	Specifics	PE		PE	
10	Time	1:00	1:00	1:00	
	Workout	Strength	E2 (z1–2)	Strength	
	Specifics	PE		PE	
11	Time	1:00	1:00	1:00	
	Workout	Strength	E2 (z1–2)	Strength	
	Specifics	PE		PE	
12	Time	1:00		1:00	
	Workout	Strength	Day off	S3	
	Specifics	PE		4–6 x 30" (2' 30" RI)	
13	Time	1:00	1:00	1:00	
	Workout	Strength	E2 (z1–2)	Strength	
	Specifics	SM		SM	
14	Time	1:00	1:00	1:00	
	Workout	Strength	E2 (z1–2)	Strength	
	Specifics	SM		SM	
15	Time	1:00	1:00	1:00	
	Workout	Strength	E2 (z1–2)	Strength	
	Specifics	SM		SM	
16	Time	0:45		1:00	
	Workout	Strength	Day off	E2 (z1–2)	
	Specifics	SM			
17	Time	1:00	1:00	1:00	
	Workout	Strength	S3	M2 (z4–5a)	
	Specifics	SM	4–8 x 30" (2' 30" RI)	4–5 x 3' (1' RI)	
18	Time	1:00	1:00	1:00	
	Workout	Strength	S3	M2 (z4–5a)	
	Specifics	SM	4–8 x 30" (2' 30" RI)	4–5 x 4' (1' RI)	
19	Time	0:45		1:00	
	Workout	Strength	Day off	M2 (z4–5a)	
	Specifics	SM		3–4 x 6' (2' RI)	

	THURSDAY	FRIDAY	SATURDAY	SUNDAY	WEEKLY TOTAL
	1:00 M2 (z3) 4-5 x 3' (1' RI)	Day off	1:15 E3 (z1-3)	2:00 E2 (z1-2)	7:15
	1:00 M2 (z3) 4-5 x 4' (1' RI)	Day off	1:30 E2 (z1-2)	2:30 E3 (z1-3)	8:00
	1:00 M2 (z3) 3-4 x 5' (1' 30" RI)	1:00 E1 (z1) (or Day off)	1:30 E2 (z1-2)	3:00 E3 (z1-3)	9:30
	1:00 E2 (z1-2)	Day off	1:00 T1 5-mile ATT	1:00 E2 (z1-2)	5:00
	1:00 S1	Day off	1:30 E4 (z1-4)	2:15 E2 (z1-2)	7:45
	1:00 E1 (z1)	0:45 E1 (z1) (or Day off)	2:00 E4 (z1-4)	2:30 E2 (z1-2)	9:15
	1:00 S1	0:45 E1 (z1) (or Day off)	2:00 E4 (z1-4)	3:15 E2 (z1-2)	10:00
	1:00 S3 4-6 x 30" (2' 30" RI)	Day off	1:00 T2 5-mile TT	1:15 E2 (z1-2)	5:00
	1:00 E2 (z1-2)	1:00 E1 (z1) (or Day off)	1:30 E2 (z1-2)	2:30 A1a (z1-3) Group ride	9:00
	1:00 E2 (z1-2)	1:00 E1 (z1) (or Day off)	1:30 E2 (z1-2)	2:30 A1b (z1-4) Group ride	9:00
	0:30 E1 (z1)	Day off	2:00 A1c Group ride	0:45 E1 (z1)	5:00

CONTINUES

PLAN 4 40 km Time Trial or Faster Group Riding (continued)

WEEK		MONDAY	TUESDAY	WEDNESDAY	
20	Time	1:00	1:15	1:15	
	Workout	Strength	S3	M2 (z4-5a)	
	Specifics	SM	4-8 x 30" (2' 30" RI)	3 x 8' (2' RI)	
21	Time	1:00	1:15	1:15	
	Workout	Strength	S3	M6 (z4-5a)	
	Specifics	SM	4-8 x 30" (2' 30" RI)	25-30 min (z4-5a)	
22	Time	1:00		1:00	
	Workout	Strength	Day off	E2 (z1-2)	
	Specifics	SM			
23	Time	1:00	1:00	1:15	
	Workout	Strength	E2 (z1-2)	M2 (z4-5a)	
	Specifics	SM		3-4 x 10' (3' 30" RI)	
24	Time	1:00	1:00	1:00	
	Workout	Strength	E2 (z1-2)	A2 (z5b)	
	Specifics	SM		4-5 x 3' (3' RI)	
25	Time		1:00	0:45	
	Workout	Day off	A7 (z4-5a)	A7 (z4-5a)	
	Specifics		4 x 90" (3' RI)	3 x 90" (3' RI)	

PLAN 5 Improve Hill Climbing

WEEK		MONDAY	TUESDAY	WEDNESDAY	
1	Time	1:00	0:45	1:00	
	Workout	Strength	S2	Strength	
	Specifics	AA	5-7 min ea. leg	AA	
2	Time	1:00	0:45	1:00	
	Workout	Strength	S1	Strength	
	Specifics	AA		AA	

THURSDAY	FRIDAY	SATURDAY	SUNDAY	WEEKLY TOTAL
1:15	0:30	1:15	2:30	9:00
E1 (z1)	E1 (z1)	E2 (z1–2)	A1c	
	(or Day off)		Group ride	
1:15	0:30	1:15	2:30	9:00
E1 (z1)	E1 (z1)	E2 (z1–2)	A1d	
	(or Day off)		Group ride	
1:00		1:00	1:00	5:00
S3	Day off	T2	E2 (z1–2)	
4-6 x 30" (2' 30" RI)		5-mile TT		
1:00	0:30	1:15	2:30	8:30
E1 (z1)	E1 (z1)	E2 (z1–2)	A1d	
	(or Day off)		Group ride	
1:00		2:00	1:30	7:30
E1 (z1)	Day off	A1c	E2 (z1–2)	
		Group ride		
	0:30	1:30	1:15	5:00
Day off	S3	Race 40K	E1 (z1)	
	3 x 30" (2' 30" RI)	Time trial	(or Day off)	

THURSDAY	FRIDAY	SATURDAY	SUNDAY	WEEKLY TOTAL
1:00		1:00	1:00	5:45
E1 (z1)	Day off	E2 (z1–2)	E1 (z1)	
(or XT)			(or XT)	
1:00		1:00	1:00	5:45
E1 (z1)	Day off	E2 (z1–2)	E1 (z1)	
(or XT)			(or XT)	

CONTINUED

PLAN 5 Improve Hill Climbing

WEEK		MONDAY	TUESDAY	WEDNESDAY
3	Time	1:00	0:45	1:00
	Workout	Strength	S2	Strength
	Specifics	AA	6–8 min ea. leg	AA
4	Time	1:00	0:45	1:00
	Workout	Strength	S1	Strength
	Specifics	AA		AA
5	Time	1:15	1:00	1:15
	Workout	Strength	S2	Strength
	Specifics	MS	7–9 min ea. leg	MS
6	Time	1:15	1:00	1:15
	Workout	Strength	S1	Strength
	Specifics	MS		MS
7	Time	1:15	1:00	1:15
	Workout	Strength	S2	Strength
	Specifics	MS	8–10 min ea. leg	MS
8	Time	1:00		1:00
	Workout	Strength	Day off	Strength
	Specifics	MS		MS
9	Time	1:00	1:00	1:00
	Workout	Strength	E2	Strength
	Specifics	PE		PE
10	Time	1:00	1:00	1:00
	Workout	Strength	E2 (z1–2)	Strength
	Specifics	PE		PE
11	Time	1:00	1:00	1:00
	Workout	Strength	E2 (z1–2)	Strength
	Specifics	PE		PE
12	Time	1:00		1:00
	Workout	Strength	Day off	S3
	Specifics	PE		4–6 x 30" (2' 30" RI)
13	Time	1:00	1:00	1:00
	Workout	Strength	E2 (z1–2)	Strength
	Specifics	SM		SM

THURSDAY	FRIDAY	SATURDAY	SUNDAY	WEEKLY TOTAL
1:00		1:00	1:00	5:45
E1 (z1)	Day off	E2 (z1–2)	E1 (z1)	
(or XT)			(or XT)	
1:00		1:00	1:00	5:45
E1 (z1)	Day off	T1	E1 (z1)	
(or XT)		5-mile ATT	(or XT)	
0:45		1:00	1:00	6:15
E2 (z1–2)	Day off	E2 (z1–2)	E1 (z1)	
(or XT)			(or XT)	
1:00	1:00	1:30	1:15	8:15
E1 (z1)	E1 (z1)	E2 (z1–2)	E1 (z1)	
(or XT)			(or XT)	
1:00	1:00	2:00	1:30	9:00
E1 (z1)	E1 (z1)	E2 (z1–2)	E1 (z1)	
(or XT)			(or XT)	
1:00		1:00	1:00	5:00
S1	Day off	T1	E2 (z1–2)	
		5-mile ATT		
1:00		1:15	2:00	7:15
M2 (z3)	Day off	E3 (z1–3)	E2 (z1–2)	
4–5 x 3' (1' RI)				
1:00		1:30	2:30	8:00
M2 (z3)	Day off	E2 (z1–2)	E3 (z1–3)	
4–5 x 4' (1' RI)				
1:00	1:00	1:30	3:00	9:30
M2 (z3)	E1 (z1)	E2 (z1–2)	E3 (z1–3)	
3–4 x 5' (1' 30" RI)	(or Day off)			
1:00		1:00	1:00	5:00
E2 (z1–2)	Day off	T1	E2 (z1–2)	
		5-mile ATT		
1:00		1:30	2:15	7:45
S1	Day off	E4 (z1–4)	E2 (z1–2)	

CONTINUES

PLAN 5 Improve Hill Climbing (continued)

WEEK		MONDAY	TUESDAY	WEDNESDAY	
14	Time	1:00	1:00 (z1–2)	1:00	
	Workout	Strength	E2	Strength	
	Specifics	SM		SM	
15	Time	1:00	1:00	1:00	
	Workout	Strength	E2 (z1–2)	Strength	
	Specifics	SM		SM	
16	Time	0:45		1:00	
	Workout	Strength	Day off	E2 (z1–2)	
	Specifics	SM			
17	Time	1:00	1:00	1:00	
	Workout	Strength	S3	M3 (z4–5a)	
	Specifics	SM	4–8 x 30" (2' 30" RI)	4–6 x 3' (1' RI)	
18	Time	1:00	1:00	1:00	
	Workout	Strength	S3	A6 (z5b–c)	
	Specifics	SM	4–8 x 30" (2' 30" RI)	4–5 x 90" (3' RI)	
19	Time	0:45		1:00	
	Workout	Strength	Day off	S3	
	Specifics	SM		6–8 x 30" (2' 30" RI)	
20	Time	1:00	1:15	1:15	
	Workout	Strength	S3	M3 (z4–5a)	
	Specifics	SM	4–8 x 30" (2' 30" RI)	4–5 x 3–4' (1' RI)	
21	Time	1:00	1:15	1:15	
	Workout	Strength	S3	A2 (z5b)	
	Specifics	SM	4–8 x 30" (2' 30" RI)	4–5 x 3' uphill (3' RI)	
22	Time	1:00		1:00	
	Workout	Strength	Day off	E2 (z1)	
	Specifics	SM			

THURSDAY	FRIDAY	SATURDAY	SUNDAY	WEEKLY TOTAL
1:00	0:45	2:00	2:30	9:15
E1 (z1)	E1 (z1)	E4 (z1-4)	E2 (z1-2)	
	(or Day off)			
1:00	0:45	2:00	3:15	10:00
S1	E1 (z1)	E4 (z1-4)	E2 (z1-2)	
	(or Day off)			
1:00		1:00	1:15	5:00
S3	Day off	T2	E2 (z1-2)	
4-6 x 30" (2' 30" RI)		5-mile TT		
1:00	1:00	1:30	2:30	9:00
E2 (z1-2)	E1 (z1)	E2 (z1-2)	A1a	
	(or Day off)		Group ride (hills)	
1:00	1:00	1:30	2:30	9:00
E2 (z1-2)	E1 (z1)	E2 (z1-2)	A1b	
	(or Day off)		Group ride (rolling)	
0:30		2:00	0:45	5:00
E1 (z1)	Day off	A1c	E1 (z1)	
		Uphill fast, down easy		
1:15	0:30	1:15	2:30	9:00
E1 (z1)	E1 (z1)	E2 (z1-2)	A1c	
	(or Day off)		Group ride (hills)	
1:15	0:30	1:15	2:30	9:00
E1 (z1)	E1 (z1)	E2 (z1-2)	A1b	
	(or Day off)		Group ride (rolling)	
1:00		1:00	1:00	5:00
S3	Day off	T2	E2 (z1-2)	
4-6 x 30" (2' 30" RI)		5-mile TT		

CONTINUES

PLAN 5 Improve Hill Climbing (continued)

WEEK		MONDAY	TUESDAY	WEDNESDAY
23	Time	1:00	1:00	1:15
	Workout	Strength	E2 (z1-2)	A2 (z5b)
	Specifics	SM		4-5 x 3' uphill (3' RI)
24	Time	1:00	1:00	1:00
	Workout	Strength	E2 (z1-2)	A6 (z5b-c)
	Specifics	SM		4-5 x 90" (3' RI)
25	Time		0:45	0:45
	Workout	Day off	A7 (z4-5a)	A7 (z4-5a)
	Specifics		4 x 1' 30" (3' RI)	3 x 30" (3' RI)

Q&A

Should I always shoot for the highest number when a range is given?
No. A range is given on some workouts to allow you to customize
the workout for how you feel. Also, if you are in a time crunch and
have to cut the workout short, go for fewer repetitions.

*If a workout prescribes two hours and I'm feeling great, can I just go
ahead and do three hours?*
In general, on long rides aim for plus or minus about 30 minutes.
On shorter weekday rides, aim for plus or minus 15 minutes.

*What happens if I get in a real time crunch and can do only 30 minutes
of a 60-minute workout, or I have to skip it altogether?*
Realistically, you will probably miss a few workouts. If you're
going to skip a workout, start with an E1 that's an hour or less.
The priority workouts are usually the long weekend rides that are

	THURSDAY	FRIDAY	SATURDAY	SUNDAY	WEEKLY TOTAL
	1:00	0:30	1:15	2:30	8:30
	E1 (z1)	E1 (z1)	E2 (z1-2)	A1d	
		(or Day off)		Group ride (hills)	
	1:00		2:00	1:30	7:30
	E1 (z1)	Day off	A1c	E2 (z1-2)	
			Group ride (hills)		
		0:30	2:00	1:00	5:00
	Day off	S3	Fastest group ride you've ever done	E1 (z1)	
		3 x 30" (2' 30" RI)		(or Day off)	

continuously building volume, weekday intervals, and strength sessions.

What if I can ride faster than the goal paces for 50 and 100 miles?
You should be able to use the workout plans as they are. You can adjust the weekend rides if you prefer. In other words, if you can average 18 mph instead of 16 mph, you can adjust the weekend ride time by about about 1.3 percent (18 divided by 16). The adjustment isn't much and is within the guidelines in the answer to the second question in this section. For example, 13 percent of a three-hour ride is about 23 minutes.

Can I rearrange the workouts within the week? I work weekends.
Rearranging the workouts is fine, with a few guidelines: Keep at least forty-eight hours between strength training sessions; try to keep high-intensity sessions separated by forty-eight hours—unless otherwise called for in the original plan; do not try to make

up missed weekday workouts on the weekend. In other words, don't try to ride for six hours on Saturday if you missed three one-hour workouts during the week and you have a three-hour Saturday ride scheduled.

I can make it to the gym only once a week. Is one strength training session really worth it?
Once a week is better than none.

I want to use the three-day tour plan, but the ride I'm going on doesn't go three hours each day. My tour is approximately two hours, four hours, and three hours. Will Plan 3 still work for me?
Yes.

Can I train if I'm sick?
If your symptoms are above the neck and minimal—runny nose, headache, scratchy throat—go ahead and work out if you feel up to it. Cut your intensity to Zones 1 and 2. Reduce the total workout time or stop altogether if you feel bad once you get the workout started. If your symptoms are below the neck or intense—cough, chills, vomiting, achy muscles, fever, sore throat—don't even start the workout. A virus likely causes these symptoms. Trying to train through the illness carries the risk of a more serious illness that can have you sidelined for months. Missing a few days of training to get well is your best investment of time.

What happens if I miss some training days due to illness?
If you miss one to three days, resume your training as shown on the plan, skipping the workouts you missed. If you miss a week or more, consider pushing your goal forward, and depending on how you recover, you may want to repeat a week or two of training to get you back on track. Whatever you do, take it easy coming back—you don't want another setback.

I want to be a faster group rider, but I can train only five hours in any given week. Will I get results if I just reduce Plan 4 to accommodate my life?

If your group rides are going between two and three hours, it will become very difficult to keep improving on only five hours of training per week.

• • •

AS I SAID IN CHAPTER 2, THE MOST COMMON MISTAKES CYCLISTS make are riding the same speed all the time, being lax about nutrition and hydration, and having no specific goals or plans. This chapter suggests goals, gives you plans, and varies the riding speeds within the plans. Most athletes tell me that not having to design their own plan is great. They can come home, look at what they're supposed to do, and get on the bike.

At first glance, the codes and plans may seem confusing. After using them a while, you'll probably find them easier to decipher. It's important to know these plans aren't gender-specific. Adults of any age can use the tests in Appendix A and the plans in this chapter. They're intended for athletes looking for a new level in their cycling or the next step. Follow one of these plans, and you might find new speed and strength on the hills. Take your riding up a notch!

chapter four

Strength Training and Stretching

One athlete I worked with came to cycling from a running background. At 5 feet 1 inch and 105 pounds, her physique was that of a distance runner: slight upper body, thin arms, and powerful legs. When she first began to cycle, she didn't have the upper-body strength to pump her tires past 80 pounds per square inch (psi); they required 120 psi.

But after gaining both upper- and lower-body strength in a weight training program, she is now capable of pumping her own tires to 120 psi. Her husband noticed her strength gains on backpacking trips because she can now handle heavier loads for longer. She notices her strength because she's capable of doing many things she couldn't do before her weight training program—and she likes the look of those new muscles!

Many female athletes turn to strength training to enhance their performance in endurance events. Others are still holdouts, fearing the gym may turn them into hulking specimens capable of powerlifting small cars and looking more like a male than a female. With the right routine, it is possible for women to build big, thick muscles. That training routine, however, is different from the training routine to build the long, lean muscles of a fast endurance cyclist. If you are reading this book, I suspect you want the strength to climb hills or ride fast. A strength training program combined with an endurance program can help you with those goals.

Consider that our natural maximal muscular strength is achieved sometime in our twenties or early thirties. That's why anyone over 30 should invest some time in a strength training program. The older you are, the more you need the gym.

On average, women tend to be about half as strong as men in their upper bodies and about 30 percent weaker in their lower bodies in terms of absolute strength. Athletic women are generally stronger than nonathletic women; however, they are generally not as strong as athletic men in the same sport. Much of this strength difference is due to hormonal factors that give males greater muscle mass. Although women may not have goals to be as strong as men within their sport, they can use a weight training program to increase their strength per pound of body mass and lean muscle mass.

Some of the adaptations that occur when we strength train are increased muscle fiber size; increased muscle contractile strength; and increased tendon, bone, and ligament tensile strength. These changes are thought to improve physical capacity, economy, and metabolic function; decrease injury risk; and help you look darn good.

We all know that cycling relies primarily on leg strength, but you also need a strong torso and upper body to climb hills, sprint, maintain balance, and bridge a gap to the cyclists ahead.

Does all this mean you'll be faster? There have been studies on trained and untrained sedentary cyclists, with both groups experiencing positive results. In one study, untrained cyclists who strength trained for 12 weeks improved their cycling endurance by 33 percent and lactate thresholds by an average of 12 percent.

In a separate study on trained cyclists, the addition of a strength training program increased their cycling endurance by 20 percent, allowing them to pedal 14 minutes longer before fatigue set in. They also increased short-term, high-intensity endurance performance in the 4- to 8-minute range by 11 percent.

Is it possible to make performance gains without a strength training program? Yes. Some cyclists make performance gains using hills as their strength training tool. However, in addition to performance increases, a weight training program can possibly help prevent bone loss and even increase bone mass, which is critical to the prevention of osteoporosis. Multiple studies have shown that cyclists have reduced bone density compared with athletes participating in weight-bearing sports such as running.

A recent study done by the Department of Nutritional Sciences (University of Missouri) found that 63 percent of a cycling group had osteopenia (bone mineral density that is lower than normal but not low enough to be classified as osteoporosis) of the spine or hip, compared with only 19 percent in the running group. Cyclists were seven times more likely to have osteopenia of the spine than runners, controlling for age, body weight, and bone-loading history.

How important a weight training program may be to endurance athletes is not quantitatively known at this time; however, experts urge athletes who only cycle to add strength training, at minimum, and to consider adding impact activities such as running, playing basketball or soccer, or doing plyometric exercises such as jumping.

STARTING A STRENGTH TRAINING PROGRAM

The benefits of strength training are sending more women to the weight room to pump iron. Men who train to be bodybuilders or power lifters, or simply to be large, may be intimidating. Most of these men are courteous, helpful, and willing to share the equipment. But if the clientele makes you feel uneasy, find a gym where you can be comfortable exercising on any piece of equipment.

Everybody needs help learning to use the equipment in the gym and to do so with proper form. When you're just beginning a weight training program, ask for help. This book is a guide, but it is also

worthwhile to ask one of the trainers at the gym to help with setting up weight training machines and with proper technique. When
seeking help, ask someone you trust to recommend a trainer, and
ask the trainer for his or her credentials.

The strength training exercises in this book are intended to augment your cycling program. If you want more body sculpting, talk to
a trainer. Because many cyclists are trying to juggle fitness, family,
and job responsibilities, this strength training program is designed
to minimize weight room time while maximizing the benefits to a
cycling program.

THE PROGRAM IN DETAIL

Table 4.1 provides a strength training program in a format that can
be copied and taken to the gym, along with the Strength Training Data Sheet, Appendix B. Whether or not you use Appendix B
to track strength gains and training program is a personal choice;
however, a journal of some sort is recommended.

Exercises

The recommended exercises are listed at the end of Table 4.1 and
are shown later in the chapter. Some exercises have more than one
option shown, which is helpful when the gym gets busy.

In addition, exercises that are slightly different, such as the squat
and leg press, stimulate muscles in different ways. The end result is
a greater number of muscle fibers stimulated by slightly varying the
routine either within a week or from week to week. For example, if
you lift on Tuesday and Thursday during the strength maintenance
(SM) phase, use squats on Tuesday and leg presses on Thursday.

In the anatomical adaptation (AA) phase, lifting can be completed
in a "circuit," meaning that you complete the first set of all the exercises before completing the second set. This might be tough in a busy
weight room, particularly for hip extension exercises. If a crowded
weight room is an issue, go ahead and complete all of the sets of an
exercise, hip extension, for example, before moving to the next.

The order of completion of exercises in the other phases is such that all sets and repetitions (reps) of each exercise are completed before moving on to the next exercise. The exceptions are the exercises in [brackets] that can be completed in "superset" format. Superset means alternating between the exercises within the brackets before moving on to the next exercise.

Tips for Strength Training

- Focus on the muscle groups that do the majority of work on the bike.
- Make multijoint exercises the priority, and do single-joint exercises as time allows. For example, squats, which are described later in the chapter, use three joints: the hip, knee, and ankle. Knee extensions use only the knee joint.
- Mimic positions and movements of cycling as closely as possible.
- Always include abdominal and lower-back exercises to strengthen your torso.
- Strength training fitness precedes on-bike fitness. Some of the training programs outlined in Chapter 3 do not include all of the strength training phases listed in Table 4.1. Generally speaking, the more time you have to prepare for an event, the greater variety of training you can do, and you'll achieve greater levels of fitness.
- Separate strength training sessions by at least forty-eight hours.
- Maintain good postural alignment whenever possible. This means standing in a normal, relaxed, neutral position with your head supported by your neck, which has a normal curvature. For example, when doing squats, your head and neck should be in a position that allows the curvature of your neck to be in a normal position–head not craned toward the ceiling or chin at the chest.
- Always, always, always maintain control of the weight on the concentric and the eccentric actions. This means using muscles, not momentum, to lift the weight, and using muscles to lower the weight, controling the speed rather than allowing gravity to do all the work.

Load

The load estimates are given in terms of 1 Rep Max, or the maximum weight you could lift only once. Estimate your 1 Rep Max by finding the amount of weight you can lift only 10 times, then divide that number by 0.75. For example, if you can leg press 150 pounds 10 times, divide 150 by 0.75 to estimate your 1 Rep Max as 200 pounds.

Another way to estimate load is to begin with a weight that is very easy. Slowly keep increasing the weight until you can only lift the number of repetitions listed for any particular phase.

Sets

This refers to the number of repeated lifting bouts done on any particular exercise.

Repetitions per Set

This is the number of consecutive times you repeat an exercise within a set. For example, during the power endurance (PE) phase, you will do a hip extension exercise one to three times, and each time you do the exercise, you will lift the weight eight to fifteen times.

Speed of Movement

The recommended speed is subjective; however, the weight must be controlled in both directions. A note about the PE phase: If you're a beginner—in your first two years of strength training—do not try for highly explosive moves.

Minutes of Recovery

Each phase has recommended recovery times between sets. These times are important for each phase. For example, the maximum strength (MS) phase is compromised if you shorten the 2- to 4-minute recovery times. A shortened recovery time means you would have to reduce the weight, not making full use of the MS phase. Stretch during your recovery time. Stretching exercises are outlined later in the chapter.

Recovery Weeks

As part of your periodization plan, you'll cut back on training some weeks to rest and recover. This might mean fewer strength training days that week, a reduction of sets within a workout, and/or using a bit less weight on each exercise.

STRENGTH TRAINING PHASES AND EXERCISES

The training plans in this book include one or more of four strength training phases. The phases summarized in Table 4.1 are described in the following sections.

As mentioned previously, Table 4.1 lists the cycling exercises (1–5). These are for when you're very busy and want the least amount of strength training that will help you reach your goals. If you typically utilize additional exercises but find yourself pinched for time, do the cycling exercises first. The optional additional exercises (6–13) are for when you have more time to train or if you have physical weaknesses that limit race performance.

If you happen to know your 1 Rep Max weight (the maximum weight you can lift one time), you can use the chart to guide the amount you lift in each phase. If you do not know your 1 Rep Max, just use the rating of exertion descriptions to estimate the weight to lift in each phase.

Anatomical Adaptation (AA)

This is the initial phase of strength training designed for the beginning of a racing season or when you are just starting a strength training program. Its purpose is to prepare your tendons and muscles for greater loads in a subsequent strength training phase. Another purpose of strength training in an endurance sport program is to prepare muscles and tendons for greater sport loads, such as moving from riding a bicycle on flat terrain to rolling and hilly terrain. In some training plans it is used as an optional third day of strength training. It is typically an "easy" day of lifting in the maximum strength (MS) phase.

TABLE 4.1 Strength Training

PHASE	AA	MS*	PE*	SM*
Total sessions/ Phase	8+	8-12	6-12	4+
Days per week	2-3	2	1-2	1-2
Exercises— minimal *(in order of completion)*	1 2 3 4 5–Circuit	[1 2][3 4] 5	[1 2][3 4] 5	[1 2][3 4] 5
Exercises— additional and optional	1 2 3 6 7 8 9 4 5 10 11 12 13	[1 2][3 6] [8 9][4 5] [7 10] [11 12]13	[1 2][3 6] [8 9][4 5] [7 10] [11 12] 13	1 2 3 4 5–additional exercises as time allows
Load Rough percentage of 1 Rep Max and how it should feel	40-60 *(light)*	80-95 *(challenging)*	65-85 *(moderate)*	Sets 1-2 at 60 Set 3 at 80 *(Sets 1 and 2 moderate, set 3 slightly challenging)*
Sets/Session	3-5	3-6	3-5	2-6
Repetitions (reps) per set	15-20	3-6	8-15	Sets 1-2 at 12 Sets 3-6 at 6-8
Speed of movement	Slow	Slow–moderate	Moderately fast or explosive**	Slow–moderate
Minutes of recovery *(between sets)*	1-1.5	2-4	3-5	1-2

CYCLING EXERCISES IN ORDER OF COMPLETION:

1. Hip extension (squat, leg press, or step-up)
2. Supine dumbbell chest press or push-up
3. Seated cable, low row (also called seated row)
4. Supine trunk flexion (also called abdominal curl or crunch)
5. Floor back extension (also called "Superman")

OPTIONAL ADDITIONAL EXERCISES:

6. Hip extension (select a different exercise than #1 above to include two hip extension exercises in your routine)
7. Standing bent-arm latissimus (lat) pull-down or seated cable lat pull-down
8. Knee flexion (also called hamstring curl)
9. Knee extension
10. Heel raise (also called calf raise)
11. Seated horizontal hip adduction
12. Seated horizontal hip abduction
13. Additional core bodywork to strengthen the trunk

CONTINUES

Strength Training and Stretching

NOTES FOR EXERCISES:

1. Do not continue any exercise that causes pain. This includes joints that "pop" or "crack" and any exercise that causes sharp pain during the exercise or lasting for days after the strength training session.

2. Before and after each strength training session, warm up and cool down with 10 to 20 minutes of aerobic activity. Easy spinning on the bike is a good choice. Running is a warm-up option. Do not use running to cool down.

3. Exercises in brackets [ ] can be done in a superset manner, alternating between the two exercises.

---

*Boldfaced exercises follow the guidelines for each particular phase for mountain bike riders. Road riders can follow the same plan as mountain bike riders or keep upper-body exercises at AA sets, weight, and reps. Exercises not in bold print are to be completed at AA sets, weight, and reps for all phases of weight training.

**Explosive movements are done only if equipment described in the chapter is available, otherwise movements are moderately fast speeds.

Routine: Complete two or three sets of 15 to 20 reps of exercises 1 through 5. Exercises 6 through 13 are optional. The weight or load you lift should feel light, as if you could lift more. The exercises can be done in a circuit fashion, doing one set of each exercise before progressing to the second set. Or complete one set of one exercise and rest 1 to 2 minutes before completing the second set of the same exercise. Rest 1 to 2 minutes before completing the third set. Move to the next exercise after completing all sets of one exercise.

In this strength training phase as well as the others, it is best to have alternative exercises to do in case the weight room is very busy. Also, don't worry if you need to rearrange the order of the exercises when pressed for time.

Maximum Strength (MS)

This phase is used to teach your central nervous system to recruit high numbers of muscle fibers. For exercises designated MS, do one warm-up set with a light weight—something you can lift around 15 or 20 times. As you add more weight, begin the first set conservatively. Use a weight you are certain you can lift 6 to 8 times.

Plyometrics

Plyometrics are exercises or drills aimed at linking strength with speed of movement to produce power. It used to be thought that plyometrics were only for sprinters and football players, but one study showed that 5 km running performance was improved in well-trained endurance athletes using plyometrics. In addition, plyometrics may help cyclists reduce the chances of developing osteoporosis.

An example of a plyometric exercise for the upper body is using a medicine ball in place of lat pull-downs. While standing, hold the medicine ball above your head and, as fast and forcefully as possible, slam the ball into the ground. A plyometric exercise to mimic rowing is difficult to duplicate. One option is to lie facedown on a bench, with your upper body extending beyond the edge of the bench. Quickly lift a medicine ball off the ground and release it at chest height. Another upper-body option includes quickly tossing a medicine ball between two people, keeping the elbows high, similar to a chest press position.

There is not enough room in this book to go into multiple, detailed plyometric programs. For more information on plyometrics, consult Donald A. Chu's *Jumping into Plyometrics*.

After a rest and stretching, add 5 to 10 pounds and lift again. Continue these sequences until up to six sets are complete. At some point, it may be impossible to add more weight and you top out, having to lift the final two or three sets at the same weight. That is fine. If you find that the last set was easy, begin the entire sequence 5 to 10 pounds heavier at the next strength training session.

As for form on the MS phase, slowly exert force on the weight to move it. Do not use an explosive force to move the weight, like a rocket booster on the leg press machine. Using explosive force to get a heavy weight up will more than likely lead to knee or back problems. Going slower may lead to a bit of a struggle to get the weight up the first time; that is okay.

Many athletes find this phase fun because strength gains come quickly as loads increase. Be cautious not to extend this phase beyond the recommended number of sessions. Continuation of this phase for too long may result in muscle imbalances, particularly in the upper leg, which could lead to hip or knee injuries.

Routine: Complete one set of 15 to 20 reps, rest, complete 3 to 6 reps, rest, and complete 3 to 6 reps again for the designated exercises. You can repeat the heavier lift for up to six sets, depending on how much time you have to strength train. The exercises that are to be done lifting heavier weight include hip extension, chest press, seated row, and lat pull-down. For all other exercises, do just two or three sets of 15 to 20 reps.

You can superset the exercises in brackets, which means to alternate between the two exercises. It is important to be fully recovered between the heavier sets.

Power Endurance (PE)

The PE strength training phase is intended to combine strength with velocity. Making fast movements with weights, however, is controversial. At least one study has shown that when lifters were asked to move a weight as quickly as possible while maintaining contact with the weight bar, power actually decreased. On a separate occasion, the same group was asked to move the weight as quickly as possible but to release the weight. Their power and speed of movement increased in the second scenario.

In theory, the body was trying to protect itself in the first scenario, attempting to keep joints from being injured. It appears that the body was using opposing muscles to slow the weight down, actually decreasing power. So, when you begin to do the PE phase, you must ask yourself if the particular piece of equipment or exercise you are using will increase or decrease your power.

Routine: On each exercise, complete three to five sets of 8 to 15 reps. Utilize the same routine of sequence and supersets that you did in the MS phase. You may have to reduce the number of exercises you do in this phase to streamline your training. Eliminate the optional exercises first, unless you have a particular weakness that needs to be addressed.

Strength Maintenance (SM)

When you're an experienced athlete, this phase of strength training is often used to maintain gains made in the MS and PE phases. When you're a beginner, this phase is sometimes included to make small gains in strength without compromising endurance performance.

Routine: Keep the same exercises you used in the AA phase, or, if you get pinched for time, decrease to exercises 1 through 5. On hip extension, chest press, seated row, and lat pull-down, begin with one set of 15 to 20 reps at a light weight. Increase the weight slightly and complete one or two sets of 12 to 15 reps. The load should feel moderate. "Moderate" means challenging, but not so challenging that you must struggle to move the load. Increase the load by a small amount on the designated exercises only and complete one to two sets of 6 to 10 reps. For all other exercises, do two or three sets of 12 to 15 reps.

Strength Exercises

The strength exercises displayed in the illustrations in this chapter are not an exhaustive list but are some of the more common exercises. Unfortunately, it is also common to perform the exercises incorrectly. For each exercise there is text that describes the start position, movement instructions, and the finish position. In addition, a description of common errors is included. If your gym doesn't have equipment that looks exactly like the equipment shown in the illustrations, try to find equipment that has you make a similar movement. You can also ask a trainer for help. Illustrations of the recommended stretches can be found at the end of the chapter.

SQUAT

Start position

–Stand with your toes pointing forward, about shoulder width apart from inside edge to inside edge.

Movement and finish position

–Keeping normal curvature of your back and head forward, squat until your thighs are about halfway to being parallel to the floor, around the same angle as the knee bend at the top of the pedal stroke when riding a bicycle. The beginning of the squat movement is similar to the movement you make to sit in a chair.

–Knees and feet remain pointed forward the entire time.

–Knees remain over the feet, not wandering in or out.

–Return to the start position.

Start

Common errors » *Looking at the floor and bending at the waist* » *Losing the normal curvature of the spine at the bottom of the lift* » *Squatting too low* » *Placing the feet about 20 inches apart with toes pointing out* » *Knees rock inward, or out, on the way up.*
Stretches » *Standing quadriceps stretch and standing hamstring stretch*

Finish

STEP-UP

Start position

–Use dumbbells or a bar loaded with weight.

–Place your left foot on a sturdy, midshin-high platform, with toes pointing straight ahead.

Movement and finish position

–Step up, using the muscles in your left leg, and touch the platform with your right foot. Pause only a moment.

–Knees and feet remain pointed forward the entire time.

–Return to the start position.

–Complete all repetitions with your left leg, then repeat with your right leg.

Start

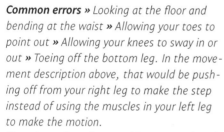

Common errors » Looking at the floor and bending at the waist » Allowing your toes to point out » Allowing your knees to sway in or out » Toeing off the bottom leg. In the move-ment description above, that would be push-ing off from your right leg to make the step instead of using the muscles in your left leg to make the motion.
Stretches *» Standing quadriceps stretch and standing hamstring stretch*

Finish

LEG PRESS

Start position

−If the seat is adjustable, make the angle of the seat so there is about an arm's length between your torso and your knees.

−Place your feet flat on the platform about 8 inches apart with toes pointing forward, aligned with your knees.

Movement and finish position

−Press the platform away from you until your legs are straight, knees almost locked.

−Lower the platform until your upper and lower leg form an 80- to 90-degree angle.

−Knees and feet remain pointed forward and about shoulder width apart the entire time.

−Keep your knees aligned with your hips and toes during the entire motion up and down.

Common errors » *Placing your feet too high on the platform so that your ankles are in front of your knee joints* **»** *Placing your feet too low so that your heels hang off the platform* **»** *Raising your heels off the platform during the lift phase* **»** *Lowering the platform so that your knees touch your chest. This generally relaxes some of the muscles that should be working, lifts your butt off the seat pad, rocks your pelvis forward, and eliminates the normal curvature of the spine.* **»** *Not controlling the weight in both directions*
Stretches » *Standing quadriceps stretch and standing hamstring stretch*

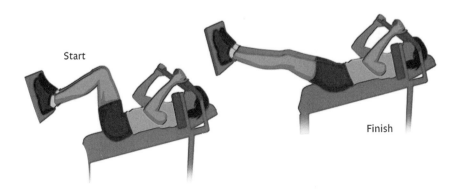

Start

Finish

SUPINE DUMBBELL CHEST PRESS

Start position

– Lie on your back on a bench with your back in a neutral position, one that allows the normal curvature of your spine.

– Feet are touching the floor or on the bench, whichever position is most comfortable.

– Weights are held in your hands, aligned with your elbows and shoulder joints. (A barbell can be used when going to heavier weight.)

Movement and finish position

– Retract your shoulders–squeeze your shoulder blades together.

– Lower the weight by leading with your elbows until your elbows align with your shoulder joints.

– Your forearm remains perpendicular to the floor throughout the movement.

– Pause for a moment and return to the start position by keeping your hands directly above your elbows throughout the movement.

Common errors » *Allowing the dumbbells to drift toward the centerline of your body or away from your body on the upward movement* » *Arching your back when lifting heavier weights* » *Not retracting your shoulders*
Stretches » *Standing upper-torso stretch*

Start

Finish

PUSH-UP

Start position

–Begin with your hands slightly wider than shoulder width, fingers pointing forward or slightly in.

–The floor contact points will be your hands and either your knees or toes.

Movement and finish position

–Keeping your body rigid, with tight abdominal muscles, push your chest away from the floor until your elbows are extended and nearly locked.

–Lower your body back toward the floor in a controlled manner, until the angle between your upper and lower arm is between 90 and 100 degrees.

–Pause for a moment before pushing back up again.

–Keep your head aligned with your body, as if you were in a standing position.

–Repeat the action until all repetitions are complete.

> **Common errors »** *Relaxing all muscles on the downward motion* **»** *Allowing your body to sag in the middle, arching the back*
>
> **Stretches »** *Standing upper-torso stretch*

Start

Finish

SEATED ROW

Start position

–Use a handle that puts your hands in a position similar to the one you use when holding the hoods of your bicycle handlebars. At gyms there are many handles to choose from: Use the widest one.

–Seated, with your torso and thighs or upper legs forming close to a 90-degree angle, place your feet flat on the footplates.

–Head and neck are upright, eyes looking forward.

–Elbows are nearly straight when handles are held at arm's length and there is tension in the cable.

–Shoulder blades are relaxed and separated (abducted).

Movement and finish position

–Initiate the pull by retracting your shoulder blades together, then pulling the bar toward your chest, leading with your elbows.

–After a brief pause at your chest, return the handle to the start position by moving first at your elbows, then your shoulders.

–After your elbows are nearly straight, allow your shoulder blades to separate slightly, returning to the start position.

–Your back should remain still throughout the entire exercise.

–Abdominal muscles remain contracted to stabilize your torso.

> **Common errors »** *Flexing or bending at your waist and using your back to initiate the movement*
> **Stretches »** *Standing upper-torso stretch*

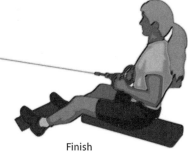

Start   Finish

ABDOMINAL CURL

Start position

–Lying on your back, bend your knees so your feet rest comfortably on the floor.

–Hands are behind your head for support (do *not* pull on your head) or crossed on your chest.

–Feet are flat on the floor.

Movement and finish position

–Contract your abdominal muscles, bringing your bottom ribs toward your hip bones.

–Your shoulders, neck, and head follow.

–You are as far as you can go when your feet begin to rise off the floor.

–Pause for a moment, keeping your feet on the floor.

–Lower yourself slowly until you are just before the point of losing the contraction on your abdominal muscles. In other words, don't relax on the floor before the next repetition.

> **Common errors** » *Pulling on your head with your hands* » *Using a rocking motion and momentum instead of controlling the movement*
> **Stretches** » *While lying on the floor on your back, stretch your hands and feet in opposite directions along the floor.*

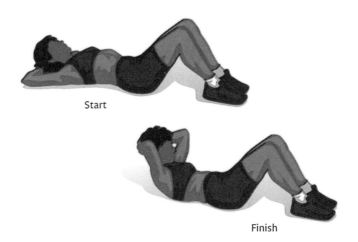

Start

Finish

FLOOR BACK EXTENSION
(Single Arm and Single Leg)

Start position

−Lying facedown on the floor, place your arms
  forward.

Start

Movement and finish position

−Using your back muscles, raise one arm and
  your opposite leg off the ground, keeping
  your pelvic bones on the floor. (*Note:* A more
  advanced move is to raise both arms and
  both legs off the floor.)
−Your neck remains aligned with your spine,
  which maintains its normal curvature.
−Pause for a moment.
−Keeping your back muscles contracted, lower
  your arm and leg back to the starting position.
−Switch to your other arm and other leg.

Finish

Common errors » *Attempting to use your head
and momentum to get your arm and leg off the
floor* » *Totally relaxing your back muscles when
returning to the start position* » *Hyperextending
your neck, pushing the chin toward the ceiling*
Stretches » *Seated back, hip, and gluteus
stretch*

STANDING BENT-ARM LAT PULL-DOWN

Start position

–Grasp the bar with arms extended, arms bent at the same angle as when riding a mountain bike.

–Step back enough to lift the weights off the stack while arms are extended in the start position.

–Knees are bent and feet are about shoulder width apart.

Movement and finish position

–Pull the bar toward your thighs by first depressing your shoulders away from your ears, then retracting your shoulder blades–pulling them together.

–Follow by pulling with your arms.

–Pause for a moment.

–Return the weight to the start position by moving your arms, then your shoulders.

Start

Common errors » Jerking the weight to begin and using a lot of torso movement to get the weight started (using your body weight instead of back and arm muscles to move the weight) » Relaxing your muscles when returning the weight to the start position and allowing the weight to jerk your arms, instead of using back and arm muscles to control the weight on the return to the start
Stretches *» Standing upper-torso stretch*

Finish

SEATED CABLE LAT PULL-DOWN

Start position

–Grasp the bar with arms fully extended and hands about shoulder width apart, using an overhand grip.

–Sit down on the bench, feet flat on the ground, and knees bent at about a 90-degree angle.

–Adjust the thigh pads so they help keep you seated.

Movement and finish position

–Leaning slightly back, pull the bar toward your upper chest by first depressing your shoulders away from your ears, followed by pulling with your arms.

–Pull down and in until the bar just touches or is very close to your breastbone.

–Pause for a moment.

–Return the weight, moving your arms, then your shoulders.

Common errors » *Jerking the weight and using a lot of torso movement* *» Leaning back to get the weight started (using your body weight instead of your muscles to move the weight)*

Stretches » *Standing upper-torso stretch*

Start

Finish

KNEE FLEXION (Hamstring Curl)

Start position

–Begin with the support pad a few inches above your heel.

–Align the center of your knee joint with the pivot point on the equipment.

–Relax your foot; don't try to flex it.

Start

Movement and finish position

–Curl one leg up as far as possible.

–Pause for a moment.

–Return the rotating arm to the start position, keeping your hamstring muscles contracted.

–Complete all repetitions in a set with one leg before switching to your other leg.

Finish

Common errors *» Stopping short by not curling your leg as far as possible » Relaxing your hamstring muscles when lowering the weight » Arching your back to complete the lift » Using momentum to complete the lift* ***Stretches*** *» Standing hamstring stretch*

KNEE EXTENSION

Start position

–Begin with both legs fully extended, lifting a weight you can lift with a single leg.

–The seat should be adjusted so you have back support and the center of your knee joint aligns with the pivotal joint on the exercise equipment.

–Keep knees and hips aligned throughout the exercise.

Movement and finish position

–Use one leg to lower the weight about 8 inches, or just before the point where your quadriceps muscles lose contraction. It is often described as a movement of 30 degrees. (Do not go all the way down.)

–Return to the starting position and pause for a moment.

–Complete all repetitions in the set with one leg before switching to your other leg.

Common errors » Lowering the weight past the point of keeping your quadriceps muscles contracted (you can put your hand on your quadriceps and feel when they are contracted and tight and when they are relaxed) » Using momentum to swing the weight up and down instead of using a controlled motion » Arching your back in the lift phase » Allowing your butt to lift off the seat pad » Allowing your knees to rotate in or out
Stretches » Standing quadriceps stretch

Start

Finish

HEEL RAISE

Start position

–Use a leg press machine, standing calf raise machine, or riser block.

–If using a leg press or standing calf raise machine, you can work both legs at once or one at a time.

–If using a riser block, you can either use your body weight or hold a dumbbell (illustrated).

–Doing single- or double-leg heel raises, point the toe of your working leg(s) forward.

–The ball of your foot is on the platform and your heel is as low as possible, allowing you to maintain an eccentric contraction in your calf muscle. (Calf muscle is not totally relaxed.)

–Knee is straight but not locked out.

Movement and finish position

–From the heel-down position, contract your calf (push up onto your tiptoes) until you are on the ball of your foot, as high as you can go.

–Pause for a moment at the top position.

–In a controlled manner, return to the start position.

–If you are doing single-leg exercises, complete all repetitions in a set with one leg, then switch legs.

Start

Finish

Common errors *» Not going as high as possible » Going too low and losing tension on your calf muscle » Relaxing your muscles on the down motion » Not doing the exercise in a controlled manner*
Stretches *» Standing lower-leg stretch*

STANDING MACHINE HIP ADDUCTION

Start position

–Stand comfortably with spine in neutral alignment. (Do not arch your back or lean forward.)

–The pad on the machine is just above your knee on the inside.

–The angle of the padded arm puts a very slight, but not excessive, stretch on your adductors (inner thigh).

Movement and finish position

–Move your leg toward the midline of your body.

–Move across the midline of your body without twisting your torso.

–Pause for a moment and return to the start position by controlling the speed of the weight.

Common errors » *Arching your back* » *Swinging and twisting your torso, not keeping hips facing the machine* » *Beginning with too much stretch on your adductors* » *Moving the weight with an explosive start* » *Relaxing muscles on the return to start position and allowing the weight to slam down*
Stretches » *Seated adductor stretch*

Start   Finish

STANDING MACHINE HIP ABDUCTION

Start position

– Stand comfortably with spine in neutral alignment. (Do not arch your back or lean forward.)

– The pad on the machine is just above your knee on the outside.

– The angle of the padded arm puts a very slight, but not excessive, stretch on your abductors (outer thigh).

Movement and finish position

– Keeping your trunk stable, move your working leg away from the midline of your body.

– Pause for a moment and return to the start position by controlling the speed of the weight.

Common errors » *Arching your back* » *Swinging and twisting your torso, not keeping hips facing the machine* » *Moving the weight with an explosive start* » *Relaxing muscles on the return to start position and allowing the weight to slam down*
Stretches » *Seated hip and gluteus stretch*

Start   Finish

STRETCHING

It seems either you are a stretcher or you aren't. Those who stretch are religious about their routine, while those who don't stretch don't see any benefit from doing so, nor do they associate any negative consequences with not stretching.

Let's address two basic types of flexibility: static flexibility and dynamic flexibility. Static flexibility is the range of motion relative to a joint, with little emphasis on speed of movement. An example is hamstring, back, and upper-back flexibility for people trying to ride in a time trial position or for those enduring a long ride.

Dynamic flexibility is resistance to motion at the joint and involves speed during physical performance. An example of dynamic flexibility is when you jump out of the saddle to aggressively climb a hill or sprint to catch an opponent. A good cyclist must have both types of flexibility.

Flexibility has been shown to improve neuromuscular coordination, improve physical efficiency, increase blood supply and nutrients to joint structure, improve balance and muscular awareness, improve performance, and even improve strength.

In a study on flexibility, swimmers, football players, and runners did contract-relax flexibility training for the knee extensors and flexors. Contract-relax flexibility training involves a passive stretch of a muscle after an isometric contraction. The athletes did flexibility training for eight weeks, three days per week.

The researchers found that flexibility training increased the range of motion of the knee joint by about 6 percent and that stretching improved knee joint torque. Eccentric knee extension torque increased by 19 to 25 percent, depending on particular velocity of measurement. Eccentric knee flexion torque increased by 16 to 18 percent, again depending on the velocity of measurement. Concentric knee flexion torque increased by 8 to 10 percent, while knee flexion isometric torque increased by 11 percent.

In short, the contract-relax flexibility training increased the strength of the knee flexors and extensors—hamstrings and quadriceps, respectively, to name two of the major muscles—during eccentric actions. The training also increased the strength of the knee flexors during concentric actions.

You should be aware that there is controversy about stretching— whether it helps everyone or not and whether it should be done at all. While the study mentioned earlier showed a positive correlation between stretching and sport strength, not all studies have shown the same results. A review of the literature indicates that there is not enough evidence to support endorsing or discontinuing a stretching routine.

Literature aside, several athletes have found themselves faced with an activity-limiting injury. Many times, the rehabilitation and future prevention routine includes a stretching regimen. Because the research literature is inconclusive and many recreational and elite athletes have benefited from a stretching protocol, I continue to recommend that you include stretching as part of your fitness routine. If you have never stretched and have not experienced any problems due to lack of flexibility, I don't see a reason to add stretching to your routine until it is needed.

How to Stretch

There are many stretching methods, but I recommend propriocep-tive neuromuscular facilitation (PNF). There are also many varia-tions on this technique.

One easy-to-follow version is this:

1. Static stretch (stretch and hold) the muscle for about 8 sec-onds. Remember to breathe.
2. Contract the same muscle for about 8 seconds. (Leave out the contraction step when stretching during the rest interval of strength training and hold static stretches for about 15 seconds.)
3. Stretch and hold the stretch again for about 8 seconds. Breathe.

4. Continue alternating muscle contractions and stretches until you have completed four to eight static stretches. End with a stretch and not a contraction.

You should find that you are able to stretch farther, or increase your range of motion, each time you repeat the stretch.

Stretches for Cycling and Weight Room

The stretches listed here can be done standing. Some of the exercises stretch multiple muscles, so they can save time for the hurried athlete. Do them in the order listed. Some of these stretches may not work for you. If you want further ideas for stretching exercises, a couple of good resources are *Sport Stretch* by Michael J. Alter and *Stretching* by Bob Anderson.

STANDING QUADRICEPS STRETCH

Movement

−While balancing against something with your right hand, grasp your left foot behind your butt.

−Static stretch by gently pulling your foot up and away from your butt.

−Stand erect and keep your hip, knee, and ankle in alignment.

−Contract by pushing against your hand with your foot. Begin with a gentle force.

−Repeat with your right leg.

Common errors » *Pulling your foot against your butt and compressing your knee joint* » *Bending over at your waist*

STANDING HAMSTRING STRETCH

Movement

–Bend over at your waist, balancing against
  something stable.

–Place leg to be stretched forward and place
  your other leg behind your front leg about
  12 inches, toes pointing forward.

–With your weight mostly on your
  front leg, press your chest
  toward your front knee-
  cap and relax your back
  muscles.

–You should feel the
  stretch in the hamstring
  muscles of your front
  leg.

–Contract the front leg by trying to
  pull it backward against the floor–there is
  no movement.

–Repeat with your other leg.

> **Common errors** » *Allowing your toes to point
> out* » *Not relaxing your back muscles*

STANDING UPPER-TORSO STRETCH

(stretches your latissimus dorsi, trapezius, pectoralis, and triceps muscles)

Movement

–Hold on to something stable for support, hands placed slightly wider than shoulder width, feet about shoulder width apart, and knees slightly bent.

–Allow your head to relax between your arms.

–For the contraction phase, push against the support with your arms, contracting the muscles in your upper back.

> **Common errors »** *Not relaxing all your muscles in your arms, chest, and upper back*

SEATED BACK, HIP, AND GLUTEUS STRETCH

(stretches your gluteus, tensor fasciae latae, and latissimus muscles as well as your iliotibial tract)

Movement

–Sit on the ground with one leg extended in front of you and your opposite hand behind your back for support.

–Cross one foot (the right foot as shown) over your opposite (left) leg and slide your right heel toward your butt.

–Place your left elbow on the outside of your right knee.

CONTINUES

–Look over your right shoulder while turning your torso. Gently pushing on your knee with your left elbow increases the stretch.

–Hold the stretch for 15 to 30 seconds.

–Contract by pushing your knee against your elbow, resisting the force with your elbow.

–Repeat with the other leg and arm.

> **Common errors »** *Keeping shoulders, back, and butt muscles tense — take a deep breath and relax.*

SEATED ADDUCTOR STRETCH

(stretches your adductor magnus, adductor brevis, adductor longus, pectineus, and gracilis)

Movement

–Sit on the ground with your spine in a natural position, not leaning forward or backward. (You can also put your back against a wall.)

–Grasp your ankles and pull them toward you enough to feel a light stretch.

–Place elbows on your inner legs and gently push your legs toward the floor.

–Contract by pushing your legs upward against your elbows, elbows resisting the push.

> **Common errors »** *Rounded back* **»** *Pushing too hard on your inner leg*

STANDING LOWER-LEG STRETCH

(stretches your gastrocnemius, soleus, and Achilles tendon)

Movement

–Lean against an immovable support object, with the leg to be stretched straight behind you and your other leg forward.

–Toes point forward.

–Press the heel of your back leg into the ground and move your hips forward, keeping your back knee straight. The farther forward you press your hips, the more stretch you should feel in your back leg's lower muscles.

–Slightly bend your back knee to stretch different calf muscles.

–Contract your calf muscles by pushing against the support object as if you were pushing it away using your back leg.

Common errors » *Pointing your toes in or out* **»** *Not putting most of your weight on your back leg*

• • •

A STRENGTH TRAINING AND STRETCHING PROGRAM SUPPLEMENTS your cycling program. A strength training program may help keep osteoporosis at bay or even build precious bone. It also can make you ride faster and more powerfully. To top it off, stretching can be a great way to relax.

chapter five

Nutrition

Nutrigenomics is the study of molecular relationships between nutrition and the response of genes. This relatively young science has a newly dedicated journal, *Journal of Nutrigenetics and Nutrigenomics*, with the first issue published in 2008. Perhaps one day we will use genetic DNA to prescribe individual, optimal nutrition for health and athletic performance. That day may be closer than we think.

Today there's a relatively new science called nutrigenomics that explores the interplay between genetics and the disease-fighting properties of certain food nutrients. But until scientists can make diet recommendations based on genetic testing, you're left to make nutritional decisions for yourself.

If you scan the shelves of your local bookstore, you'll find hundreds of so-called diet books. A search for "diet" in a popular online bookstore came up with nearly 271,000 book choices. Plug the words "diet plan" into an Internet search engine and you'll get more than nine million entries. I wish I could recommend one golden diet that always delivers results, but all my research on nutrition for health and athletic performance has made it clear to me that no single plan works for everyone.

If we talk about diet in very general terms, maybe a perfect one does exist: Eat and drink enough of the right foods to build and maintain a healthy body. It's not as easy as it sounds. The difficult part comes when people want to know exactly what to eat. How many carbohydrates? How much fat and protein? How many calories? Which foods should we eat each day to guarantee optimal health? An appropriate diet for an individual depends on:

- **Genetics.** Some people are born with faster metabolisms than other people. Also, some people have inherited health issues that require medication, and some medications affect basal metabolism.
- **Gender.** Men have a greater percentage of muscle mass than women do, so they have a greater basal metabolic rate.
- **Body surface area.** Given the same weight for two individuals, one tall and one short, the tall person has a greater body surface area and therefore has a greater basal metabolism.
- **Daily routine activity level.** If your job has you sitting at a desk all day long, your caloric needs are different from those of someone who does physical labor.
- **Lifestyle and personal preferences.** Some people have a lifestyle of eating only home-prepared foods, whereas others are dependent on food prepared by others. Choosing the right foods in either scenario can be challenging. All of us have food preferences.
- **Exercise activity level.** Duration, intensity, and specific type of exercise burn calories and can affect basal metabolism.
- **Food quality.** Highly processed foods tend to have fewer nutrients than whole foods. Athletes who want to maximize health and performance need to maximize the nutrient quality of their food.

The most important message is: You're a study of one. Your unique genetics, history, and lifestyle all contribute to your nutritional status. You need to take responsibility for your health and track your health status with the help of your health care professional.

When your health status markers are out of line with what you expect for optimal health, take action. Seek the advice of your family doctor and sports medicine specialists to help you improve your situation.

A Story of Change

Windy Ann was a competitive racer, trying to get better. She wanted to lose some weight to help her edge toward faster race speeds and more podium spots. It seemed the women who were faster than she were also thinner. Maybe if she were lighter she would be able to race even faster. She was well-read on diet and nutrition. Literature throughout the 1980s told her she could lose weight by following a low-fat diet, going no lower than 1,200 calories per day, and exercising. So that's what she did.

Windy monitored her calories and opted for high-value foods, those chock-full of vitamins and minerals but low in fat. Foods fitting this description were fruits and vegetables. She knew she needed protein, but she was also aware that the average person consumes too much protein. She got most of her protein from nonfat dairy products and fish or poultry.

After several years of competition and training, she was unable to change her body weight. Why? She exercised between six and ten hours each week, worked between forty-eight and fifty-five hours each week, and watched what she ate. How could she not lose weight? She worked hard at her job, and was athletic and conscious of food intake. Why didn't her body look like the body of a fit athlete? She had no energy, and she always had a nagging injury each year that kept her from developing her full speed potential.

In the early 1990s, frustrated with her situation, Windy sought the help of a registered dietitian, who asked her to keep food logs for a week. Keeping a food log was easy for Windy; she had meticulously counted calories for

CONTINUES

CONTINUED

years. She could estimate portions without weighing them and would occasionally check her expertise against a measuring cup or a scale. The dietitian found Windy's diet to be very high in vitamins and minerals; low in fat—only 10 percent of total caloric intake; low in protein—only 10 percent of total calories; and high in carbohydrates—80 percent of total calories. Her daily intake averaged around 1,300 calories. Perfect for wanting to lose weight—well, maybe one hundred calories per day too high. It was the perfect diet for an endurance athlete and for someone trying to keep their 195-198 cholesterol from getting any higher. Yet, if this diet were so perfect, why wasn't she thinner? Why didn't her body have that svelte, strong, athletic look advertised in magazines? She would later discover that she had other problems, which she didn't even realize were diet-related.

Chris, the registered dietitian, told Windy that she thought her caloric intake was too low. Based on Windy's work and exercise routine, Chris recommended that she increase her daily caloric intake to around 2,300 calories. What? Increase calories? How was Windy ever going to lose weight? Surely not by eating more food!

Chris also thought Windy's fat and protein intake was too low. Windy suspected this as well. She had read about the work that Barry Sears did with the Stanford swim team. He helped them change their diet to 30-30-40: 30 percent fat, 30 percent protein, and 40 percent carbohydrates. Windy wanted Chris's opinion about a 30-30-40 diet.

Chris had also read about this new diet and they agreed to move forward and give it a try. Windy would eat more food, more fat, more protein, and fewer carbohydrates. After one week, Windy returned to Chris's office to find she had lost three pounds. She physically felt better, although it felt like she was eating a ton of food.

Now convinced she should make changes to her diet, Windy continued eating more calories, and the macronutrient split of those calories would include more fat and more protein.

CONTINUES

CONTINUED

It was November when Windy began her diet change. In the weeks and months that followed, she began to take notice of some big changes. She had more energy and was sleeping through the night, not getting up three to five times–sometimes for a snack. Her hair was growing faster and needed to be cut more often. She simply felt good, and her menstrual cycle had resumed.

Three years before starting the new diet, Windy had quit taking birth control pills. After that, her menstrual cycle was never regular. She just thought it was due to being on the pill for so long. Within five months of changing her diet, Windy had regular menstrual cycles.

By the time the next racing season arrived in May, Windy was feeling better than ever. She made it through a winter of training with regular menstrual cycles, no nagging injuries, no winter injuries to haunt her all race season, but still no significant weight loss. The initial three pounds was all Windy lost, but the numbers on the scale were meaning less and less to her. They meant less because she felt better and she was racing faster. The entire race season following her diet change, her racing times improved.

During the race season, she found she could consume a diet near 30-30-40, but she needed to change that regimen during races. She found she needed to consume a sports drink during longer races, or she felt terrible. She also found she needed more carbohydrates in the hours following a hard workout or race in order to speed her recovery.

Windy had faster race times, regular menstrual cycles, no injuries, and, in general, she felt better, but she was worried about her cholesterol level. If this new diet was good for her athletics but was putting her at risk for heart disease, she decided she would head back to the old, low-fat diet. Fourteen months after changing to a 30-30-40 diet, Windy had blood tests from which she found her total cholesterol to be improved at 160–she was surprised.

After two years of her new eating habits, Windy lost an additional seven pounds. It was a slow process, but worth the time.

CONTINUES

CONTINUED

> Although she no longer keeps food logs, Windy tries to balance her snacks and meals by eating some protein, fat, and carbohydrates. She no longer lives on nonfat yogurt, bagels, fruits, and vegetables. She hasn't given up the fruits and vegetables, but now she consumes lean meats and nuts as well. And fat is no longer an enemy.
>
> **Note:** No one mentioned, or the author, has any affiliation with Barry Sears, financial or otherwise.

I share Windy's story with the athletes I coach because it illustrates many of the nutrition rules this chapter will cover in depth. On a positive note, Windy knew something was wrong and took action. She had too many things she wanted to do and had no time for injury or illness. Windy's story shows how:

- Both extreme calorie restriction and chronic dieting slow metabolism.
- Very-low-fat and/or very-low-protein diets are correlated with amenorrhea in women. (Many studies correlate amenorrhea in female athletes with loss in bone density.)
- A body that receives inadequate nutrition will break down. This can mean more frequent colds and flu, or it can mean more serious physical injuries. The ill and injured cannot train or burn as many calories as they'd like, nor can they reach their full potential as competitive athletes.

The beginning of Windy's story is common among athletes, both female and male, who want to lose weight to increase speed. The first thing they do is cut calories. No one wants to diet for any extended time, so they cut a lot of calories for a short period of time to get the "diet thing" over with. But when athletes cut significant calories to lose weight, the results are often counterproductive.

A study conducted by J. A. Frentsos and J. T. Baer (1987) at Xavier University in Cincinnati, Ohio, analyzed the dietary habits of four male and two female elite triathletes. The study found that they consumed too few calories and carbohydrates to support their estimated daily requirements. Their diets were also found to be low in zinc and chromium. The researchers recommended diet changes to increase food intake. Follow-up seven-day diet records found the athletes had increased average daily calories, had increased carbohydrate consumption, and met their daily requirements for zinc, chromium, and all other nutrients. Their race results also displayed an improvement in performance.

In a separate study on trained cyclists by E. V. Lampert et al. (1994) at the University of Cape Town Medical School, a high-fat diet was found to increase endurance. Five trained cyclists followed either a high-fat diet (70 percent fat, 7 percent carbs, 23 percent protein) or a high-carbohydrate diet (74 percent carbs, 12 percent fat, 14 percent protein) for two weeks. Endurance at 60 percent of VO_2max was measured before and after the dietary changes; the high-fat diet was associated with "significant" increases in endurance.

If performance is not your only concern—perhaps you want to live to be 100 years old—consider the people who live in Lerik, Azerbaijan, a small mountain town near the Iranian border. This village is famous because of the many residents who live 100-plus years. How do they do it?

Most of the villagers are uneducated, receive inadequate medical care, and do a considerable amount of physical labor. They eat very little—mostly vegetables, fruit, and sour cheeses. When Azerbaijan was part of the Soviet Union, doctors visited the town and took numerous blood samples, looking for the secret to their long lives. The tests were inconclusive. Researchers theorized that the villagers' longevity was related to genetics and clean, stress-free living.

Confused yet? How can athletes who follow completely different diets all have improved or sustained high performance? Some of the athletes studied ate a 30-30-40 diet, others simply increased calories, and still others ate a high-fat diet, yet they all had performance improvements. Then there are the Lerik "athletes," toiling each day and outliving most people, displaying sustained high performance.

Most of us don't live like the people in Lerik, so maybe that's an unfair comparison. People living in modern cities deal with pollution, job-related toxins, plenty of stress, and processed food. So, given the variables, how do we know what our own optimal diet is?

The remainder of this chapter gives information you can use to evaluate and improve your diet. A single chapter can't cover all the information necessary for understanding nutrition (and as technology develops, you will want to consider new and more accurate information). But this chapter gives a good overview of macro- and micronutrients, some nutritional concerns common to athletes, and some tools to evaluate diet. Let's begin with macronutrients.

MACRONUTRIENTS

Depending on which book you read, there are either three or four macronutrients. The commonly agreed-upon macronutrients are carbohydrates, fat, and protein. Some sources consider water to be a fourth macronutrient, so I'll discuss it in this section.

Carbohydrates

Carbohydrates are almost exclusively found in plants and their processed by-products. Fruits, vegetables, beans, peas, and grains are sources of carbohydrates. The only animal sources that have significant carbohydrates are milk and yogurt.

Carbohydrates are made of sugar molecules and are divided into two major groups: complex carbohydrates and simple carbohydrates. Complex carbohydrates consist of many sugar molecules linked together. Foods in the complex group include vegetables, whole grains, beans, and peas. These foods contain fiber and starches and are made of long, complex chains of sugar molecules; thus, they are more difficult for the body to break down into fuel.

Simple carbohydrates, sometimes referred to as simple sugars, include fructose (fruit sugar), lactose (milk sugar), sucrose, and glucose. Notice that all of them end in the suffix "-ose," which identifies "carbohydrate." A food product that has several "-ose" ingredients listed separately on its label actually contains that many simple sugars or combinations of sugars of different origin.

The body absorbs sugars and eventually converts them into glucose, the body's usable form of sugar. Sugar is absorbed into the blood, heart, skeletal muscle, and liver—in that order. When blood sugars reach homeostasis, or a state of balance in the blood, the heart and skeletal muscles accept glucose. The always-working heart uses glucose for energy, and the skeletal muscles can also use it for energy. Skeletal muscles also have the capacity to store glucose as glycogen for later use. The liver can also absorb glucose from the blood and convert it into glycogen. The glucose not immediately needed or stored by functioning body parts is converted to fat.

Insulin is a pancreatic hormone that regulates blood sugar, and its effects are most beneficial when it does so at a moderate pace. When insulin continuously spikes and dips or is produced in inadequate quantities, health problems arise, including hypoglycemia (low blood sugar), diabetes (high blood sugar), and some of the health issues related to coronary heart disease. It's preferable to maintain blood sugars at an even level to minimize ups and downs in insulin response.

The rate at which carbohydrates are digested and their effect on the rise of blood glucose are described by the food's glycemic index. Foods that are easily digested and cause a pronounced rise in blood sugar have high glycemic index values. This pronounced rise of blood sugar initiates an insulin surge and stimulates body cells to store glucose as fat.

Foods that are more slowly digested have lower glycemic index values and do not cause the paired glucose and insulin spikes. The glycemic index values of some common carbohydrate foods are shown in Table 5.1. It is important to note that foods containing fats and proteins have lower glycemic index values because fat and protein take more time to digest.

High-glycemic-index foods are most valuable during exercise and post-exercise recovery. Otherwise, they should be used in moderation or in combination with fat and protein to slow their absorption rate.

TABLE 5.1 Glycemic Index of Foods

HIGH GLYCEMIC INDEX (80% OR HIGHER)	MOERATE GLYCEMIC INDEX (50-80%)	LOW GLYCEMIC INDEX (30-50%)	VERY LOW GLYCEMIC INDEX (LESS THAN 30%)
Apricots	All-bran cereal	Apple	Cherries
Banana	Baked beans	Apple juice	Grapefruit
Carrots	Beets	Apple sauce	Plums
Corn	Garbanzo beans	Barley	Peanuts
Corn chips	Orange juice	Black-eyed peas	
Corn flakes	Navy beans	Dates	
Crackers	Oatmeal	Figs	
French bread	Oranges	Grapes	
Grape-Nuts	Pinto beans	Kidney beans	
Honey	PowerBar	Lima beans	
Mango	Potato chips	Peaches	
Molasses	Spaghetti	Pears	
Muesli	Yams	Peas	
Oat bran		Rye bread	
Pastries		Sweet potato	
Potatoes		Tomato soup	
Raisins		Yogurt	
Rice			
Rye crisps			
Shredded Wheat			
Soda pop			
White bread			
Whole wheat bread			

Fat

Fat is essential for normal body functions. It also makes food taste good, is enjoyable to eat, and makes us feel satisfied. Fats are constructed of building blocks called fatty acids. The major categories of fatty acids are saturated, polyunsaturated, and monounsaturated. The body can use all three kinds, but, as with carbohydrates, there are some fats that should be consumed in moderation.

Some of the fatty acids necessary for good health are called essential fatty acids (EFAs). EFAs contribute to a healthy body by improving hair and skin texture, reducing cholesterol and triglyceride levels, preventing arthritis, and contributing to healthy hormone levels. EFAs are found in large quantities in the brain, where they aid in the transmission of nerve impulses and overall brain function. EFAs are also essential for rebuilding and producing new cells.

Since the body cannot manufacture EFAs, they must be obtained from food. Omega-3 and omega-6 fats are the two basic categories of EFAs. Omega-3 fats are found in oily cold-water fish, such as salmon, mackerel, menhaden, herring, and sardines, and are also found in canola, flaxseed, and walnut oils.

Omega-6 fats are found primarily in raw nuts and seeds and in grapeseed, sesame, and soybean oils. To supply EFAs, omega-6 fats must be consumed in raw or supplement form or as pure liquid; they can't be subjected to heat in processing or cooking. Wild game, not subjected to chemical-laden, fatten-them-up, feedlot-style diets, is rich in both omega-3 and omega-6 fats.

The fats that should be consumed in moderation are the saturated variety. Excess consumption of saturated fats can raise cholesterol levels, particularly low-density lipoprotein (LDL), or "bad" cholesterol. Saturated fats are found in animal products and some tropical oils, such as coconut and palm. Also, when some unsaturated oils are partially hydrogenated (a process that turns a liquid fat into a solid one), the new fat is more saturated. Hydrogenated fats contain trans-fatty acids, believed to contribute to coronary artery disease. Hydrogenated and partially hydrogenated fats are prevalent in many processed foods, such as crackers, cookies, and some canned products. Food manufacturers are now required to list trans fat on nutrition labels, but beware: Under U.S. Food and Drug Administration rules, up to 0.5 gram can be listed as "0" grams. Read labels carefully, and look for the word "hydrogenated."

Polyunsaturated fats are found in corn, safflower, soybean, canola, and sunflower oils. Consumption of the polyunsaturated family may actually lower total cholesterol; however, it appears that large amounts of polyunsaturated fats also lower high-density lipoprotein

(HDL), or "good" cholesterol. Some of the polyunsaturated oils do contain EFAs.

Monounsaturated fats are also thought to positively influence health. They are found in nuts and some vegetables and also in the oils of those foods, such as almond, avocado, olive, and canola oils.

Protein

Protein in the diet is absolutely necessary for growth and development of the body. Next to water, protein makes up the greatest portion of our body weight. All of our cells contain protein. Some food protein sources are considered "complete proteins" because they include all of the amino acids the body cannot manufacture on its own (the "essential" amino acids). These amino acids are histidine, isoleucine, leucine, lysine, methionine, phenylalanine, threonine, tryptophan, and valine.

Complete protein foods include meat, milk, eggs, poultry, fish, cheese, and yogurt. Some sources consider soybean products to be complete proteins. Other sources, however, consider soy products to be incomplete because they are very low or deficient in the amino acid methionine.

Vegetarians need to be well educated on combining foods to achieve complete proteins, because most plant products are incomplete proteins, meaning they are missing or are deficient in one or more of the essential amino acids. If a diet consistently omits one or more of the essential amino acids, a deficiency will develop, resulting in illness or injury.

Water

Between 40 and 60 percent of an individual's body weight is water. Water is typically 65 to 75 percent of the weight of muscle and less than 25 percent of the weight of fat. This water is essential to a functioning body. A body can survive many days without food but only a few days without water.

Many people don't stay well hydrated. Most literature recommends drinking eight to ten glasses of water each day. If you are drinking eight to ten glasses each day and your urine is dark yellow in color and strong-smelling, you're still not drinking enough. Rather than aiming for a certain number of glasses of water per day, a better guideline is to drink enough water so that your urine is light in color and has minimal odor. Other signals of dehydration are constipation, fatigue, and headaches.

Caffeinated coffee, tea, and soft drinks can have a diuretic effect, which means they increase the normal urinary output, leaving less fluid in the body for normal functioning. It appears, however, that individual responses to caffeine vary. Routine caffeine consumption can cause tolerance and minimize caffeine's effect. In some studies, caffeine has been shown to increase calcium loss, so limiting its intake can help preserve precious bone. Depending on caffeine's effect on you, limiting daily intake of caffeine can keep the body hydrated.

A well-hydrated athlete also performs better. Dehydration levels as low as 2 percent of body weight are thought to impair athletic performance, perhaps by as much as 20 percent.

MICRONUTRIENTS

Vitamins and minerals are considered to be micronutrients because they are needed in smaller quantities than the macronutrients—water, carbohydrates, fat, and protein. Some vitamins and minerals are coenzymes, enabling the body to produce energy, grow, and heal.

Vitamins regulate metabolism and assist in the biochemical processes that release energy from digested food. Some vitamins are known for their antioxidant, cancer prevention, and cardiovascular disease protection properties. Vitamin E and vitamin C are two of the vitamins scientists believe we should supplement in our diet because we probably do not get enough of these from our food.

Some sources of vitamin E are nuts, seeds, whole grains, cold-pressed vegetable oils, and dark green, leafy vegetables. Vitamin C is found in green vegetables, citrus fruits, and berries, to name a few sources.

Minerals are necessary for the correct composition of body fluids, the formation of blood and bone, the regulation of muscle tone, and the maintenance of healthy nerve function. Calcium and iron are two of the minerals of most concern. Adequate calcium helps maintain bone density and can be found in dairy products, tofu, fortified orange juice, soymilk, and canned fish with bones (such as sardines and salmon). Iron is incorporated in hemoglobin and myoglobin and aids in the oxygenation of red blood cells and muscle. It is found in the largest quantities in the blood. Menstruating women lose blood and iron each month during their menstrual cycles, so care must be taken to consume adequate iron to avoid becoming anemic. The best dietary sources of iron are red meat, eggs, and beans.

ANTIOXIDANTS AND PHYTOCHEMICALS

Scientists have recognized for years that diets rich in fruits, vegetables, grains, and legumes appear to reduce the risk of a number of diseases, including cancer, heart disease, diabetes, and high blood pressure. Researchers have found that these foods contain antioxidants, which protect cells against oxidation. Oxidation is the damage to cells that is similar to rust on metal.

Phytochemicals are another group of health-promoting nutrients thought to prevent a number of diseases and aid in the repair of cells when disease strikes. Phytochemicals give plants their rich color, flavor, and disease-protection properties. There are literally thousands of phytochemicals—tomatoes alone are thought to contain over ten thousand different varieties.

The recent discovery of phytochemicals illustrates how science continually discovers more and more about whole foods and their valuable properties. As the scientific community and nutritionists continue to explore and discover new properties of phytochemicals, there may come a time when individuals will know exactly which phytonutrients are necessary for maintaining their optimal health, but in the meantime, dietary supplements cannot replace the value of whole foods. Eating a balanced diet and avoiding overprocessed foods is still the best goal in terms of nutrition.

DISORDERED EATING AND EATING DISORDERS

Before discussing diet specifics, it's important to talk about disordered eating and eating disorders. The social pressures to be thin are everywhere. Thin, beautiful models stare out from magazine covers; publishers hope consumers will like their looks, pick up the magazine, and eventually buy it.

Women are becoming savvier about the visual stimuli that come out of Hollywood and the media. Often young teens are made up to look like adults, and those images are used to sell products. Products are purchased, and inevitably there are readers in pursuit of attaining the same standards. This environment is especially difficult for younger girls to navigate.

Even the photographs are illusions. Digital photography and computers allow us to manipulate any image. Want a few flowers in the foreground? No problem. Want to get rid of facial lines, cellulite, or skin blemishes? A push of a button, and they're gone. With the right software, it's easy to turn a size 10 into a size 2. If you've ever watched a good magician , you know about this power of illusion. But if the illusions are exposed, the magic disappears. So before you attempt to imitate a model, remember that what you're looking at has been altered by technology. Perhaps illusions contribute to the estimated 65 percent of female athletes with disordered eating behaviors. Disordered eating can be the precursor to eating disorders.

If you feel yourself aiming for a body that appears to be thin and beautiful, like the bodies displayed in magazines, consider rethinking your goals. Rather than striving for the rail-thin body found in a modified magazine photograph, wouldn't you rather aim for the

Poisonous Beliefs

The *Reporter-Herald* newspaper, in Loveland, Colorado, conducted a survey on body image and received comments from seventy-seven seventh-graders and thirty-three fourth-graders. When asked how they felt about the way they looked, half of the girls didn't give positive answers. Forty-two percent of the fourth-graders and 46 percent of the seventh-graders said they wished they were thinner. At the tender, young age of ten, 42 percent of the girls are worried about gaining weight. That number climbs to 53 percent in the twelve-year-old group.

Many of the girls—90 percent—read fashion magazines, and a full 64 percent of them admire the women in the magazines, and many aspire to look like them. Considering the average model is 5 feet 11 inches and weighs 114 pounds, this is a near-impossible goal for the majority of the female population, which averages 5 foot 4 inches tall and 140 pounds. A few of the girls did believe the models were too thin; however, they were the minority.

Sadly, many of the girls are passing up opportunities to be active for fear of being ridiculed. For example, they may avoid the swimming pool altogether. Others wear heavy, bulky T-shirts at the swimming pool to cover their tummy, thighs, and butt. Both of these behaviors discourage girls from activity—the very thing that can help them have fit, healthy bodies.

It is apparent from this survey, done in the spring of 1998, that unhealthy attitudes about body image start at an early age. Although there is growing awareness that fit, healthy bodies and minds are valuable assets, the cultural drive to correlate thinness with self-worth is poisoning another generation of women.

healthy body and the lifestyle that accompanies that body? Are you really aiming for a long and strong athletic life?

Your perfectly healthy and athletic body will likely look different from that of the woman next door. Those differences should be celebrated. Realistic, achievable goals and body image help you lead a balanced and happy life. If you begin to notice that you are stressing about your body image and food, see if any of your current habits are signals of disordered eating.

Unfortunately, the desire to be thin can transform into a full-blown eating disorder. Two of the most common eating disorders are anorexia and bulimia. Anorexia is characterized by restricting food to the point of near starvation. Anorexics see themselves as fat, although their outward appearance to others is emaciated.

They usually have an incredible amount of nutritional knowledge that is used to categorize foods as either "good" or "bad." Fat and calories are considered evil. People with anorexic behaviors will often prepare elaborate meals for others or give food as gifts but will not eat the foods themselves. If they do sample a forbidden food, the quantity would be too small to equal one bite.

Bulimia, in contrast, is characterized by episodes of bingeing on high-calorie foods. A bingeing person can consume 2,000 to 20,000 calories in a single sitting. The consumption is followed by guilt, and a purging behavior follows. Purging takes the form of vomiting, fasting, laxative or diuretic abuse, or excessive exercise.

Recognizing Eating Disorders

Some behaviors signaling disordered eating are:

- Obsessive talk about food, calories, fat grams, and body weight.
- Constant awareness of weight and food intake of other people.
- Not eating in public.
- Often talking about being overweight.
- Consistently skipping meals.
- Classifying some foods as "bad" and totally forbidden from the diet.
- Consumption of "bad" foods causing bingeing, purging, or other self-punitive behaviors.
- Self-diagnosed allergies to foods based on a single or few adverse reactions. Food group elimination can cause unnecessarily restrictive eating behavior and may lead to vitamin and mineral deficiencies.

Disordered eating or an eating disorder can lead to amenorrhea and, eventually, bone loss. When this occurs, an athlete sacrifices her health. No weight-loss scheme, short- or long-term, is worth your long-term health.

DIETING

It's not hard to see how dieting can be misguided or ultimately detrimental to your health and fitness. However, for many athletes, being 5 or 10 pounds lighter could improve fitness and overall health. Speaking of weight loss, there are a gazillion diets out there. Go into any bookstore and browse the health and nutrition section, and you will see how abundant weight-loss schemes are. But before embarking on any dietary protocol, ask yourself:

- Who are the subjects being discussed
  in the dietary plan?
- Is my background similar?
- Is my lifestyle similar?
- Are my goals similar?
- How restrictive is this diet?

Some years back, there was a popular diet that involved eating a huge amount of vegetable soup. The diet originally was designed to reduce the weight of obese patients preparing for open-heart surgery. These people probably had some genetic conditions that predisposed them to heart disease. They probably were not very fit or active. And their goal was to lose weight fast to prepare for open-heart surgery.

Now, unless you have the same lifestyle and background as these people, and you're planning a trip to the hospital for an operation, why would you follow their diet? To lose weight fast?

If that logic works, then anyone wanting to be a top cyclist should eat like a Tour de France rider. They average anywhere from 5,800 to

9,000 calories per day (about 62 percent carbohydrates, 15 percent protein, and 23 percent fat). Why would few people consume a Tour de France cyclist's menu to be stronger, faster riders—calories and all—and more people follow a diet designed for obese heart patients? This is faulty logic. If you're not one of the people the diet is designed for, following it would be unhealthy.

While it is not the fast fix to get your scale to read back that magic number, the best diet for you comes with a basic understanding of what your body's nutritional needs are, especially as a woman and an athlete. Know that finding the lifelong eating habits that are best for your body may require some patient trial and error. Later in this chapter we'll take a closer look at what your nutrition should look like, in terms of both caloric intake and macronutrients, if you are trying to shed a few pounds.

HOW MUCH OF WHAT?

Before changing your diet, evaluate what you're eating. A dietitian would ask you to keep a food diary, and if you decide to analyze your diet on your own, you'll need to do the same thing. Use a reference book such as *The NutriBase Nutrition Facts Desk Reference* to measure the calories and macronutrients in your current diet. Log what foods you eat, how much, and when. Begin with tabulating just calories, or log the grams of carbohydrate, fat, and protein as well.

Record your information honestly, and try not to change your eating behaviors just because you're keeping a food log. It might turn out that you have been maintaining a healthy weight and eating 3,000 calories per day, and there's no reason for you to change anything. Or you may constantly feel weak and tired while eating 3,000 calories per day; in this case, something needs to change. For now you're just recording, so suspend your judgment.

Next, fill out the "Health Questionnaire" in Appendix C. It will give you important information to help determine whether you're healthy. If you're not as healthy as you'd like to be, consider changing your diet or lifestyle—or both—in consultation with a dietitian who specializes in sports nutrition.

PUTTING IT ALL TOGETHER

Now things get sticky. We need carbohydrates, fat, and protein to sustain good health, but how much of each? How many calories are enough? How can a woman lose weight without compromising health? Should we take vitamin and mineral supplements? Long bouts of exercise need calorie supplementation, but how much and from what kinds of food? Long or exhausting exercise requires quick recovery—how is that best accomplished?

If you first establish your dietary and fitness goals, prioritize those goals, and determine how to measure them, then the answers become more clear. If you eat with the main goal of building a healthy body, chances are good you will live a full and active life.

Consider the following goals, prioritized here in order of importance, for achieving long-term wellness. Consume a diet that:

- Builds and maintains a healthy body in the short term and minimizes the risk of disease in the future.
- Allows you to feel good physically and mentally.
- Considers your genetic makeup.
- Takes into account your lifestyle, fitness, and activity level.
- Enhances your athletic capabilities.

BENCHMARK FORMULAS

So far, we've established a set of nutrition rules, prioritized the goals of a healthy diet, determined what you are currently eating, and recorded your current health status. You know where you are and, in general, where you want to go. Now how do you get there?

If your current diet meets both your needs and the goals of a healthy diet, celebrate! If you think your diet needs fine-tuning, or if you just want more information about measuring your intake of macro- and micronutrients, read on. Some people prefer general dietary guidelines, while others want numbers. What follows is a bit of both.

Daily Caloric Intake

One of the common formulas used to determine now many calories are needed daily to maintain body weight is 30 calories per kilogram of body weight. To find your weight in kilograms, divide your weight in pounds by 2.2. For example, if your weight is 140 pounds, your weight in kilograms is

$$140 ÷ 2.2 = 63.6 \text{ (or 64 kilograms)}$$

Your daily caloric needs are

$$64 × 30 = 1,920 \text{ calories}$$

At 140 pounds, it takes roughly 80 calories per hour (1,920 calories/24 hours) to fuel your body. Of course, the exact value changes depending on whether you are awake and active or sleeping, but 80 calories per hour is a good start.

Modify this formula as appropriate:

- **Add** 100 to 300 calories to the daily total if you lead a highly active lifestyle.
- **Subtract** 100 to 300 calories from the daily total if your lifestyle or job is sedentary.

The following modifiers include both resting energy expenditure and exercise expenditure.

- **Add** about 0.15 to 0.17 calorie per minute per kilogram of body weight for cycling. (For example, 0.17 calorie per minute-kilogram × 60 minutes × 64 kilograms equals 653 calories needed for one hour of fast cycling.)
- **Add** about 0.14 to 0.29 calorie per minute (roughly the range from an 11-minute pace per mile to a 5-minute, 30-second pace

per mile) per kilogram of body weight for running. (For example, 0.2 calorie per minute-kilogram × 60 minutes × 64 kilograms equals 768 calories needed for an hour of fast running.)

• **Add** about 0.1 calorie per minute per kilogram of body weight for strength training. (For example, 0.1 calorie per minute-kilogram × 60 minutes × 64 kilograms equals 384 calories needed for an hour of strength training.)

So the 140-pound person in our example would need to consume somewhere between 1,620 and 2,820 calories each day to maintain her weight, maybe more if training for an ultradistance event. This athlete needs to consume more calories on active training days and fewer calories when her body doesn't need them.

What if You Want to Lose Weight?

When I first began my coaching career, I often heard women express concern about weight, but men seldom did. Times have changed. Now I hear as many men as women discussing weight loss and maintenance. Before heading into your weight-loss program, know that severe caloric restrictions can decrease resting metabolic rate by 45 percent. Decreasing your metabolism is the last thing you want to do when you are trying to shed pounds.

A commonly suggested ways to lose weight is to decrease your daily caloric intake by 200 to 300 calories without dropping below 1,500 a day. You can calculate how many calories it takes to maintain your current weight from your food log, assuming your weight has been constant. This slow approach to weight loss, through reduced food intake, reduces the risk of compromising health.

Here's the strategy I recommend to athletes: Begin eating now the way you plan to eat at your new weight. After all, this is a long-term strategy for success. Athletes who plan to "go on a diet" to lose weight, do lose weight, and then return to old eating habits, will not keep the lower weight for long.

To illustrate how easy it is to eat for your new weight, let's look at an example: If you currently weigh 135 pounds and want to weigh 125 pounds, what is the difference in the daily caloric needs to maintain body weight, without looking at exercise?

At 135 pounds (61.4 kilograms), your maintenance level is 1,842 calories per day (61.4 × 30). At your goal weight of 165 pounds (75 kilograms), you need 1,705 calories per day (56.8 × 30). Yes, that's right—a difference of only 137 calories per day!

What Source for Calories?

Most experts agree that there is no one specific number value for the consumption of each macronutrient that will maintain or improve health and athletic training for every individual. Many experts, however, agree that there is a range for each macronutrient that has been found to work very well for almost everyone. When you are designing your diet, aim to be within these ranges (see Figure 5.1):

- **Carbohydrates:** 40 to 65 percent of total calories
- **Fat:** 15 to 30 percent of total calories
- **Protein:** 15 to 30 percent of total calories; between 1.5 and 2.0 grams per kilogram of body weight

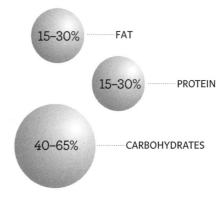

FIGURE 5.1
Macronutrients in Your Diet: Suggested Ranges of Consumption of Total Calories

Note: The protein range is between 1.5 and 2.0 grams per kilogram of body weight.

15–30% ········· FAT

15–30% ········· PROTEIN

40–65% ········· CARBOHYDRATES

Exactly how much of each macronutrient to consume depends on your health risks, dietary goals, and current mode of training. Your health and athletic training needs are constantly changing, so your diet must also change. Don't try to lose weight and race at the same time. This combination can result in emotional instability or decreased performance. Consider the following suggested diet modifications:

- **Intense training or high volume of training:** Carbohydrate consumption should be on the higher end of the range when you are training fast miles (Zones 4 and 5) or long miles (90 minutes or more). Protein consumption should be higher when training hard, building muscle mass, or doing very long rides (over three hours). (See Figure 5.2.)
- **Moderate training:** Carbohydrate consumption should be in the middle range when you are training in Zones 1 to 3 (see Figure 5.3). Also recall from the Cape Town study mentioned earlier in the chapter that an increased level of fat consumption improved endurance. Increased fat during moderate aerobic training may improve your endurance.
- **Weight loss:** Carbohydrate consumption should be at the lower end of the range when you are trying to lose weight. Protein consumption should be greater when you are trying to maintain muscle mass while dieting. (See Figure 5.4.)

There are different ways to estimate calorie and nutrient needs. Some sources refer to macronutrient consumption as a percentage of calorie intake, while others talk about consuming a certain number of grams of each macronutrient. It can get confusing when the measuring systems are talked about interchangeably. It helps to know that not all food grams have equal energy value. As you can see in Figure 5.5, alcohol and fat add on calories much faster than the same portions of carbohydrate or protein.

FIGURE 5.2
Micronutrients for
High-Volume or
Intense Training

Note: Some athletes perform
better with a higher percentage of protein, others wtih
higher fat.

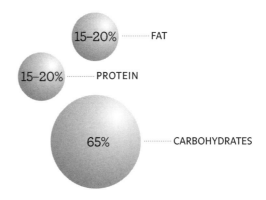

FIGURE 5.3
Micronutrients for
Moderate Training

Note: As training becomes
more moderate, carbohy-
drates can be reduced while
increasing fat and protein.

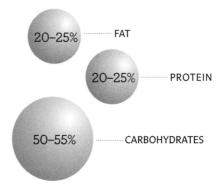

FIGURE 5.4
Micronutrients for
Weight Loss

Note: Most athletes find they
are more successful with
weight loss when carbohy-
drates are reduced. Generally,
reduced carbohydrates means
reduced training intensity.

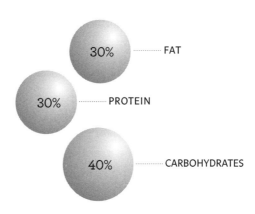

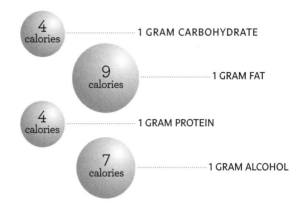

FIGURE 5.5
Energy Value
Contained in
Macronutrient
Food Grams

The Rules of Optimal Nutrition

- Eat adequate calories to maintain weight.
- Don't try to lose weight with extreme calorie restriction.
- Eat a balance of macronutrients.
- Drink adequate fluids.
- There are no "bad" foods, but you may consume some with discretion.
- Dietary fat is essential to optimal health.
- A healthy diet should contain a wide variety of minimally processed foods.
- Eat. Eat often. Eat variety. When cycling long, eat early–don't wait. Most importantly, eat!

ENERGY NEEDS DURING EXERCISE

It can be tricky to change your diet based on your training, but it is even more difficult to find the key to nutrition during exercise and recovery. If you are an experienced cyclist, it could be that you have it figured out. If you are satisfied with your current health and athletic performance, don't change for the sake of change.

If you are not happy with your health or performance, you may be a cyclist who is performing below your potential because your body lacks either adequate nutrition or hydration. If you are looking for more help defining energy needs during exercise, see the following sections to defining what you need based on the demands of your event or ride. We'll consider the specific ergogenic aids you might use to fuel your exercise and recovery after figuring out the basic numbers.

Determining Caloric Needs Based on Event

Consume a minimum of 30 to 60 grams of carbohydrate (which is equivalent to 120 to 240 calorie) per hour of intense or long exercise. For exercise lasting less than about three hours, many athletes find that consuming 150 to 250 carbohydrate calories works just fine. For exercise over three hours, anecdotal evidence suggests that many athletes need a minimum of 250 to 350 calories per hour. On rare occasions, athletes report consuming as many as 500 or more calories per hour. To determine how many calories per hour your body can process and utilize will require some experimentation.

How much you need to consume depends on body size, pace, pre-event muscle glycogen storage, and individual metabolism. The exact optimal breakdown of carbohydrates, fat, and protein in your fuel is very individual. Your fuel can be taken in through fluid or solid sources. Be certain to consume adequate fluids as well, which we'll explore in the next section on hydration.

Athletes who compete in events that last from six to seventeen hours will tell you that nutrition can significantly influence the outcome of a race. Nutrition, in effect, becomes an event within the event. Some of these ultraendurance athletes prefer to include fat and protein in their exercise nutrition. The exact macronutrient proportions necessary for optimum performance are not clear and appear to vary by individual.

Maintaining Hydration

During training and racing you should hydrate at a rate of 4 to 8 ounces every 15 to 20 minutes. There are significant variations in individual sweat rates, with some individuals losing more fluid than they can replace or absorb. Fitness, environmental conditions, acclimatization to heat, and genetic differences are some of the factors influencing individual fluid losses.

One way to estimate your individual sweat rate is to weigh yourself without clothes before and after a one-hour running session. Monique Ryan, sports nutrition expert and author of *Sports Nutrition for Endurance Athletes,* tells us that "every pound of weight loss represents 500 ml (16 oz) of fluid loss." Repeat the test for a one-hour cycling session. Repeat the test for different environmental conditions, such as cool winter training and hot summer training. For each test, note how much fluid you lost and your exercise intensity during the session. From these tests, you can estimate your sweat rate and adjust fluid intake to keep your body in balance.

It's important to note that excessive hydration with water can dilute the sodium content of the blood and cause a dangerous condition called hyponatremia. Hyperhydration and dehydration are both undesirable—your body seeks balance.

For long exercise sessions or excessive sweat rates, there is a loss of electrolytes. The electrolytes lost in sweat that cause the most concern are sodium and chloride, which combine to form salt. Once again, there are individual variations in the amount of sodium lost and how much sodium needs to be ingested to keep an athletic body in balance.

For long exercise sessions, a rule of thumb to follow is to include 250 to 500 milligrams of sodium per hour, along with your fluid replacement strategy. Some ultraendurance athletes may need to supplement at rates higher than 500 milligrams per hour. It is best to begin on the low end of supplementation and make gradual adjustments as needed.

Other electrolytes of note are potassium, magnesium, and calcium. Many energy drinks include a combination of these electrolytes. You will need to experiment to determine which fluid and electrolyte replacement strategy is best for you.

Enhancing Recovery Through Replenishing Proper Fuel

To speed recovery, consume liquid or solid fuel within 20 to 30 minutes of completing a long or exhausting workout. This fuel should contain 1.5 to 1.6 grams of carbohydrate per kilogram of body weight and 0.4 to 0.5 gram of protein per kilogram of body weight. To further enhance recovery over the twenty-four hours after exercise, consume liquid or solid fuel that contains 6 to 8 grams of carbohydrate per kilogram of body weight.

Recovery-type foods include milkshakes, chocolate milk, bagels, cottage cheese, lean meat, fruit and protein-powder smoothies, yogurt smoothies with fruit, and beef jerky combined with a sports drink. Some studies indicate that regular snacks of approximately 50 grams of carbohydrates, eaten every two hours, may optimize recovery. (Of course an evening meal containing adequate carbohydrates would be necessary to get you through a night's sleep. In other words, don't try to set an alarm to wake up every two hours to eat.)

Putting It Together

Back to our 64-kilogram athlete: Let's say she is doing a big day of training. She needs about 2,800 calories. If her protein intake were 1.8 grams per kilogram of body weight, that would be 115 grams of protein, or about 460 protein calories.

On her three-hour ride, she'll consume 200 carbohydrate calories per hour—600 calories total. And she will consume a post-ride recovery food containing 1.5 to 1.6 grams of carbohydrate per kilogram of body weight. So, say 1.6 × 64 = about 102 grams of carbohydrate, or 102 × 4 = 408 carbohydrate calories. These 1,008 carbohydrate calories meet her cycling needs.

Since her ride was a very fast group ride, she'll need 6 to 8 grams of carbohydrate per kilogram of body weight over the next twenty-four hours to restore her glycogen levels. At 6 grams, she would need 384 grams of carbohydrate (including the post-ride recovery drink), and at 8 grams, she would need 512 grams of carbohydrate.

Choosing 512 grams, she needs to consume about 2,000 carbohydrate calories over 24 hours to replenish her glycogen. She can consume some of those calories today and some tomorrow.

If today's caloric needs are about 2,800:

- Protein calories are 460 (115 grams), or 16 percent of the total (460/2,800).
- Carbohydrate calories are 1,680 (420 grams), or 60 percent of the total mean.
- The remaining calories are fat: 2,800 − 460 − 1,680 = 660 calories (about 73 fat grams), or about 30 percent fat.

The perfect diet and nutrient breakdown depends on many factors. The best place to start is to simply log what you are doing now and review your current health and performance status. If your diet doesn't meet your needs, make a change.

ERGOGENIC AIDS

An ergogenic aid is something that can increase muscular work capacity. Most questions I receive concerning ergogenic aids are about sports drinks, energy bars and drinks, and caffeine, so let's take a look at the pros and cons of each of these.

Sports Drinks

The simple rule of thumb is to drink the one that tastes best to you and doesn't cause extra potty stops or an upset digestive system. If you select a drink that tastes good and use it for workouts that are more than an hour long, generally it's beneficial. Be aware that some athletes have gastrointestinal problems with fructose-based sports drinks. If you're having difficulties, check to see if fructose is one of the main ingredients.

Some sports drinks include protein. Common carbohydrate-to-protein ratios range from 4:1 to 7:1. In general, I recommend sticking to a product that contains only carbohydrates for shorter, faster

Keeping Your Diet in Check

Now that you have formulas to estimate caloric needs, macronutrient break-downs, fueling during a long ride, and post-ride fueling strategies, here are some words of caution:

- The word "estimate" is critical. Don't worry about getting the exact numbers when consuming calories. There is a margin of error on food product labels, and there is a margin of error when estimating personal nutrition needs.
- If you've determined that you need 100 grams of carbohydrate and 33 grams of protein for post-ride recovery and a food source has 115 grams of carbohydrate and 25 grams of protein, don't worry–it will work fine.
- Don't become a food log addict. Use food logs to establish good eating behaviors or as spot checks to see what is going on with your diet. It is possible to drive yourself nuts weighing and counting everything. Let food logs serve their purpose, then give them a rest.
- Just because you exercise doesn't mean you can eat unlimited quantities of food. Everyone's body has an energy balance system. You need to learn to manage your own body and its special needs.
- Body weight is a number. Don't weigh yourself every day and look for changes. In fact, if you lose several pounds from one day to the next, it's probably due to dehydration. Try to remedy that by drinking additional fluid and putting some numbers back on the scale. At most, weigh yourself weekly–at the same time, on the same day, and on the same scale. Your overall health status is a better measure of nutritional success than numbers on a scale.

events. For events longer than about three hours, many athletes find that some protein seems to help. How much protein can be tolerated seems to vary by individual. Some athletes do fine with a 4:1 mix, while others experience gastrointestinal distress at this level. Test your sports drinks during training events.

Energy Bars

Energy bars aren't one of the major food groups. They're useful for long rides, pre- and post-workout snacks, and pre-race snacks. Some athletes use them as a major source of calories, choosing them over fruits and vegetables because they're a grab-and-go food.

Use them as supplements for sporting activities; they are not appropriate as meals. Eat minimally processed foods and, whenever possible, choose whole foods over highly refined foods—including energy bars.

Energy Drinks

Energy drinks such as Red Bull, Rockstar, and Redline can contain as little as 3 milligrams or as much as 30 milligrams of caffeine per ounce, and most cans contain 8 to 16 ounces. That means you're getting up to 480 milligrams of caffeine in one can, the equivalent of two to four cups of coffee. Caffeine can be useful in training and competition, but these drinks also might contain other stimulants, such as guarana and yerba maté, and some have lots of added sugar. If you plan to use them, read the labels carefully to make sure you know what you're ingesting.

Caffeine

Caffeine may be the most widely used drug in the world. It stimulates the central nervous system, the adrenal system, the metabolic system, and the muscular system. While some studies have shown that it influences the metabolic system by stimulating fat metabolism and sparing glycogen during aerobic exercise, the research on this theory is not conclusive.

For example, some studies show that glycogen sparing is limited to the first 15 to 20 minutes of exercise. Additional studies in which the focus is on the measurement of free fatty acid metabolism, which spares glycogen, show that the response to fat burning may not be optimal until three to four hours after ingestion.

Another theory is that caffeine lowers the level of perceived pain at a given pace, so athletes have the ability to produce more work, or work for longer periods, with the use of caffeine. Several studies support the notion that caffeine, when used in conjunction with exercise, appears not to have the diuretic effect it has when consumed in a nonexercise situation.

There are conflicting opinions about whether regular caffeine users need to abstain from caffeine use for some period prior to an important event to optimize the effects. At least one study (Graham 2001) suggests that caffeine nonusers and regular users respond similarly to caffeine when taken before exercise, so the theory of regular users needing to abstain from caffeine before important events may not be necessary.

A second study, by D. G. Bell (2002), shows that the ergogenic effect following a dose of 5 milligrams of caffeine per kilogram of body weight for regular caffeine users and nonusers produced greater effects in nonusers than in users during exercise one to three hours after ingestion. Some studies show that ingesting caffeine as coffee is ineffective compared with ingesting pure caffeine, although the reason isn't clear.

A dose of 5 to 7 milligrams of caffeine per kilogram of body weight, given one hour prior to exercise, has been the typical protocol for most studies; however, doses as low as 3.3 to 4.4 milligrams of caffeine per kilogram of body weight have been shown to be effective.

There can be negative side effects to caffeine consumption. Some people don't tolerate caffeine well and become shaky, jittery, and unable to focus. It also is bothersome to some gastrointestinal systems, producing stomach pain, abdominal cramps, and diarrhea. The U.S. Olympic Committee once banned caffeine at levels measuring 12 micrograms/milliliter of urine, but this restriction was removed in January 2004.

Although the exact mechanisms that cause caffeine to be an ergogenic aid are unclear, all the studies I have found show that it can be effective. If you decide to use caffeine, experiment with it during training sessions. Don't wait until a race or big event to test your tolerance and advantage levels. For racing, consume the caffeine approximately 30 to 60 minutes before race start. Refer to Table 5.2 for the major sources of caffeine.

TABLE 5.2 Caffeine Content of Beverages

PRODUCT	SERVING	CAFFEINE
Coffee	8 oz	100–250 mg
Espresso	1 oz	35–60 mg
Cappuccino	8 oz	35–60 mg
Latte	8 oz	35–60 mg
Mountain Dew	12 oz	55 mg
No-Doz, regular	1 tablet	100 mg
Excedrin	2 tablets	130 mg
Go Fast	11.9 oz	120 mg
Red Bull	8.2 oz	80 mg

SUPPLEMENTS

The word "supplement" is defined as something added to complete a thing or to make up for a deficiency. Notice this definition does not say "a substitute for . . ." No amount of vitamin and mineral supplementation will make up for a crummy diet, something people don't seem to understand. A recent case in point: The young man sacking my groceries expressed curiosity about the volume and variety of vegetables I was buying. "Are you a vegetarian or something?" he asked.

"No, at our house we eat lots of different vegetables because they taste good and their vibrant colors make an exciting plate," I replied.

"Oh, I don't like vegetables, so I just eat meat and potatoes and take vitamins," he said. "Anyway, one vitamin pill has all the stuff

I really need, so I don't have to worry about it. I'm training to be a boxer, so I need all the vitamins."

His thought process is all too common. While he continued sacking the groceries, I explained about fiber; phytochemicals; and the unknown, healthy substances probably also contained in real food. I explained how recent the discovery of phytochemicals is and that although we humans are pretty smart, we are a long way from knowing everything. I further explained that supplements are meant to complement a diet high in whole foods but that no supplementation plan will make up for a diet high in processed foods, saturated fat, sugar, and salt and low in fiber and variety. The young man asked if I would let him take my groceries to the car so he could ask more questions. I answered, "You bet!" I don't know if he'll change his habits, but at least he was thinking.

Nutrition is still a young science. Researchers are continually discovering more information about vitamin and mineral supplementation. A survey of top researchers asked what they themselves take for vitamin and mineral supplementation, and the answers were not uniform. Some of the supplements that continue to receive attention among scientists are multivitamins, vitamin C, vitamin E, calcium, and iron.

Multivitamins

Most experts recommend a multivitamin and mineral supplement. Some experts still strongly believe we should be able to meet all of our vitamin and mineral needs from food, but more research suggests that it doesn't happen that way for most folks.

U.S. Department of Agriculture data indicate that at least 40 percent of Americans routinely consume a diet containing only 60 percent of the recommended daily allowance (RDA) of ten selected nutrients. We would fare worse if more nutrients were evaluated.

There continues to be controversy as to whether athletes' requirements for vitamins and minerals exceed those of the average population. If athletes are consuming a balanced and varied diet and taking some supplements, that might be enough.

Vitamins C and E

The current recommendation is to supplement a multivitamin with 500 to 1,000 milligrams of vitamin C and 400 IU of vitamin E. Both of these are antioxidants, substances that block oxidative damage to the body's cells. To maintain constant concentrations of vitamin C in the blood, it's best to take two doses eight to twelve hours apart.

Calcium

The current recommendation is to consume somewhere between 1,000 and 1,500 milligrams of calcium daily. This is particularly important for postmenopausal women. After menopause, women no longer produce as much estrogen. Reduced estrogen production is associated with increased bone loss. Protein, some minerals, and vitamins C, D, E, and K all play a role in calcium absorption. For example, too much magnesium, sodium, and/or phosphorus (found in many soft drinks and processed foods) can inhibit the absorption of calcium.

Just supplementing the diet with calcium isn't a cure-all. Weight-bearing exercise plays an important role, though more is not necessarily better. For example, even men, who seem to be less prone to bone loss, can suffer when exercise levels are excessive. One study of University of Memphis male basketball players found that they were losing about 3.8 percent of their bone mass from preseason to midseason in a single year.

Bob Klesges, the head scientist, discovered that the basketball players were losing substantial amounts of calcium in their sweat. He reached this conclusion by collecting the sweaty T-shirts of the players and carefully wringing out their contents to be analyzed.

(Yuck!) He found that the players gained back 1.1 percent of their bone mass during summer, but they lost an additional 3.3 percent when practices resumed, making their total losses about 5.8 percent. With supplemental calcium, they were able to regain the losses.

For exercising women and postmenopausal women, it is important to get an adequate supply of calcium. Make a solid effort to get 1,000 to 1,500 milligrams of calcium from your diet (an 8-ounce glass of milk contains 290 milligrams). If you're not getting enough through your diet, consider a supplement on the days when your food consumption does not give you the recommended requirements.

The superior supplement is calcium citrate malate, which can be found in many calcium-enriched juices. On average this supplement allows people to absorb 35 percent of the calcium in calcium citrate malate, compared with 30 percent of the calcium in other supplements.

Iron

Iron is an essential component of hemoglobin and myoglobin and functions in the oxygenation of red blood cells and muscle. Women, especially, can have low levels of iron and develop anemia.

One of the common causes of anemia is excessive menstrual flow coupled with inadequate dietary iron. Good food sources of iron are fish, meat, beans, whole grains, enriched breads, and enriched cereals. Iron supplements should be prescribed by a doctor.

Constant fatigue is one of the common symptoms of anemia. Anemia can be easily identified with a simple blood test. In fact, blood tests can detect many problems associated with diet, health, and wellness. For athletes serious about wellness and competition, an annual blood test—in the restorative or off-season—is an excellent source of information. This baseline test can then be used to diagnose changes in blood chemistry when a competitive season seems to have gone awry.

• • •

MY GREAT-UNCLE CALLED ME WINDY ANN—THE STORY AT THE BE-ginning of this chapter is about me. I'll be happy if I can prevent other people from repeating my journey. And don't be fooled into thinking this is only a problem for women. I coach many men, and highly competitive male athletes are also prone to extreme calorie restriction.

I hope this brief introduction to nutrition will encourage you to learn more about the subject. Read information and recommenda-tions carefully to determine whether they apply to you. If you have special needs or deficiencies that aren't discussed in this chapter, take care of them and learn as much as you can about their treat-ment.

Remember—it's critical to overall good health to consume enough calories and a wide variety of foods to ensure adequate absorption of macro- and micronutrients. Not consuming enough calories can slow metabolism and cheat the body of nutrients needed for nor-mal menstrual cycles and healing, both of which are critical to good health and athletic performance.

chapter six

Mental Tools

Courage is resistance to fear, mastery of fear—not the absence of fear. —MARK TWAIN

We all have a little voice inside our heads, and it's not always a helpful one. On a bad day on the bike, it says, "I hate hills. I'm the worst hill climber. Everyone is going to leave me in their dust." It's time to start paying close attention to how your little voice influences your attitudes and actions. This critical step underlies all the concepts and tools in this chapter.

Some people spend their entire lives waiting for "just the right time" to try something new, stretch their wings, or take a risk. They want to wait until they are rich enough, thin enough, strong enough, or confident enough. If you have a dream, you have enough right now to make it come true, even if moving toward that dream requires work and patience.

As you read through this chapter, you will notice the concepts are framed for athletic performance. While framed for your cycling world, the concepts are just as useful in your work and everyday life. Strong mental fitness is just as valuable off the bike as it is on the bike. Practice in both arenas.

KEY CONCEPTS FOR MENTAL TRAINING
Key Concept 1: Play to Win

This means to go as far as you can using all that you have. Playing to win is different from "playing not to lose," which is a defensive strategy to maintain security and comfort (see Table 6.1). It's important to be honest about your motives and insecurities in order to realize your potential. If you do your best on any given day, under any given circumstances, you're a winner—regardless of what place you finish in the race. If you give it all you've got, you owe no apologies. Your focus is on you, your performance, and what you can control.

TABLE 6.1 Mental Fitness

PLAYING TO WIN	PLAYING NOT TO LOSE
Show up and do your best.	Don't show up if you can't do well at a race or lead a ride.
Focus on yourself and your performance.	Focus on others and their performance.
Take responsibility for what you can control. Be accountable.	Blame your performance on the weather, equipment, or other people.
Embrace discomfort for growth.	Stay in your comfort zone.
Stretch your skills.	Avoid new situations.

Key Concept 2: Tolerate Discomfort but Treat Pain

Becoming a faster cyclist is going to be uncomfortable. There will be times when your legs are burning and you feel as if you can't go another second—and then you go 10. (By the way—you just played to win.) Tolerating this type of discomfort, both physically and mentally, is part of becoming a faster cyclist.

As you increase your fitness level, you'll increase your tolerance for discomfort, and embracing discomfort is part of growth and improvement. There is, however, a real difference between discomfort and pain. The physical discomfort I'm referring to is typically muscular and goes away as intensity decreases. A second type of physical discomfort is the kind that shows up a day or two after a hilly ride or a tough weight room workout. This is called delayed onset of muscle soreness. Both of these types of physical discomfort are common to athletic training.

Pain, on the other hand, comes in various forms, some of which need a doctor's attention. Pain after a ride is probably nothing to worry about—take, for example, when you get a kink in your neck, but it goes away within twenty-four hours. Various home treatments may be appropriate when pain flares up, including gentle stretching; icing the injured area; and taking anti-inflammatories such as aspirin, ibuprofen, or naproxen sodium. Pain during the ride that doesn't force you to stop can be treated the same way as after-ride pain. In this case, you might consider taking a day or two off the bike to reduce further injury.

But for pain that occurs throughout the ride, interferes with your ability to complete the ride, or persists when you are off the bike, stay off the bike for a few days, ice the injured area, perhaps take an anti-inflammatory—and get medical attention. Athletes often try to train through an injury, making it worse. It's important for you to be able to distinguish among discomfort, minor pain, and injury.

Much as physical pain comes from doing an activity that is somehow foreign or challenging, mental discomfort comes from doing something you've never done before, something that makes you feel vulnerable. What happens if you don't meet your goal? What happens if you can't keep up with the group? What will people say? It is important that you determine your own definition of success or failure. Stretching beyond your comfort zone and taking some risks will move you toward new levels of skill and confidence.

Key Concept 3: Train Your Mind

Just as you practice and improve physical aspects of cycling, you need to practice the mental aspects of training. Seek new sources to increase your mental skills, and keep adding to your abilities. I liken this effort to a stash of multipurpose tools. This mental training toolbox will work not only in athletics but in other aspects of your life as well.

BUILDING YOUR MENTAL TOOLBOX
Tool 1: SET

- **S**top the little voice.
- **E**valuate the situation.
- **T**ake a course of mind.

That little voice can be so helpful and encouraging, urging you on when you're struggling, but it can work against you too: "This wind is horrible. You ride poorly in the wind. Why even start the ride?" When the little voice turns negative, it's time to silence it and evaluate the situation. Say it warns you not to travel through a dark, wooded park at night. Stop the voice and decide whether the unlit park is a safe situation. If your voice makes sense, listen and change your route.

However, if the voice says you're not up to a ride in the wind, stop and evaluate. Sure, it's windy, but maybe you can use the wind to simulate hills and enhance your training. If you're riding with other people, form a pace line to rotate a lead position so that you alternate work and rest. How about riding out in a headwind and back in a tailwind? Wouldn't it be fun to see how fast you can go on the way back?

When that little voice starts talking to you, pay attention. If the talk is negative or makes you feel fearful, evaluate all options and then take a course of mind action. Is there really something to fear, or can you forge on to "make lemonade out of lemons"? Whatever your mind decides, your body will follow. The wind and hills can be valuable training tools if you let them.

Tool 2: Kill the Mental Monsters

When I was a child, I believed I could stay out of the "Monster Zone" by getting a good running start from the hallway and jumping into bed. The monster, a large, brown, hairy creature with dust bunnies stuck to his fur, lived under my bed. He hated light and became active at night, trying to grab my leg if I allowed it to dangle over the side of the bed. But if I could leap over his realm, get my feet under the covers, and lie in the center of my bed, I was safe. The monster was closely related to the "Closet Ghost," a transparent creature who stared at me with glowing eyes if I left the closet door open at night. Sometimes the eyes were between hanging clothes, and other times they seemed to float near the top shelf. I remember fearing those eyes and making rules that would keep me safe.

I can now admit that I made the whole thing up—yet the memory is so vivid that if I close my eyes, I can still see both of them. I can also admit that I still make things up sometimes, along with rules to keep me safe. Some days I get on the bike and think I will never be a hill climber. Using Tool 1, I ask myself, "Will I never be a hill climber?" If I never ride the hills and work to get better, I probably won't be very good. But if I work at being a better climber and make myself stronger, maybe I can improve. And maybe that hill isn't as big as it looks.

It's also common to look at other people and think they're thinner, faster, stronger, better, taller, shorter, and more athletic than you are. Really? Is that true? Or have you imagined this person, perhaps your competition in a race, as being larger than life? Again, ask yourself if there's any truth in what your little voice is saying. Are those monsters real or imagined? If you can't completely eliminate monsters, at least turn on the light and have a good look at them. Maybe you will find they are no more than small, harmless trolls with blue hair.

Tool 3: Celebrate Small Successes Every Day

This tool ties in with the goal setting mentioned in Chapter 2. Set subgoals to mark your progress toward the larger goal. Close each day by recalling at least one good thing about your day. Finish your workouts by identifying something positive that better prepares you for the ultimate challenge. Even if the workout was tough and you survived it, the mental and physical test has left you better equipped for the demands of your event. This sort of positive self-recognition builds self-esteem and confidence, propelling you to reaching your goals.

Tool 4: Hang Out with Positive People

Have you ever noticed that spending time with a positive person makes you feel better? Have you ever noticed that hanging with a negative person wears on your nerves? Research has found that a simple grimace will raise the level of adrenaline and lower the level of serotonin in your system, producing all the physical symptoms of fear. Those symptoms include an elevated pulse, shallow breathing, and slowed digestion. Negative thoughts turn into negative emotions, which then turn into negative physical symptoms.

A positive outlook on any situation contributes to a healthy physical and emotional state. Surrounding yourself with positive, supportive people is an advantage. There is one catch, though: Positive people prefer to be around positive people as well, so they will expect the same from you.

Tool 5: Collect Positive Affirmations

Keep a notebook with positive comments about yourself. Are you a good hill climber? Jot it down. Are you improving your average speed? Write it down. Are you good at keeping your cool when tempers flare? Make a note. A brief review of any and all of your positive attributes can boost confidence. When the going gets tough and you can't muster a single positive thought, go back and read what you have written about yourself. It will help you reframe your thoughts.

Tool 6: Measure Success Based on *Yourself*, Not Others

This tool was also mentioned in Chapter 2. You can't control anyone else's performance or fitness level. You can use other people's performances as points of reference, but don't base your entire measure of personal success or failure on others.

Some good measures of personal success include aerobic and all-out time trials, average speed on a particular ride, or simply how strong you feel on the bike. Record that information on a sheet of paper and then transfer it from logbook to logbook each year. Then you can look back to earlier in the season and at past years to review how your performance has improved.

Tool 7: Enough Rules!

Some people overdo the work, and sometimes enough is enough. It's easy to get caught up in goals, schedules, plans, and training logs. Athletes will ignore pain signals and risk injury or ignore bad weather to get those final training miles in this week. Enough is enough! Relax, enjoy family and friends, or take a nap. There's time to train tomorrow.

Tool 8: Recognize a Learning Opportunity When You See One

Some of us have a tough time distinguishing between doing something wrong and making a mistake. Doing something wrong implies intent. We know before we do the action or say the words that it's not the right thing to do. If you were to intentionally swerve your bike and force another cyclist off the road, it would clearly be wrong.

On the other hand, if you look over your shoulder and steer your bike to the side as a consequence, nearly causing an accident, that's a mistake. Learn to ride a straight line when looking over your shoulder. Use errors and their corrective action to help improve performance. Forgive yourself for making a mistake, and use it as an opportunity to learn.

Tool 9: Use Music as Motivation

Music can set a mood, influence thoughts, and offer a bit of solitude. Many athletes prepare for a race by listening to music they find motivational or calming. Pay attention to music and see what it does for your mood. Would music help you prepare for an event or a race? Or maybe listening to music after a long day at work would help you clear your mind, allowing you to sleep better and feel more rested for tomorrow's ride.

Tool 10: Focus on What You Can Control

As you train and compete, there will be many things over which you have no control: weather, other people's performance or actions, accidents, flat tires. You can control only your attitude, your outlook on the situation, and your actions. Before thoughts become caught in a downward spiral or you become physically impaired by some kind of monster, use Tool 1 to take a course of mind action. Evaluate the situation and begin brainstorming options. Many times you have several choices. You can choose to quit and go home, which is a valid option, or continue as best you can on that given day—and play to win. To the extent that you can keep this perspective in other aspects of your life, your training and racing will benefit.

• • •

I'VE SHARED THE CONCEPTS AND TOOLS PRESENTED IN THIS CHAPTER with athletes and businesspeople. I was first introduced to the "play to win" concept by Pecos River Learning Centers, and as I mentioned at the beginning of the chapter, I believe these concepts have value in sports and everyday life. In work and in play, I encourage you to hone your mental skills. The body will follow the mind, but an unwilling mind can't force the body to realize its full potential.

Part II

Cycling as a Woman

From the Greek goddesses to modern-day cycling superstars, women have proved their athletic mettle time and again. And ever since they hopped on bikes in the late nineteenth century, they've never stopped pedaling.

In the early days, people wondered whether women should be encouraged to do such things: Would it affect childbearing? Wasn't it entirely too much for the weaker sex? Wasn't it unwomanly?

It's been a long struggle to change those attitudes, but we're definitely going in the right direction. The 1984 Olympic Games included women's road racing for the first time, and American Connie Carpenter, a thirteen-time U.S. Women's National Cycling champion, took the gold. Today, great female cyclists can be found the world over–riders like Jeannie Longo of France, Italian Fabiana Luperini, and German sprinter Petra Rossner.

In Part II, we'll look at some of the special challenges women cyclists face because of their physiology and the impact of menstruation and pregnancy, and we'll consider ways to stay as safe and comfortable as possible, no matter what kind of cycling you're doing.

We'll also look at the aging process and strategies to keep riding like Linda Miller, Marsha Macro, and Martha Hanson. I like to refer to these women because they embody strength of character and physiology, and because as of the writing of this book they own national records in their age categories. Linda has the record for the Track Time Trial–Standing Start 500 m in both the 55+ (8/09/06) and 60+ (8/27/07) categories. Marsha has records in both the Track Time Trial–Flying Start 200 m and the Track Time Trial–Standing Start 2 km in the 60+ categories, set at two different times (8/09/06 and 8/04/04, respectively). Martha Hanson owns the Road Time Trial (20 km) records in three age categories, 75+ (9/03/95), 80+ (9/03/00), and 85+ (9/03/07).

But you don't have to be a champion to be the best female cyclist you can be. Just keep riding, and read on!

chapter seven

The Physiology of a Cyclist

My opinions may have changed, but not the fact that I am right.

—Ashleigh Brilliant

No two athletes are exactly the same, particularly if only one of them is female. But what do those differences really mean? We do have some answers. Women who have unexpectedly succeeded at athletic endeavors have piqued scientific curiosity, resulting in a slew of research into how female physiology reacts differently from male physiology to the same activity.

While it's true that measurements of human performance have limits, and there's much that can't be explained, science does offer some studies that can be useful to the female cyclist. These include research into questions about the impact of genetic influences on athletic ability, the effects of altitude training, outstanding female performance in ultraendurance events, the importance of retaining bone mass, the influence of the menstrual cycle on injuries, and gastric emptying rates. Let's examine each of these questions to get a better understanding of our physiology.

TO WHAT DEGREE DO GENETICS DETERMINE ATHLETIC POTENTIAL?

You might be several years into cycling and asking whether you picked the wrong parents. Several scientific studies have been conducted to determine if genetics are responsible for great athletic performances. Claude Bouchard, PhD, and a team of researchers at Laval University in Montreal, Quebec, Canada, put 10 pairs of identical twins on a twenty-week training program. The twins trained fouror ive times per week for 45 minutes per session at an average intensity of approximately 80 percent of maximal heart rate.

The result? Identical twins responded nearly identically to the training program. One pair gained 10 and 11 percent on their VO_2max, while a second pair gained 22 and 25 percent. Most of the variation in performance gains was between sets, rather than within sets, of twins.

Although the study on twins revealed that 82 percent of the variation in VO_2max was due to genetics, it also showed that only 33 percent of the differences found in ventilatory threshold (another benchmark of improvement) was attributed to genetics. This is important, since ventilatory threshold and the closely related lactate threshold (covered in Chapter 2) are frequently found to be the best predictors of actual performance. In other words, lactate threshold speeds tend to be more "trainable" than VO_2max, which is good news for all of us.

The researchers at Laval conducted other studies in addition to the one already mentioned here, and, in short, they concluded that genetic factors account for only 20 percent of the variation in performances of endurance athletes. Nongenetic factors—including nutrition, lifestyle, past exercise patterns, age, socioeconomic status, and mental skills—influence twice as much, or 40 percent of the variation. Gender differences accounted for 10 percent. The final 30 percent was in how a particular set of genes reacts to a particular training program (some people will respond to one training program, but not another). The bottom line: Roughly 70 percent of your performance is under your control; what works for you won't necessarily work as well for the cyclist next to you.

What about the differences between athletes on the same program? The Laval researchers conducted another study to determine how much variation there would be in fitness gains if people followed the same training program. In this study, 24 similar subjects who were initially sedentary followed the same training program for twenty weeks. After that time, there were some big changes. The average gain in VO_2max was 33 percent, and one person in the group gained a whopping 88 percent. Unfortunately, another individual, sweating on the same plan, increased VO_2max by only 5 percent.

Within the same study, scientists measured power output on a bicycle ergometer. Subjects pedaled away for 90 minutes, and their mean power output was measured before the training program began and again at the end. The average power improvement was a nice 51 percent. One happy person gained a gigantic 97 percent, while another gained only 16 percent.

Why do some people seem to make big gains and others make minimal gains? And do they make their gains at equal rates? The studies at Laval led researchers to believe that there are "responders" and "nonresponders." Those who are considered to be responders make big improvements in aerobic capacity and power as a result of their training, while nonresponders barely show a gain, even after twenty weeks of hard work. The scientists estimated that about 5 percent of us are high responders who can make improvements of more than 60 percent, while nearly the same number are nonresponders and may expect only a 5 percent improvement.

In addition to responders and nonresponders, the studies revealed a difference in response rates—a scale of responsiveness. Some people made nice gains after just four to six weeks of training but seemed to plateau and made minimal gains in weeks 7 to 20. Others were late bloomers and were at a standstill for six to ten

Where VO$_2$max Originates

Speaking of genetics, some speculate that you get your aerobic capacity from your mom. When you were being formed, your mother's egg (ovum) contained a large amount of mitochondria–which provide most of the energy required for endurance performance–and your father's mitochondria were limited to the tail portion of the sperm .

By viewing the fertilization process through electron microscopy, it's clear that sometimes a portion of the sperm's tail makes it into the egg, but not always. If mitochondria from the sperm do make it into the egg, they are not believed to influence the mitochondrial DNA of the new being.

So although individual mitochondrial DNA appear to be maternally de-termined, both parents may influence the total number of mitochondria. We also know that training can increase the number and size of mitochondria, and there could be a potential doubling of aerobic system enzymes. How much this training effect is governed maternally or paternally is unknown.

Mitochondria are just one parameter contributing to the complex issue of aerobic capacity. Examples of other parameters that influence aerobic capacity and can improve with training are heart rate, stroke and blood volume, muscle size, metabolic activity, respiratory exchange rates, and exercise economy.

There's a lot left to be learned about genetic influences on athletic performance. There remains uncertainty as to which genes are critical in predicting or improving athletic performance. Undoubtedly, there will come a day when DNA samples can be used to determine how to optimize each individual's performance.

weeks, but then blossomed, improving their aerobic capacities by 20 to 25 percent after ten weeks of additional training.

It's important to realize that not everyone will react exactly the same way to any single training program. Some people will make big gains, while others may make marginal gains. You will need to learn how your body responds to training, then make adjustments. Chapter 3 outlines training programs to help you on your path to new levels of fitness. You may need to modify the programs based on your personal needs. Tips on how to modify the programs are included.

WILL ALTITUDE TRAINING REALLY BENEFIT PERFORMANCE?

If you are a lowlander and have traveled to the mountains to bike, hike, ski, race, or sightsee, you may have experienced uncomfortable symptoms of high altitude. You may have gotten a rip-roaring headache, nausea, or just felt lousy all over. Still, you have heard that high-altitude training is good for you. Is altitude training really worthwhile?

The truth is, the density of oxygen in the air decreases in direct proportion to increasing altitude. In other words, when you take a normal breath of air at altitude, you will have less oxygen in your lungs than you would if you were to take the same-size breath at sea level. Being an aerobic animal, you know your muscles want and need lots of oxygen to operate a bicycle. To compensate for less oxygen and reduced pressure, the body tries to adjust, occasionally rebelling. The most important compensations include an increase in respiratory drive (which means you breathe faster and may hyperventilate) and an increase in blood flow at rest and during submaximal exercise.

Additional responses to changes in altitude can include increased resting heart rate, light-headedness, headache, insomnia, nausea, and loss of appetite. As altitude increases above 15,000 feet, people may experience vomiting, intestinal disturbances, dyspnea (labored breathing), lethargy, general weakness, and an inability to make rational decisions.

In the first few days of altitude adaptation, cardiac output and submaximal heart rate may increase 50 percent above sea-level values. No wonder people feel like their hearts are going to leap from their bodies! Because your body requires the same amount of oxygen to work at altitude as it does at sea level, the increase in submaximal blood flow partially compensates for reduced oxygen levels.

In terms of total oxygen circulated in the body, at rest and moderate levels of exercise, a 10 percent increase in cardiac output can offset a 10 percent reduction in arterial oxygen saturation. In other words, your heart can pump 10 percent faster to compensate for 10 percent less oxygen in your bloodstream.

It is beyond the 10 percent range where things get tough. The greatest effects of altitude on aerobic metabolism seem to be during maximal exercise. At top intensities, the ventilatory and circulatory adjustments to altitude cannot compensate for the lower oxygen content of arterial blood. This means the athlete has to slow down to reduce the demand for oxygen.

Adaptations to Altitude Stress

With all the seemingly negative effects, why would someone want to train at altitude? The biggest reason to train at altitude is the body's long-term adaptation, which is an increase in the blood's oxygen-carrying capacity. This is partially due to an altitude-induced increase in erythropoietin (EPO), the key chemical that stimulates increased red-blood-cell production. Altitude exposure also causes an increase in 2.3 DPG, the chemical that makes oxygen more available to the muscles.

During the first few days at altitude, there's a decrease in plasma volume. Because of this decrease, red blood cells become more concentrated. For example, after about a week at 7,400 feet, the plasma volume is decreased by 8 percent, while the concentrations of red blood cells and hemoglobin are increased by 4 and 10 percent, respectively. The changes observed after a week cause the oxygen content of arterial blood to increase significantly above values observed immediately upon arrival at altitude.

Following this adaptation of decreasing plasma volume is an increase in red-blood-cell mass. Through responses initiated by the body, reduced arterial oxygen pressure stimulates an increase in the total number of red blood cells. For example, a healthy high-altitude native may have a red-blood-cell count that is 50 percent greater than that of a native sea-level dweller. These two adaptations to altitude have an effect that translates into a large increase in the blood's capacity to transport oxygen.

Just How High Is "Altitude"?

Elevations between 10,000 and 18,000 feet are generally considered high altitude. Scientists refer to moderate altitudes being between 4,000 and 10,000 feet. Generally, there is minimal scientific discussion about elevations between sea level and 4,000 feet, although some believe altitude effects may show up as low as 2,000 feet.

Speed and Power at Altitude

Having lots of red blood cells that flood the body with oxygen-carrying capability sounds great, right? People ought to be aerobic animals after they adapt to high elevations. But here's the bad news: When exposed to higher altitudes, it's nearly impossible for athletes to train at the same intensity as they were able to train while at sea level.

In other words, if you are a lowlander capable of averaging 20 miles per hour for a 40 km time trial, at a heart rate of 175 beats per minute and a perceived exertion of 17 on the Borg Scale (breathing hard), your average speed (assuming a duplicate course profile) could be decreased by 5 to 10 percent for the same heart rate and perceived exertion when exposed to even moderate altitudes. This means your speed will decrease by 2 miles per hour, which is quite a reduction.

What if people who already live at high altitude travel to sea level? Is there an automatic gain in speed? That's a good question, and there's no easy answer. Since people living at a higher altitude are not able to train at the same intensity levels they would train at as lowlanders, they have not trained their bodies to perform at higher speeds. Though this theory is unproven by science, perhaps the highlanders don't have the neuromuscular programming, in addition to the metabolic speeds, necessary to cycle fast at sea level.

How long is it before the benefits of high altitude disappear when that athlete travels to race at sea level? Estimates for an athlete to lose her native, high-altitude adaptations are in the six- to eight-week range.

Living or Training at Altitude

One training theory suggests that you should live at a moderately high altitude and train at a lower one. This notion is commonly expressed as "live high and train low." Theoretically, this means living in the mountains to gain more oxygen-carrying capacity and driving to sea level to do your speed work to achieve maximum power.

While nobody wants to spend that much time or money driving, scientists have researched this kind of training using a "high-altitude house" that simulates living at 8,200 feet. In one experiment, athletes spent sixteen to eighteen hours living inside the high-altitude house and did their training outside at sea level. These athletes showed the physiological improvements typical of living at high altitude, and they had performance breakthroughs as well. In contrast, other athletes doing the same training but not living at high altitude showed no gains either in physiology or performance.

If living at or simulating high altitude is not a reality for you, can gains be made by taking shorter trips to high altitude? Unfortunately, for the average cyclist who just wants to ride faster, studies on short-term high-altitude exposure (one to six weeks) are inconclusive. Some studies suggest that performance increases after a period of high-altitude training, while others indicate that training at sea level will yield faster race times. Anecdotal evidence on high-altitude training indicates that many athletes feel it helps. This may indicate that high-altitude training really does improve

Individual and Gender Differences When Training at Altitude

A study that was detailed by Joseph Verrengia in the column "Peak Condition" examined the effects of high altitude on women. The study was conducted on Colorado's Pikes Peak at 14,111 feet above sea level. As with numerous other areas of medical and physical research, many studies assumed that women's bodies reacted the same way to high-altitude stress as men's. However, this assumption may not be accurate.

Previous studies had shown that men's metabolism at high altitude increases around 17 percent, and their bodies burn more carbohydrates. Traditional high-altitude information has recommended that people increase their consumption of carbohydrates upon arrival at a higher elevation. The Pikes Peak study revealed that women's metabolism increases between 17 and 29 percent. In addition, a woman's body burns more fat at a higher altitude. At least two other studies (Tarnopolsky 1995 and Braun 2000) have confirmed the observation that women burn more lipids at altitude. Though no detailed literature exists, this result may indicate that women require a different nutritional strategy than men at high altitude. We can watch for more research using a wider variety of test subjects.

performance. Some people think athletes just feel so terrible and stressed while training at high altitude that when they return to sea level, they feel great!

However, we do know a few things about high altitude for certain. Exercise physiologist Dave Morris (formerly with USA Cycling) says, "We know that when people are exposed to altitude and adapt, their red-blood-cell count increases, and along with it so does the oxygen-carrying content of the blood. We know that myoglobin increases, which is inside muscle and gives the muscle an affinity for oxygen. At the same time, altitude decreases the buffering capacity of the body, which decreases its ability to work at lactate threshold and translates to slower speeds."

As you can see, studies on altitude can result in confusing recommendations. This is partially due to the lack of studies on short-term exposure to altitude, though one such study done by Burtscher (2006) indicates an improvement in performance when racing at high altitude if test subjects give themselves time to acclimatize. Just three days of exposure to high altitude gave participants a 50 percent recovery from the aerobic losses experienced at their initial arrival.

So what should you do if you are planning a bicycle tour at high altitude or a high-altitude hill climb? In my personal experience, I've noted significant improvement in race performance when given a few extra days to adjust to high altitude. If your travel plans are flexible, give your body a chance to build up those red blood cells before starting your high-altitude adventure.

ARE WOMEN BIOLOGICALLY BETTER SUITED FOR ENDURANCE EVENTS?

Our skeletal muscle is made of different types of fibers with different metabolic and functional properties. Classified by contractile and metabolic characteristics, type I fibers are commonly called slow-twitch fibers, and type II fibers are commonly called fast-twitch fibers. Slow-twitch fibers generate energy primarily by means of long-term aerobic (with oxygen) energy transfer. They are fatigue resistant and well-suited for endurance events—prolonged exercise at moderate intensity.

The fast-twitch fibers are activated in sprint-type activities and activities requiring forceful muscular contractions, such as short hill climbing. These type II fibers are divided into three categories:

1. *Type IIa fibers* are considered intermediate in that they have a capacity to transfer energy by aerobic and anaerobic means.
2. *Type IIb fibers* are the real anaerobic engines and are considered the true fast-twitch fibers.
3. *Type IIc fibers* are rare and won't be covered here.

Sedentary men, women, and young children exhibit 45 to 55 percent slow-twitch fibers. The remaining fast-twitch fibers are usually equally distributed between type IIa and type IIb.

Among competitive athletes, those in sports requiring a large amount of endurance will have a higher percentage of slow-twitch fibers. Distance runners and cross-country skiers will have slow-twitch fibers occupying as much as 90 percent of their total. Weight lifters and sprinters tend to have more fast-twitch fibers and lower relative VO_2max numbers.

With training, can we change the percentage of slow-twitch fibers we have? Right now, it appears that with the proper training, muscle fibers can switch from one group to another. Several studies (Allemeier 1994; Howald 1985; Jansson 1978; and Simoneau 1985) have shown that proportions of muscle fibers changed with training. In the Simoneau study, 24 sedentary subjects were given no training or controlled training. The control group with no training included 10 subjects: 4 women and 6 men. After fifteen weeks of training, the training group significantly increased the proportion of type I fibers (from 41 percent to 47 percent) and decreased the proportion of type IIb fibers (from 17 percent to 12 percent). In the Howald study, the percentage of type I fibers increased by 12 percent and type IIb fibers decreased by 24 percent. The other studies produced similar results.

A composite study (Staron 2007) representing data collected over ten years on muscle fiber type composition of the vastus lateralis muscle of young men and women revealed that type I fibers tended to be larger for women, while type II fibers were larger for men. Though we cannot make a leap to assuming all muscle fibers have the same distribution in both genders, it does raise the question of whether muscle fiber type is one contributor to the success women enjoy in endurance events.

In 1993, women ran their way to victory and won 12 ultraraces held in the United States. Granted, it was 12 of 223, yet women were placing first—overall—in some prestigious races. Research conducted at South Africa's Comrades Marathon found that women outperform men at the 90 km distance.

In a specific study (Speechly et al. 1996) conducted by the Department of Physiology at the University of the Witwatersrand Medical School in Johannesburg, South Africa, scientists matched men and women for performance in the marathon (42.2 km). These performance-matched runners, 10 men and 10 women, were then examined at running distances of 10 km, 21.1 km, 42.2 km, and 90 km.

The women's group weighed less than the men's, but the women had significantly higher body fat at 22 percent, compared with 16 percent for the men. The women had lower VO_2max than the men when the measure was expressed relative to body mass and corrected for altitude. There were no significant differences in running economies or lactate threshold between the men and women. The two groups were also similar in training volume and intensity.

The scientists measured VO_2max, running economy, lactate accumulation, and running speeds at 10 km, 21.1 km, and 42.2 km, and the matched men and women performed about the same. At the 90 km distance, however, the women's performance was significantly better than that of the men, as were their average run times. The men's performance declines at 90 km were attributed to a decline in their fraction of VO_2max workload. It appears women are able to exercise at higher percentages of their VO_2max for longer amounts of time, allowing them to maintain a higher work rate over longer distances.

Critics of the Speechly study point out that all the world records for men are faster than those for women at the same distance and event. Women have relatively smaller hearts than men and have up to 10 percent less hemoglobin on average, meaning less oxygen-carrying capacity. Other critics note that the men used in the study were not built for longer distances; they were much larger than the women.

The Speechly study, admittedly, is not suggesting that elite women will soon outperform elite men. There are, however, some exceptional elite women athletes as well as exceptions to the preceding statement. As mentioned previously, women are winning some ultradistance running races. One notable example is Ann Trason, who finished more than 4 miles ahead of the nearest male competitor when she won the USA twenty-four-hour running championships.

Women are able to better utilize fats while using fewer carbohydrates than men who are equally trained and nourished. Women make better use of their fat stores, a real advantage in moderate-intensity, long-duration exercise.

Another fascinating contributor to a woman's endurance ability is estrogen. The female hormone acts as a natural antioxidant and may help women deal with central fatigue. Additional research suggests that estrogen may be a defense against muscular injury caused by overuse. Better fat utilization and estrogen may help women be well-suited endurance athletes.

DO WOMEN FACE A HIGHER RISK OF INJURY DURING OVULATION?

While some researchers have found estrogen to be helpful to endurance exercise, researchers at the University of Michigan Medical Center have linked high levels of estrogen and relaxin, found in a woman's body during ovulation, to increased ligament injury (Hewett et al. 2007). The researchers studied 40 young women with acute anterior cruciate ligament injuries and found the injury rate to be nearly doubled when the women were ovulating. The speculation is that higher levels of estrogen and relaxin affect soft tissues like tendons and ligaments as well as the neuromuscular system.

Since the Michigan study, several other studies have found that women are more susceptible to knee injuries than men. Additionally, the menstrual cycle does have an influence on the laxity of ligaments, particularly in the knee. Several studies found an increase in laxity and knee injury susceptibility in the preovulatory and ovulatory stages of the menstrual cycle. While there are a few studies that concluded ligament laxity does not vary during the menstrual cycle, they are in the minority.

More research is needed to determine the exact role of estrogen, relaxin, and other hormonal changes present during the menstrual cycle and their relationship to athletic training in endurance sports, power sports such as basketball, and strength training. The risk of injury to the knee ligaments is higher in sports that require side-to-side and torsional movements of the knee. Women who choose cycling as their primary sport may have a lower risk of knee injury than those who do sports such as alpine skiing, basketball, and soccer.

If you are a multisport athlete and notice differences in knee stability during the different phases of your menstrual cycle, it may be important for you to add a focused strength training program for strengthening the tendons and ligaments that support the knee, and one that is specifically geared toward your noncycling sports.

BONE MASS

Osteoporosis is a major health concern for women. Osteoporosis occurs if bone isn't replaced as quickly as it is lost, allowing the bones to become thin, brittle, and easily broken. A gradual loss of bone mass—beginning at about age 30—occurs in both men and women. The concern for women is that they may lose up to 30 to 50 percent of their bone density. Men may lose only 20 to 30 percent.

Although science has yet to determine the cause of osteoporosis, a number of factors increase risk. These include a calcium-poor diet, high sodium intakes, physical inactivity, reduced levels of estrogen, heredity, excessive cortisone or thyroid hormone, being Asian or Caucasian, being underweight, some medications, smoking, and excessive alcohol use.

A major preventive measure against bone loss is regular weight-bearing exercise. The exercise should be one that combines movement with stress on the limbs. Several recent studies have indicated that road cyclists have lower bone mineral density (BMD) than athletes in impact sports such as running, rugby, and jumping rope (Duncan et al. 2002; Maïmoun et al. 2004; Nevill et al. 2004; Rector et al. 2008; and Sabo et al. 1996). More disturbing was that one study (Sabo's) found endurance cyclists to have lower BMD than the control group doing no exercise.

A study looking at recreationally competitive road racers and mountain bike racers (Warner 2002) found that the mountain bike group had higher BMD than the road racers. The study suggests that the loading associated with mountain bike racing causes enough weight-bearing activity to perhaps stimulate an osteogenic effect. One consideration, however, is that the mountain bike racers were younger than the road racers. More research needs to be done on mountain bike riding and osteogenic effects.

It was once thought that women over 30 were unable to add calcium to their bones, but researchers from a study at Tufts University at the Human Nutrition Research Center (Nelson et al. 1994) have found that strength training at any age can actually increase bone mass. Their research looked at a group of 39 women ages 50 to 70: 19 did no strength training, while 20 did a strength training workout twice a week. After one year, bone density measurements in the spine and hip of the strength training group revealed an increase of 1 percent. The sedentary control group had lost 2.9 percent of their bone mass. A healthy balance of cycling and strength training can significantly influence a woman's bone mass.

Maintaining a healthy lifestyle by eliminating smoking and excessive alcohol use will also contribute to keeping healthy bones. Some individuals may require the help of a physician to determine whether calcium and vitamin D supplements are necessary. A physician may also prescribe hormone replacement therapy for postmenopausal women to aid with reduced estrogen levels.

There is currently no "cure" for osteoporosis. The U.S. Food and Drug Administration has approved bisphosphonates (alendronate, ibandronate, and risedronate), calcitonin, estrogens, parathyroid hormone, and raloxifene for the prevention and/or treatment of osteoporosis. The good news is that BMD scans are widely available. With this completely painless test, you can determine your risk for osteoporosis. Early diagnosis is critical.

To summarize, there are four key areas that we need to consider to minimize the possibility of osteoporosis:

1. **Weight-bearing exercise.** Currently, it does not appear that if you restrict your exercise to cycling and do not include weight training, plyometrics, running, or other impact sports, you may be at risk for decreased BMD.
2. **Diet.** Minimize items that are known to leach bone from your body and increase items that are calcium-rich.
3. **Excessive sweat.** As discussed in Chapter 5, excessive sweating may lead to calcium losses—even if the exercise is weight-bearing.
4. **Supplementation.** Nutrition experts currently recommend supplementing your diet with 1,000 to 1,500 milligrams of calcium each day.

DIGESTION, SUBSTRATE UTILIZATION, AND POST-EXERCISE SUBSTRATE RESPONSE

Some athletes are ravenous throughout a training ride or race, while others can't make themselves eat because they always feel full. In a study by Hermansson et al. (1996), researchers looked at the differences in gastric emptying rates of solid meals between 16 men and 14 women. In the study, men had faster emptying rates than women. The men's half-empty time averaged 47 minutes faster than the women's.

A second study (Sadik et al. 2003) utilizing newly developed radiological techniques looked at 83 subjects, 43 of whom were women, to examine gastric emptying, small intestine transit, and colonic transit. For all measures, the average values for women were significantly slower than for males at 30 minutes, 1 hour and 12 minutes, and 4 hours and 48 minutes, respectively. In this study, when males and females consumed the same fuels, gastric empty times varied from 1.6 to 4.9 hours in the women. In the male subjects, times varied from 0.7 to 3.7 hours. With these values, it is easy to see why there is such variation in the optimal fuel and fueling techniques among individuals. While a few studies were inconclusive or found little difference, more studies found a statistically significant difference, resulting in recommendations for separate medical reference values for young men and women.

If men and women have different rates of fuel movement through their digestive systems, these differences may influence how

Evaluating Research Claims

How do you know when to believe the results of a scientific study? It's helpful to ask the following questions:

- Was the study published in a reputable scientific journal?
- Who were the researchers and did they have financial incentives to gain by the results of the experiment?
- What are the limitations of the study? Were the studies done on animals and not humans? Were the studies done on populations that are significantly different from those being questioned by the hypothesis? For example, if we want to determine the effects of 60-second interval training on masters- level women cyclists, we don't want the study group to be twenty-year-old sedentary men. At best, the experiment may lend suggested relationships between the question and the results from the study group.
- Is the study "an amazing discovery"? Are there studies that directly contradict the amazing find? Or does the study, in some way, support research that is already known? This particular point will need to be reviewed, simply due to the lack of past research on women and women athletes.
- What was the size of the study group? A study on hundreds of people will carry more weight than a study of ten people.

athletes consume foods prior to, during, and after events. In addition, the different digestion rates may have an effect on substrate fuel utilization as well as post-exercise substrate response. Several studies concluded that during moderate-intensity, long-duration exercise, women utilize more fats and fewer carbohydrates as fuel when compared with men. Some of this may be related to the menstrual cycle, as discussed in Chapter 8.

More recently, at least one study (Vislocky et al. 2008) examined men and women in the 3.5-hour recovery period following an endurance run. The study found that females experienced increases in glucose, lactate, and insulin during the recovery period. Utilizing this information to maximize recovery is the next challenge.

What should you take away from this information? Although current recommendations for fueling are general in nature, several studies indicate there may be gender-related strategies to optimize fueling endurance athletes. In addition, it is good to know that there were some wide individual variations in some of the studies. This means even if a particular fuel and fueling strategy work perfectly for one athlete, they may not work for you. For now, you will need to fine-tune your own fueling prior to, during, and after exercise. Unfortunately, this will require some trial and error until science and technology give us better prescriptive tools.

• • •

IN THE PAST, THERE WERE DIFFERENT STANDARDS FOR TRAINING men and women athletes. Some of these differences were based on the areas in which men had an edge, such as strength and power. Although much more research is needed, perhaps we have missed some opportunities to capitalize on the differences between men and women—differences that might be advantageous.

New research is being done all the time, and the sidebar gives tips on how to evaluate its validity. Knowledge is always increasing, and you'll need to keep abreast of current research through books, magazines, television, and online resources. Not all information will work for you. You're responsible for deciding what actions are best for you. Become your own research project.

chapter eight

Menstrual Cycles

Some take "gearing-up" seriously, as women have won medals and set world records at every phase of their menstrual cycles.

—NADIA CONSTANTINI, MD

A blessing or a curse? How you view your cycle may depend on what your mother told you, what peers say, whether you're trying to get pregnant, or whether your period coincides with a long bicycle tour. I include the menstrual cycle here because it's critical to every woman's health.

This chapter will explain how a "normal" cycle is supposed to work, what hormonal changes affect the cycle, how hormonal changes may affect athletic performance, why there should be concern if menstrual cycles cease, tools for tracking a cycle, and tips for making things as comfortable as possible.

HOW IT ALL WORKS

The average menstrual cycle is typically twenty-eight days, plus or minus eight days. What is "normal" for one woman isn't necessarily normal for another, so it's in your best interest to know what's normal for you. You can do this by keeping track of the length of your cycle, your physical and psychological symptoms, and anything that seems out of the ordinary. A tracking tool is discussed later in the chapter.

Figure 8.1, which has been greatly simplified, shows a twenty-eight-day cycle and various changes occurring within the body. As

The Four Phases of Menstruation

The menstrual cycle can be divided into four functional phases on the basis of structural, physical, and hormonal changes:

1. *Menstruation* is marked by the first day the uterine lining begins to shed as menstrual blood. This "bleeding" is actually sloughing tissue, which is expendable and needs to be cycled out of the body. The tissue sloughing helps prevent endometrial cancer. Menstruation is also the transition from the luteal phase to the follicular phase.

2. The *follicular phase* is the period of time when the ovarian follicle is preparing to ovulate. A key ovarian hormone, estrogen, is on the rise. The endometrium, or uterine lining, is building in preparation for a fertilized egg.

3. *Ovulation* is marked by high peaks of luteinizing hormone (LH) and follicle-stimulating hormone (FSH). LH levels increase rapidly, doubling within two hours, with the mean duration of this surge being forty-eight hours. The exact timing of ovulation is still unknown; however, it is thought to occur between thirty-five and forty-four hours after the onset of the LH surge.

4. The *luteal phase* gets its name from the corpus luteum–Latin for "yellow body"–which is formed by cells left behind in the ovary after the ovum (egg) is released. In this phase, the cycle shifts from an estrogen dominance to progesterone dominance. Progesterone "ripens" the endometrium.

FIGURE 8.1 28-Day Menstrual Cycle

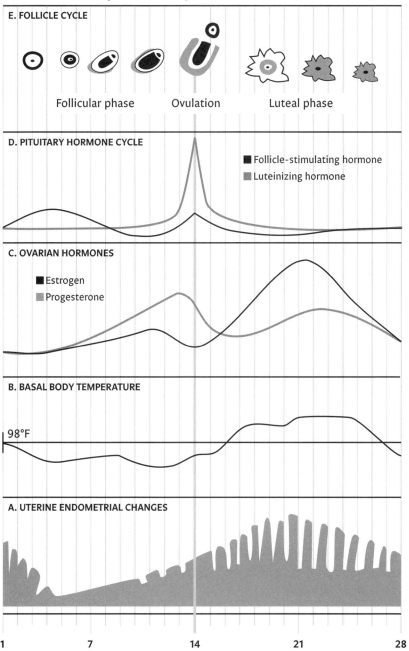

seen in part C of the figure, estrogen and progesterone—ovarian hormones—are at their lowest levels just prior to and during the first few days of menstruation. The low levels of these hormones just prior to the beginning of menstruation are a signal to the body that an egg has not been fertilized. The time of bleeding—menses—typically is three to seven days.

Menses, when the uterine lining is shed, takes place during the first few days of the follicular phase. During this time, estrogen levels are on the rise. Ovulation occurs shortly after estrogen levels are at the highest, somewhere around thirteen to fifteen days into a twenty-eight-day cycle.

After ovulation, in the luteal phase, estrogen levels decrease, increase slightly, then decrease again to their lowest level just prior to menstruation. Meanwhile, progesterone levels rise during the luteal phase to thicken the lining of the uterus in preparation for a fertilized egg. Progesterone then decreases, and if no fertilization has occurred, bleeding will begin, marking the start of a new cycle.

Let's look at each phase in a bit more detail.

Menstruation

Menstruation, "menses," "having a period," and countless slang expressions are all terms for the time of the month when postpubescent women experience uterine bleeding. The few days prior to and the first day or two of menstruation can be uncomfortable for some women. Common complaints include lower abdominal cramps, headache, backache, fatigue, breast soreness or tenderness, weight gain, gastrointestinal problems, diarrhea, and unpredictable bowel movements.

The degree of discomfort and the number of symptoms experienced vary from woman to woman. Extremely painful menstruation is called dysmenorrhea.

Many women cyclists agree that beginning their period right before a race or during a multiday tour can be depressing. Others, however, refuse to let their period affect their performance. "If the

Technically Speaking

Here is some additional terminology that might come up when discussing your menstrual cycle with your doctor.

Menarche: First occurrence of menses

Late menarche: Delayed age at the onset of first menses

Eumenorrhea: Regularly occurring menstrual periods

Dysmenorrhea: Difficult or painful menses

Oligomenorrhea: Irregularly occurring menstruation

Menorrhagia: Profuse flow

Metrorrhagia: Spotting or bleeding between menses

Amenorrhea: Absence of menses

Primary amenorrhea: Menses have never occurred

Secondary amenorrhea: Cessation of menses after menarche has occurred

---

race is important to me, and I've put a season of training into this event, I gear up, focus on the matter at hand, and give my all to the race," they say. "I can't let it bother me." Some take "gearing up" seriously, as women have won medals and set world records at every phase of their menstrual cycles.

Great performances can happen at any phase of the cycle, but being as comfortable as possible can make the performance more enjoyable. To help alleviate premenstrual and early menstrual symptoms, some health care providers recommend a balanced diet, eliminating bingeing behaviors, cutting down on caffeine, reducing salt intake, exercising, and using relaxation techniques. While these recommendations work for some, others may need additional help.

For example, women with extreme cramping may need prescription drugs. Others might be able to use over-the-counter, nonsteroidal anti-inflammatory drugs (NSAIDs) and find relief. NSAIDs, such as ibuprofen and naproxen sodium (trade names such as Advil and Aleve), work to inhibit prostaglandins, which are substances released by your body to cause your uterus, intestines, and other smooth muscles to contract.

NSAIDs seem to work best if taken the day before or as soon as flow begins, before prostaglandin levels are high enough to produce cramping. NSAIDs may also help reduce those emergency trips into the bushes for a bowel movement. Don't take NSAIDs on an empty stomach, as they may irritate the stomach lining or cause gastrointestinal distress. Diuretics, which reduce water retention, may also help relieve menstrual cramping, but this remedy isn't recommended for women riding and racing multihour events in which hydration is critical.

As for exercise helping to relieve menstrual aches and pains, the studies yield conflicting results. Most women report that exercise doesn't seem to make a difference. But for relieving premenstrual symptoms (PMS), such as depression and mood swings, exercise does seem to have a positive effect.

It's ironic that a woman might turn in a personal best performance at the time of the month when she feels as personable as a saber-toothed cat, as fast as a snail, and as sleek as an elephant. Just before and during menstruation, when estrogen levels are at their lowest, aerobic capacity is at its peak. This increase probably won't make a difference for recreational athletes. But for elite athletes seeking a competitive edge, the change might be enough to mean the difference between first and second place. The increase in aerobic capacity is also significant enough to make scientists control menstrual cycles when they do experiments to test physical performance in females.

Follicular Phase

The follicular phase typically lasts seven to twenty-one days, with the average being fourteen. As the follicular phase progresses, estrogen levels continue to rise and aerobic capacity decreases. The other function that decreases is spatial visualization, or the ability to judge distances.

Common Symptoms of the Premenstrual and Menstrual Phases

Emotional	Physical	Other
Anger	Acne breakouts	Alcohol cravings
Anxiety	Backache	Clumsiness
Confusion	Bloating	Forgetfulness
Crying easily	Breast	Lack of
Depression	tenderness	concentration
Insomnia	Fatigue	Salt craving
Irritability	Headache	Sweet craving
Mood swings	Light-headed	
Nervous tension	Swollen feet	
Withdrawal from others	Swollen fingers	
	Unpredictable bowel movements	
	Weight gain	
	Yeast infection	

While these two functions are on the decline, carbohydrate metabolism, mental capacity, mental focus, problem-solving capabilities, and fine-motor function all increase. There is also an increase in perceptual speed, or how quickly women notice things. If you happen to be a female road racer, and problem solving and quick decisionmaking become critical, any increases in estrogen may be helpful.

Ovulation

Women are born with about two million underdeveloped eggs. For women with normal cycles, an egg is released about once per month. It is possible to have a menstrual cycle in which no egg is released. This type of cycle is anovulatory. Anovulatory cycles are usually those cycles free from cramping during menstruation and in which PMS symptoms are less noticeable.

Estrogen levels peak just prior to ovulation, then drop off significantly. Two other hormones released by the anterior pituitary gland rise to peak levels, causing the mature ovarian follicle to release an egg. These additional hormones are FSH and LH.

Fluid-filled chambers—follicles—in the ovary are prompted by FSH to begin growing. Within each follicle, a single ovum is growing as well. An LH surge triggers a follicle to rupture, releasing its egg.

FIGURE 8.2 The Menstrual Cycle's Impact on Training

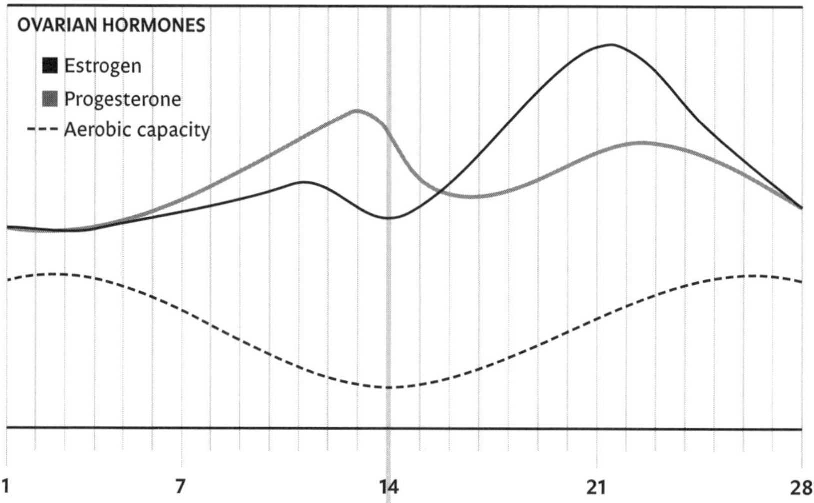

Follicular Phase
Your metabolism, mental focus, and fine-motor function are increasing, and your aerobic capacity is peaking during your period.

Luteal Phase
Your ventilation typically increases, making you feel you are working harder. Still, this is the optimal time for burning fat.

Ovulation
You have good mental focus and fine-motor function, but aerobic capacity and spatial perception are decreased.

During ovulation, while mental focus and fine-motor function remain high, aerobic capacity and spatial visualization are decreased.

Luteal Phase

The luteal phase follows ovulation and usually lasts twelve to fourteen days. During the luteal phase, estrogen declines, increases slightly, and then proceeds to its lowest level near the end of the phase. While estrogen is declining, progesterone rises to its peak around the midluteal phase and declines to low levels at the end of the phase.

Declining estrogen levels mean that aerobic capacity and the ability to conceptualize are improving, and glycogen storage rises a bit. But memory, perceptual speed, and fine-motor ability are not at their best during this phase.

Studies on runners have shown that ventilation during the luteal phase can increase by around 8 percent, which makes any given pace feel harder. Running economy—the percentage of VO_2max the runner is able to work at—dips by about 3 percent; mental vigor or toughness declines; and near the end of the phase, depression and fatigue increase.

With all these seemingly "bad" conditions, studies on runners have shown the luteal phase to be good for fat burning. Studies on normally menstruating runners have shown that fat furnished 70 percent of the energy at 35 percent VO_2max, 58 percent of the energy at 60 percent VO_2max, and 46 percent of the energy at 75 percent VO_2max. Compare those values with the midfollicular phase, in which 52 percent of the energy is provided by fat at 35 percent VO_2max, 43 percent of the energy at 60 percent VO_2max, and 39 percent of the energy at 75 percent VO_2max.

The last few days of the luteal phase are premenstrual—the few days prior to menstruation and the start of a new cycle. Some women have multiple premenstrual problems, while others have minimal difficulties. For roughly 10 percent of women, premenstrual symptoms are enough to disturb their life.

There's controversy about what PMS is and what causes it. If you suffer from PMS problems, it's best to keep a log of physical and psychological problems and when they occur within your cycle. If the symptoms become problematic, a record of the problems and when they occur will be helpful to a physician if you feel that you need to seek medical help.

Cervical Mucus

The cervical mucus changes during the course of the menstrual cycle. Tracking these changes can help you determine where you are in your menstrual cycle.

During menses, it is difficult to determine the consistency of cervical mucus. In the follicular phase, the mucus tends to be yellow and tacky. During ovulation, mucus is clear, stringy, stretchy, and very fluid. But during the luteal phase, the mucus returns to a yellow color and more of a tacky texture.

Prior to menstruation, a yellow-tinted mass of mucus will be excreted; this is called the cervical plug. Infections, contraceptive creams, and douching cut down on mucus, possibly changing its color and texture.

ABNORMAL MENSTRUAL CYCLES
Amenorrhea

There is a tendency to mix the terms "amenorrhea" and "oligomenorrhea." Oligomenorrhea signifies few periods, but periods still occur. Amenorrhea is classified into two categories: primary and secondary. Primary amenorrhea means menses have never occurred. Young girls who have been in a heavy exercise program may experience primary amenorrhea. Secondary amenorrhea is the cessation of menses after menarche has occurred.

Some of the studies considered three or fewer periods per year to be amenorrhea, although amenorrhea literally means that periods have stopped. Using either term, if a woman hasn't had a period for ninety days, it's time to seek help.

Understanding Secondary Amenorrhea

There are conflicting studies and opinions regarding the exact cause of secondary amenorrhea. Some believe it is a combination of factors, including:

- Low body weight
- Low body fat
- Obesity
- Sudden increases in training volume or intensity
- Low-calorie, low-fat, low-protein, or low-nutrient diets
- Psychological stress
- Hormonal imbalances
- Physical disorders
- Perimenopause or premenopause

Amenorrhea doesn't necessarily mean ovulation has stopped, so it's unreliable birth control. You might ovulate when you least expect it, and it's also possible to ovulate and not menstruate. One unprotected moment of passion can result in an unintended pregnancy. That moment might arise from increased estrogen levels, which also increase libido. Studies have shown that women have increased libido around ovulation and near menses.

How do you know when you're ovulating or when your luteal phase is shortened? The overall length of your cycle isn't a good measure because it may remain constant, but you may not be ovulating, or your luteal phase may be decreasing in length. Body temperature is a common way to track ovulation, the length of the follicular phase, and the length of the luteal phase. Taking a basal body temperature measurement means taking your temperature before getting out of bed in the morning. A chart of basal body temperatures for a normally menstruating woman will generally reveal temperatures less than 98°F during the follicular phase. Just prior to ovulation, body temperature will decrease, then increase over the next day or two. During the luteal phase, body temperature tends to climb above 98°.

The best way to determine what is normal for you is to chart body temperature for a few months. If body temperature fluctuates widely or doesn't vary much at all, the cycle was probably anovulatory. Women who are trying to conceive are certainly concerned with anovulatory cycles and may also experience fertility problems with cycles having a short luteal phase.

For women not trying to conceive, the biggest concern with anovulation and shortened luteal phase is long-term health. Some types of anovulation and short luteal phase are related to low estrogen levels. Low estrogen is a contributing factor to bone loss and osteoporosis because the body does not as readily absorb calcium when estrogen levels are low.

Even women who have amenorrhea and resume normal menstrual cycles have lower bone mass than those who have always had normal menstrual cycles. Osteoporosis is a serious condition, and its symptoms and effects don't show up until well into the future. Keeping a normal menstrual cycle is one way to prevent the risk of bone loss.

It's unknown whether anovulation or low estrogen levels adversely affect athletic performance. If low estrogen levels create an out-of-balance situation for all hormones, does it affect a woman's ability to recover from exercise? Does hormonal imbalance affect mental as well as physical aspects of training? Although some athletes consider amenorrhea to be a good thing, perhaps they don't understand all of the ramifications. More research needs to be done to determine the effects of anovulation and its associated low estrogen levels on athletic performance.

Getting Back to Normal

Some of the possible causes for amenorrhea include low body weight and low body fat—two entirely different things. You can have low body weight and not have low body fat. Studies on both of these issues are conflicting as to whether they're directly linked to amenorrhea.

Studies on how training volume and intensity relate to amenorrhea are also conflicting. While some have found that women will adapt to new levels of training and resume a normal menstrual cycle after some irregularities, others have found that a reduction in training and/or intensity is necessary to solve abnormal cycles. In a study done by Drinkwater et al. (1984), training mileage was found to be the only difference between 14 amenorrheic athletes and 14 regularly menstruating controls. Researchers found no significant differences in their nutritional status.

In a separate study by Pedersen et al. (1991), dietary habits and nutrition did affect the menstrual cycle. Researchers found menstrual irregularity to be 4.9 percent among nonvegetarians and

Physician Visits: What to Bring

When you're concerned about your menstrual cycle, or the lack of a cycle, talking to a sports-savvy doctor might help, and it also helps the physician if you bring along the following information regarding your past menstrual cycles:

• Typical length of the cycle, before any changes

• Basal body temperatures, if available

• Typical menstrual flow patterns and any changes

• Bodily changes such as insomnia, hair loss, skin changes, and night sweating

• Changes in training, diet, or body weight

• Family history

This information, in addition to an exam, can rule out concerns that the irregularity is caused by something more serious, such as an unwanted growth in the uterus or a pituitary tumor. Knowing the cause of menstrual dysfunction will alleviate stress, further enhancing health.

26.5 percent among vegetarians. Kaiserauer et al. (1989) found that amenorrheic runners consumed significantly less fat, red meat, and total calories than did the regularly menstruating runners. This study also included nonrunning controls. The study concluded it was not the exercise that caused menstrual irregularity.

Stress may also affect the balance of hormones and the menstrual cycle. Stress can stem from the rigors of training and competition, a lack of support systems, interpersonal relationships, and self-image. Although a certain amount of stress can spur good performance, too much stress is thought to be detrimental to overall health and can disrupt a normal menstrual cycle.

After physical disorders and disease are ruled out, an athlete experiencing amenorrhea can work with her doctor to make changes that may include reducing exercise or taking hormonal supplements. Diet-related changes may include increasing food intake, changing the macronutrient profile (the amount of carbohydrate, fat, and protein of foods eaten), or changing the diet to include more whole foods and fewer processed ones.

GETTING TO KNOW YOUR CYCLE

Many doctors recommend that you track or chart your cycle. This makes it easier to find answers should menstrual problems arise. It can also help separate bodily changes associated with your menstrual cycle from the aches and pains associated with your athletic training. Having personal knowledge of how your body works may help alleviate stress, as you are more able to predict PMS and menstrual problems, enabling you to take measures to eliminate or significantly reduce symptoms. As a matter of convenience, being able to predict the beginning of menstruation allows you to be prepared—for instance, taking tampons along on a bike tour.

Figure 8.3 is an example of how to chart your menstrual cycle. This woman recorded the number of days since her last period, her menstrual flow pattern, her cervical mucus pattern, PMS symptoms, menstrual symptoms, treatments applied, and a few notes. Her period began on March 20, twenty-six days after the beginning of her last period. Her period began with one light day, two heavy flow days, and so on. Her PMS symptoms included tender breasts and generally feeling blue. She noticed back pain and cramping on the second day of her period and began taking ibuprofen to relieve the discomfort. She also made a note to herself to begin the ibuprofen one day earlier in the hope of completely eliminating menstrual cramping.

Other notes on her chart include cervical mucus and race-day comments. She raced on March 22 and had a great race. She began charting her cervical mucus changes to help predict the beginning of her period. Although there is space on this chart to track body temperature, this woman did not take her basal temperature at this time. Daily temperature measurements may cause this particular chart to be too busy for some women. If you already know what your temperature typically does in a month's time, you can take occasional temperature samples and record them on a chart similar to Figure 8.3.

If you want to track basal temperature each day, a sample basal body temperature chart is shown in Figure 8.4. Due to its graphical nature, it's easier to "see" what is happening to body temperature as the menstrual cycle progresses. The format is the same as that of Figure 8.3, so the two can be aligned by the day of the month. Changes in temperature may correlate well with other changes occurring during the month.

You will find blank templates for charting and reading your menstrual cycle, including your PMS and menstrual symptoms, in Appendix D.

CONTRACEPTIVES

Birth-control pills are perhaps the most common form of contraception. They come in two forms: combination pills containing estrogen and progestin, and "minipills" containing progestin only. Progestin is the synthetic version of progesterone. The amount of

FIGURE 8.3 Sample Menstrual Recording   Month: *March*

DATE	1	2	3	4	5	6	7	8	9	10	11	12	13
Days since last period	*8*	*9*	*10*	*11*	*12*	*13*	*14*	*15*	*16*	*17*	*18*	*19*	*20*
Basal body temp.													
Menstruation													
Cervical mucus				*CH*	*CH*	*CH*			*YH*		*YH*		
PMS SYMPTOMS													
Tender breasts													
Feeling blue													
MENSTRUAL SYMPTOMS													
Backache													
Cramps													
TREATMENTS													
Advil													

Menses: S = Spotting   L = Light flow   M = Medium flow   H = Heavy flow

PMS or menstrual symptoms: S = Slight, hardly noticeable   L = Light, but noticeable
M = Moderate, aware of problem   H = Problem, high aggravation, affecting
activities/lifestyle

Cervical mucus: C = Clear, stringy   Y = Yellow, tacky   L = Limited mucus
M = Moderate mucus   H = Heavy flow, copious mucus

14	15	16	17	18	19	20	21	22	23	24	25	26	27	28	29	30	31
21	*22*	*23*	*24*	*25*	*26*	*1*	*2*	*3*	*4*	*5*	*6*	*7*	*8*	*9*	*10*	*11*	*12*
						L	H	H	M	L	S						
VL																	
				M													
			S	S													
							M										
							M										
							X	X									

FIGURE 8.4 Basal Temperature Chart   Month: *May*

DATE	1	2	3	4	5	6	7	8	9	10	11	12	13
Days of menstrual cycle				1	2	3	4	5	6	7	8	9	10
Temp. > 100°F record here													
100													
99.9													
99.8													
99.7													
99.6													
99.5													
99.4													
99.3													
99.2													
99.1													
99.0													
98.9													
98.8													
98.7													
98.6													
98.5													
98.4													
98.3													
98.2													
98.1													
98.0				X	X	X							
97.9													
97.8							X		X			X	
97.7								X	X				
97.6							X						X
97.5													
97.4													
97.3													
97.2													
97.1													
97.0													

14	15	16	17	18	19	20	21	22	23	24	25	26	27	28	29	30	31
11	*12*	*13*	*14*	*15*	*16*	*17*	*18*	*19*	*20*	*21*	*22*	*23*	*24*	*25*	*26*	*27*	*28*
														X			
									X								
					X		X		X		X	X	X		X		
						X				X						X	
				X													
			X														
X	X																X
		X															

estrogen in birth-control pills suppresses ovulation. The progestin blocks the release of an egg during ovulation and creates an environment in the uterus that makes pregnancy unlikely.

The newest generation of hormonal contraception can shorten, lighten, or completely suppress a woman's period, which can be a real boon to athletes. In May 2007, the government approved Lybrel, a birth-control pill designed for daily use that completely suppresses a woman's period. The first continuous-use drug product for prevention of pregnancy comes in a twenty-eight-day pill pack with low-dose combination tablets that contain 90 micrograms of a progestin, levonorgestrel, and 20 micrograms of an estrogen, ethinyl estradiol.

Some pills, such as Seasonique, reduce the menstrual cycle to once every three months, while Yaz and Loestrin 24 promise shorter, lighter periods, fewer cramps, and PMS relief.

Other birth-control methods that suppress, shorten, and/or lighten periods are:

- Implanon, a flexible, matchstick-size rod inserted in the upper arm
- Mirena, an intrauterine device that reduces monthly bleeding by 90 percent in most women and eliminates bleeding in about 20 percent of women after a year
- Depo-Provera, an injection containing only progestin, which prevents pregnancy for three months
- Ortho Evra, a plastic patch placed on the buttocks, stomach, upper outer arm, or upper torso once a week for three weeks in a row
- NuvaRing, a flexible ring inserted into the vagina once a month

The decision whether or not to take birth-control pills depends on each individual situation. The current, lower-dose formulations may decrease many of the undesirable side effects. Your family

Benefits Versus Risks

There are a number of benefits and risks associated with taking hormonal contraceptives.

BENEFITS

- Regular, lighter, shorter menstrual cycles, reducing PMS and cramps
- Reduction of bleeding, helping protect against anemia
- Protection against ovarian cancer and cysts, uterine fibroids, cancer, endometrial cancer, and ectopic pregnancy*
- Protection against osteoporosis and cardiovascular disease, two of the reasons why postmenopausal women are prescribed estrogen replacement therapy
- Possible lower risk of Alzheimer's disease
- Less acne
- Generally greater convenience, allowing athletes to train more predictably

RISKS

- Links to certain types of cardiovascular disease
- Increased risk of blood clots
- Increased risk of stroke
- Increased risk of certain types of breast cancer**
- Estrogen may slightly lower aerobic capacity and promote fluid retention, potentially affecting athletic performance

---

* An ectopic pregnancy is one in which a fertilized egg implants somewhere other than the uterus. This misplaced, fertile egg can begin to grow within the fallopian tube, on the surface of the ovary, within the abdominal cavity, or within the pelvic cavity.

** One study has shown a link between the use of oral contraceptives and certain types of breast cancer. Other studies have not been able to confirm this finding.

history and current health status, including alcohol consumption and smoking, are all factors to consider when making the decision to take oral contraceptives.

Generally speaking, women should not take oral contraceptives if they have any of these risk factors:

- Smoke and are over age 35
- Have a history of stroke or blood clotting
- Suffer from uncontrolled high blood pressure
- Have diabetes with vascular disease
- Have high cholesterol
- Suffer from active liver disease
- Have any cancers believed to be hormonally sensitive, such as endometrial or breast cancer

• • •

A NORMALLY FUNCTIONING MENSTRUAL CYCLE IS ESSENTIAL TO your health. Low levels of estrogen associated with amenorrhea and oligomenorrhea decrease bone mass and contribute significantly to osteoporosis, even in active athletic women.

Each phase of the menstrual cycle appears to have physical and emotional advantages and disadvantages. Women are taking steps to reduce or eliminate the disadvantages at any phase and have gone so far as to break world records at various phases of the menstrual cycle.

You should do what you can to help alleviate uncomfortable menstrual cycles, and some of the latest forms of birth control can help tremendously. At the same time, you can do a great deal to recognize and reduce some of your own difficulties by tracking your cycle, noting what makes you feel better and what makes you feel worse, and taking action on future cycles.

Estrogen is a powerful hormone and should be celebrated.

chapter nine

Pregnancy and Exercise

The "right" answer is the one that's right for you—it may not be the same answer as the one for the world-class athlete next door, or the woman down the street having complications with her pregnancy.

When an active woman becomes pregnant, she has many decisions to make. Should she continue her current exercise or training program? How much exercise is too much? Should she reduce her training intensity? Can exercise hurt her baby?

While questions are multiplying, well-meaning but unsolicited advice can make an expectant mom even more insecure: "Maybe you should just rest and concentrate on growing a baby." "All that exercise can't be good for a developing fetus, can it?" "You exercise too much anyway; this is a good time to take a break from all that." Those kinds of comments haunt the expectant mother's every pedal stroke. "What if I fall or crash?" may become a question that adds to the growing list of concerns. "I don't want to risk any fallings, but

I don't want to stay home lying on the couchwant to remain active and I love to ride. What should I do?" A visit to the obstetrician early in pregnancy will likely make women aware of the risk of engaging in any activity that could result in mild abdominal trauma. Everyone wants the best for the mom and the unborn child. The question is, what is best?

The short answer is that healthy, pregnant women benefit from at least 30 minutes of moderate activity on most, if not all, days of the week, according to the American College of Sports Medicine (ACSM) and the American College of Obstetricians and Gynecologists (ACOG). General benefits can include more controlled weight gain, less fatigue, and possibly even shorter labor. This is especially true for women who were active prior to becoming pregnant. Unfit pregnant women will also benefit from exercise during pregnancy, but they need to ease into a more active lifestyle. Women who are pregnant with multiple babies or women with high-risk pregnancies should consult with a doctor, as it could be recommended that they avoid exercise altogether.

For women specifically interested in riding during pregnancy, taking some simple precautions can increase confidence on the bike. Riding a hybrid with wider tires can provide greater stability, and getting on and off the bike safely is easier without clipless pedals. When cycling, women may feel less susceptible to collision if they avoid group rides and descents, instead sticking to bike paths and even terrain. Women with extensive cycling experience may not find it necessary to abandon their road bikes and clipless pedals right away, but they still need to discuss their plans with their doctor throughout the changes of the pregnancy and adjust the intensity of their training as needed.

Recommended intensity levels during exercise are more difficult to pinpoint. It's obviously unethical to ask pregnant women to endure a nine-month study of the impact on the fetus of repeated exercise to exhaustion, but there are still a number of useful studies of exercise during pregnancy that can help define appropriate exertion. We'll consider these findings in this chapter. It can also be valuable to hear the stories of active women who have already made the journey.

WOMEN WHO HAVE BEEN THERE

Many women have remained active right up to the day of delivery. Mary Jane Reoch, a world-class road racer who became pregnant at 35, pedaled from conception to delivery and raced a criterium during her fifth month. Although she was criticized for "hurting the baby," her doctors were supportive of her exercise program. Mary Jane was active literally right up to the end: She actually rode her bike the 10 miles to the delivery room, where she gave birth to a healthy 7-pound, 12-ounce baby girl.

Blaine Bradley Limberg completed four triathlons, a biathlon, and a cross-country ski race before he was born. Blaine's mom, Barb, found out she was pregnant in the months just prior to the Hawaii Ironman World Championships, a race including a 2.4-mile swim, 112 miles of cycling, and 26.2 miles of running. After consulting her team of health care providers, including midwives, an obstetrician-gynecologist, and others who had information about exercise and pregnancy, she decided to go ahead with training and the race. She completed the event when she was three and a half months pregnant.

In training and racing, Barb decided there were three critical areas. First, she kept her core body temperature below 101°F. Second, she stayed hydrated. And third, she took action to reduce fatigue by cutting her training in half. Although she wasn't able to achieve her original time goal of 12 hours, she completed the event and did not drive herself into a deep state of fatigue. At a respectable 14 hours, 30 minutes, Barb completed the event long before the cutoff time of 17 hours.

What about after a woman delivers? Will she be able to compete at high levels? Numerous women have come back after delivering a child to even higher levels of performance. One example: Susan

Notorangelo, who was the only female finisher in the 1989 Race Across America two years after the birth of her daughter. In this transcontinental bicycle race, the clock never stops. Notorangelo covered the distance in 9 days, 9 hours, and 9 minutes, coming closer to the first-place male finisher than any woman competing in the previous five years. Overall, she finished seventh amid 13 male finishers, 24 hours, 24 minutes behind the first-place time.

An example of running through pregnancy and posting great performances after pregnancy is England's Paula Radcliff, who won the 2007 New York City Marathon a mere nine months after giving birth to daughter Isla. When she was pregnant, she kept her heart rate below 160 beats per minute (bpm), roughly 89 percent of the heart rate (180 bpm) she would typically hold for more than two hours in a race.

In a study of 30 elite athletes from Finland participating in long-distance running, speed skating, cross-country skiing, and/ or orienteering, 53 percent of the pregnant women did not notice any change when they sustained their exercise regimen during pregnancy, 10 percent subjectively felt they were in better condition, and 23 percent felt they were in worse condition (Penttinen and Erkkola 1997). After the births of their children, 18 of the 30 athletes surveyed continued to compete. Of those, 11 percent achieved better performances, 61 percent reached the same level as before pregnancy, and 28 percent did not achieve the same performance level. Researchers found that the endurance training had no harmful side effects on the pregnancies or the deliveries and concluded that the effect of pregnancy on exercise performance is individual.

Most of the women in these examples are professional athletes, so they bring to their pregnancy a high level of fitness that allows them to maintain a greater volume of training at healthy exertion levels. Of course only a small percentage of women will choose to complete an ultraendurance event during pregnancy. But there is evidence to support the benefits for women of remaining active throughout their entire pregnancy, in spite of the body's changes.

PLANNING FOR AN ACTIVE PREGNANCY
Physical and Mechanical Changes

Some changes occur during pregnancy that have minimal effect on a cycling program and may be eliminated or reduced by exercise. They include varicose veins; swelling in the hands, legs, and face; muscle and leg cramps; and hand numbness or tingling in toes and fingers. Promoting circulation helps alleviate some of these problems, but other changes occur that are probably not influenced by exercise. They include skin changes, gums that bleed more easily, and thicker hair growth. These changes generally return to pre-pregnancy condition after the birth. Women who opt to exercise regularly can expect different changes over the course of the pregnancy, many of which vary for each individual.

Early pregnancy may bring restless nights, fatigue, vivid dreams, morning sickness (nausea and vomiting), and the onset of a higher resting heart rate. Over the course of pregnancy, a woman's resting heart rate can ultimately rise to 15 to 20 bpm higher than before she was pregnant. All of these symptoms can make "this should be easy" exercise require greater effort. Many women who were active before pregnancy find some relief by cutting back on pre-pregnancy exercise volume and intensity and resting more. To reduce morning sickness and gaggy feelings, never ride on an empty stomach, and eat several smaller meals throughout the day.

Despite a higher resting heart rate, it is possible for aerobic capacity to increase throughout pregnancy because the increased heart rate is complemented by an increase in blood volume. Compared to pre-pregnancy levels, blood volume increases by nearly 50 percent by the end of the pregnancy. With more blood and a higher heart rate, cardiac output and stroke volume (ml/beat) both increase (Ireland et al. 2002).

As the pregnancy continues past the third month, the mother continues to gain weight, which affects her center of gravity and balance. Larger breasts and abdomen move her weight forward, which can mean lower-back pain and instability. A higher handlebar and more upright riding position may help. Reducing time in the saddle may also relieve some of the discomfort. Although overall riding time may have to be reduced at some point, some women find that breaking their ride into smaller segments helps: for example, going for two 45-minute rides instead of a single 90-minute ride.

Pregnant women secrete the hormone relaxin, which causes the body's connective tissues to soften and stretch. While this is a great help during delivery, it also affects joints such as the ankle and knee. Usually this is not as much of a concern in cycling as it is in a sport such as running, but pregnant cyclists should still be aware of the changes and any new joint pain that was not present before the pregnancy and is not attributed to increased mileage or bike-fit changes.

Pregnancy may cause a once comfortable bike seat to be too narrow and generally ill-fitting. As mentioned in Chapter 1, the selection of the most comfortable bike seat is highly personal. During pregnancy, a woman may be more comfortable with a seat that is wider in the back than her regular saddle.

The pressure of the uterus on the bottom of the diaphragm can cause shortness of breath during the third trimester. Again, a more upright riding position might help; that would mean raising the stem on a road bike or perhaps switching to a mountain or cyclo-cross bike that can be used on both roads and trails. Late in the third trimester, the fetus usually drops and relieves this feeling. For smaller women, this change may have little effect on the amount of pressure on the diaphragm. This is why some women have difficulty drawing a deep breath until after they deliver. The feeling of breathlessness may also be related to an increase in progesterone during pregnancy, which makes the body more sensitive to carbon dioxide (Jensen et al. 2005).

The urinary frequency that accompanies pregnancy, particularly during the first and third trimesters, can mean more time out of the saddle, but it's critical to stay well hydrated, as dehydration has been associated with premature labor. Staying well hydrated will help the exercising mom to perspire more readily, in turn better regulating her body temperature.

Emotional and Sexual Changes

Pregnancy brings not only physical changes but emotional changes as well. The emotions vary according to the individual woman and the number of children she already has. Some common emotions for the mother-to-be include reminiscing about her own childhood,

Exercising at Altitude

Pregnant women should be cautious about exercising at elevations over 5,250 feet (1,600 meters), especially if they are accustomed to living at sea level. Like any athlete, a pregnant woman may find she needs to decrease her volume and intensity of exercise upon arriving at higher elevations to give the body time to adjust–typically four or five days. A 2003 study in the *Canadian Journal of Applied Physiology* found that with proper hydration, moderate exercise at elevations up to 8,250 feet (roughly 2,500 meters) above sea level does not appear to significantly affect the well-being of the baby or the mother. However, there is little research to be found on this topic, so it is best to be conservative. Women experiencing the following warning signs should stop exercising and seek medical attention (Davis et al. 2003):

- Excessive shortness of breath
- Chest pain
- Dizziness or feeling faint
- Painful uterine contractions
- Vaginal bleeding

In the same way that women who are fit prior to pregnancy can handle a higher volume or intensity compared to unfit women, women who live at higher altitudes are less likely to experience difficulty.

becoming more focused on the baby's father and home life, and feeling big and less desirable.

In contrast, some women embrace pregnancy and its positive changes to their skin, hair, and sexual desire. For some women, the increased levels of hormones accompanying pregnancy increase their libido. Although some parents-to-be are concerned about sex during pregnancy, in most cases there is no harm to the fetus, which is cushioned by the sac of amniotic fluid.

Exercise can help some women keep a positive attitude about their changing bodies. In studies conducted by the Melpomene Institute, women reported that remaining physically active was positive for their emotional health. Exercise has also been shown to help the body change and take on extra weight in the healthiest way possible—meaning women who exercise during pregnancy gain less weight and deposit less subcutaneous fat (Clapp et al. 1995), which is fat that is just below the skin's surface.

Benefits to the Baby

There are several benefits to the mother if she maintains an exercise program while she's pregnant, but what about the baby? Numerous studies have followed the offspring of mothers who exercised during pregnancy and have found the babies to be healthy, with normal growth and development.

In an interesting study conducted at the University of Vermont, head researcher James Clapp, MD, matched two groups of pregnant families for socioeconomic status, education, marital stability, and body size. The fathers were also included in the body size data. The two groups were matched for pre- and post-pregnancy exercise habits; both groups of mothers breast-fed, had similar child care arrangements, and had comparable parental weight change over time.

The only difference between the two groups was exercise *during* pregnancy. One group exercised "vigorously" by running, doing aerobics, cross-country skiing, or some combination of all three. They exercised at least 30 minutes three times per week throughout their pregnancies. The second group ceased all exercise except walking.

The researchers found that by age five, the children of the vigorous exercisers had less body fat than the children born to the walking group. The children born to the second group were called "a bit on the fat side." In addition, the vigorous exercisers' children scored significantly higher on the Wechsler test of general intelligence and coordination as well as on tests of oral language skills.

General Guidelines for Exertion during Pregnancy

Not everyone will be able to maintain a regular exercise program during pregnancy. Some exercise, however, is better than none. ACOG and ACSM revised the recommendations for pregnant women in 2002 to make them less restrictive. ACOG now suggests that women use perceived exertion as a guideline rather than limiting themselves to a specific heart rate: Generally speaking, if you can carry on a conversation while you exercise, your heart rate is in the right place. This equates to RPE 12–14, or 60 to 80 percent of aerobic capacity for most pregnant women, according to ACSM (2006). (Refer to Chapter 2 for more information on exercising heart rates.) This guideline may be overly conservative for well-trained athletes. It's important that every woman establish her personal guidelines in consultation with her medical professionals.

It will be easier to be physically active if you allow yourself some flexibility. Don't set goal times for races or events, and be willing to turn around and go home when you're not feeling well. Listen to your body, and exercise at an intensity that feels comfortable. Seek support from family and friends, and talk to other women who have exercised or who are exercising during their pregnancy. Studies show positive physical and emotional benefits for women who begin an exercise program after becoming pregnant. If you decide to start a program, talk with your health care provider.

In the end, you're the only one who can decide how much exercise is too much. The "right" answer is the one that's right for you—it may not be the same answer as the one for the world-class athlete next door or the woman down the street having complications with her pregnancy.

Exercise Guidelines for During and After Pregnancy

With the ACOG changes in mind, the following is a collection of general guidelines for women who want to exercise during and after pregnancy:

- Consult with a health care provider about exercise programs. This is especially true for women who were less active prior to pregnancy.
- For maximum benefits, exercise should be mild to moderate and regular–at least three to five times per week is preferable to intermittent activity.
- Use good judgment and reduce intensity, or stop exercise, when fatigue sets in.
- Low-impact exercise, such as cycling and swimming, decreases risk of injury to mother and fetus. In the case of cycling, avoid situations that increase risk of falling. Women experiencing loss of balance, particularly in the third trimester, should limit cycling to a stationary trainer.
- Eat adequate calories. Pregnant women require roughly 300 calories per day in addition to their normal intake. "Normal" includes calories necessary for exercise (keeping in mind that 300 calories is probably less than you think–for example, a sizable salad or a whole-wheat English muffin with peanut butter).
- Drink adequate fluids to avoid overheating and dehydration.
- Wear proper clothing and exercise in a cool environment to help avoid overheating. This may mean exercising in cool morning or evening conditions, indoors in air conditioning, or indoors in front of a fan. This is especially important in early pregnancy (the initial two to three weeks).
- Exercise in the supine position (lying on the back) for a prolonged period should be avoided after the fourth months of pregnancy to prevent restricting blood flow to the fetus.

POSTPREGNANCY: FINDING THE FASTEST TO RECOVERY ROAD

Many of the physical changes associated with pregnancy last four to six weeks postpartum, so women should work into their post-pregnancy routine gradually. Consultation with an obstetrician-gynecologist is just as important after the baby is born as it is in early pregnancy. Women who experience complications in labor or have stitches (due to a tear or episiotomy, i.e., an incision through the perineum) may need more time to resume their active lifestyle. Before sitting on a regular bicycle seat, tears and episiotomies need to be healed. Women who have had cesarean sections should avoid vigorous exercise for six to eight weeks after delivery and follow their doctor's advice once they begin exercising again.

Avoid Episiotomy

You'll speed your postpartum recovery and get back on your bike faster if you avoid episiotomy during childbirth. An episiotomy is a surgical incision made through the perineum, the area between the vaginal opening and the anus. Obstetricians once justified its routine use in uncomplicated births by alleging that it sped up the second stage of labor; reduced perineal tearing; and helped avoid postpartum urinary incontinence, pelvic-floor problems, and sexual dysfunction.

Research has shown, however, that episiotomy offers no benefit in a normal vaginal birth and delays recovery, increases postpartum pain, and makes sexual intercourse problematic. Tears in vaginal tissue that might occur during delivery generally are much more superficial and heal more quickly than an episiotomy, which cuts through actual muscle. ACOG has recommended that episiotomy no longer be a routine procedure.

Although episiotomy rates have dropped in recent years—not long ago, it was used in nearly 100 percent of first-time births—it's still one of the most common obstetrical procedures. Pregnant women should talk to their medical providers well in advance about their desire to avoid an episiotomy if at all possible.

The perineum stretches naturally, but you can help prepare it for birth by practicing squatting, doing perineal massage during the last six weeks of pregnancy, and strengthening your pelvic-floor muscles.

Strengthen the Pelvic Muscles

Dr. Arnold Kegel developed exercises to strengthen the pelvic floor, or the muscles surrounding the urethra, vagina, and anus, to help women with stress incontinence and uterine prolapse. Kegel exercises strengthen the pubococcygeus (PC) muscle, the slinglike band from the vaginal opening to the anus.

Doing these exercises during and after pregnancy has myriad benefits. In childbirth, it makes the pushing stage of labor faster and easier and helps to avoid episiotomy by making it possible to push with greater control. Kegels also reduce problems with urinary incontinence (the involuntary loss of urine) caused by an unstable bladder (urgent need to urinate accompanied by a fear of leakage and a high frequency of urination) or stress incontinence (leaking urine after a cough, sneeze, or any maneuver that increases the abdominal pressure exerted on the bladder). Best of all, strong pelvic muscles enhance sex.

To locate the PC muscle, sit on the toilet with your legs apart and stop the flow of urine. You just did your first Kegel. If you're a beginner, start by contracting the PC for 3 seconds, then releasing. If you've been doing Kegels for a while, try the "elevator exercise": Imagine the muscle is an elevator and try to raise it a floor at a time—three levels—until you reach the top. That's the easy part. Now try to lower it a floor at a time—much tougher! Repeat the exercise as often as you can but at least forty times a day. You can do it while driving to work, sitting at your desk, or watching television, and no one's the wiser.

Dr. Kegel's patients were very grateful to him, and not just because he helped with incontinence and uterine prolapse. They discovered that strengthening the PC muscle enhanced sexual pleasure; it's the muscle that creates the vaginal tightness that can be lost after pushing out an eight-pound baby. To regain muscle control, start doing Kegels immediately after giving birth—and never stop. Should you continue to struggle with incontinence problems, see a physical therapist for further exercises, some of which can be performed with a vaginal device that provides resistance or feedback.

Breast-Feeding

Breast-feeding your baby is great for his or her health—and for yours. Your milk, made specifically for your child, can help prevent disease, enhance development, and provide other health benefits that follow your child into adulthood. The World Health Organization recommends exclusive breast-feeding (no formula, milk, juice, or water) for at least the first six months and solid foods with continued breast-feeding up to two years of age or beyond.

Breast-feeding burns 500 to 1,000 calories a day, making it easier for new mothers to return to their pre-pregnancy weight. However, women still have to monitor postpartum weight loss to ensure that the pounds don't come off too quickly after the first six weeks. One study found that women could safely lose about one pound a week without compromising their baby's growth.

A common breast-feeding myth says that exercise will "sour" mother's milk, causing the baby to feed less or refuse to nurse altogether. Research, however, shows that even the most intense exercise has no impact on infant feeding patterns.

A University of New Hampshire study analyzed the breast milk of 24 women one hour before and one hour after three test sessions: a maximal oxygen uptake test that exercised the women to exhaustion, 30 minutes of moderate exercise 20 percent below lactic acid threshold, and a resting control session (Carey et al. 2002).

Breast-Feeding Benefits

FOR BABY

- Decreased risk of bacterial meningitis, diarrhea, respiratory infections, ear infections, and urinary tract infections
- Reduced rates of sudden infant death syndrome in the first year of life
- Lower rates of diabetes, lymphoma, leukemia, Hodgkin's disease, obesity, high cholesterol, and asthma in later childhood
- Superior cognitive development

FOR MOM

- Decreased postpartum bleeding and more rapid uterine involution, which is the return of the uterus to its pre-pregnancy size
- Decreased menstrual-blood loss and increased child spacing attributable to lactational amenorrhea
- Earlier return to pre-pregnancy weight
- Decreased risk of breast and ovarian cancers (specifically for women who lactate prior to age 30)
- Potential for a decreased risk of hip fractures and osteoporosis in the postmenopausal period

The mothers expressed their milk, fed it to their babies, and rated the babies' acceptance of the milk. Three lactation consultants who watched videotapes of the feeding sessions also rated infant acceptance. Researchers found that the milk's lactic acid levels rose only following the maximal exercise session, but the moms and lactation consultants observed no difference in the babies' willingness to nurse.

Other studies have found that even maximal exercise had no impact on concentrations of calcium, phosphorus, magnesium, potassium, and sodium. Researchers also found no difference in breast-milk volume or composition—plasma hormones, milk energy, lipid, protein, and lactose content—or in infants' weight gain among mothers who exercised vigorously compared with sedentary moms.

Breast-feeding mothers who exercise regularly must be careful to consume adequate nutrition and remain hydrated. In contrast to the modest increase in caloric intake during pregnancy, lactation requires two to three times this amount. With inadequate nutrition or dehydration, breast milk volume and composition can suffer.

While sedentary women have to be more cautious than active women about exercise duration and exertion during pregnancy, their postpartum weight loss efforts will be helped with regular exercise and modest calorie restriction (500 calories/day).

• • •

FOR HEALTHY WOMEN, CONTINUING OR BEGINNING AN EXERCISE program during pregnancy appears to benefit both the mother and the unborn baby. Women continue to comment that exercise makes their pregnancy more enjoyable by helping them maintain a positive attitude, good self-esteem, and a sense of control. Exercise can help with the management of gestational diabetes, depression, and other problems that occasionally accompany pregnancy.

Many women who are competitive athletes and become pregnant have found they are able to return to competitive levels after having the baby, if competition is a priority for them. Some comment on a newfound strength and mental toughness in their training and competition after they've given birth. Others have found a new balance that allows them to put athletic training in perspective with other priorities in their lives.

In exercising during pregnancy, the health of the unborn baby is always the top priority, but the motion is important too. Each woman needs to determine what level of exercise is appropriate for her and her unborn child. A well-informed health care provider can furnish information to assist a woman in the fitness-during-pregnancy journey—and a supportive network of family and friends makes the journey easier.

The author wishes to give special thanks to Dr. Pauline Entin at the University of Northern Arizona for her thoughtful contributions to this chapter.

chapter ten

The Masters Cyclist

I still remember one of the strongest female athletes I've ever met. I don't remember her name, but she made a lasting impression on me. I vividly recall her looks because she resembled my great-grandmother. She was a short woman with broad shoulders and a sturdy body, much like the German farmers in my family. Heavy brows and a strong nose accentuated her friendly eyes. She proudly told me she was 74, her German accent spicing each word.

"They only let me enter five events," she said. "I can do more, you know."

She began her first event, diving off the starting blocks in a masters swimming meet. When she finished, I told her the time on my clock. She smiled as though she knew a secret. Raising one eyebrow she asked, "Good, eh?"

Good? No . . . great!

As a child, my concept of an old person was someone who was at least 30. I'm finding that the older I get, the older "old" becomes. The things that so impressed me about the 74-year-old German woman were her commitment to exercise and how much fun she seemed to be having. When she was growing up, exercise was the manual labor associated with earning a living. Now she was diving into a swimming pool and racing as fast as she could for the sheer joy of it. I want to do the same thing.

As we age, what can we expect? Was this German dynamo the exception, or can we all be just as active as we age? While it's possible to remain highly active and fit as we age, our bodies do change. The rate of change appears to be individual, but changes are inevitable.

Women tend to live longer than men, and the average life expectancy for both genders has been increasing. People born in the United States in 1900 could expect to live to be about 47, with women living about four to ten years longer than men. For people born in the United States in 1946, women could expect to live 78.5 years and men 71. Experts disagree about the average life expectancy for those born in the 1980s or 1990s. There are also plenty of theories as to why women and men have different life expectancies, but those won't be covered here.

The average life span, differing from average life expectancy, is defined as the age by which all but a very few members are deceased. Although average life expectancy has been increasing, the average life span has remained stable at 85. This chapter covers the aging process: what we can expect in general and, in particular, the changes we'll encounter as we go through menopause.

THREE STAGES OF MENOPAUSE

There was a time when some women would commit suicide or submit to alcoholism to escape the physical and mental hell they were experiencing during midlife. Their bodies and minds seemed to turn against them. At the time, science, much less husbands, didn't understand the process of menopause, and doctors weren't able to help patients comprehend what was happening as their bodies changed. Furthermore, some doctors believed the symptoms were not real.

Fortunately, medical science continues to discover more about menopause and can offer advice to women so they may continue to lead healthy lives during and after "the change of life." The knowledge supplied by science, coupled with simply discussing menopause with women who have experienced it, can help younger women be better prepared.

Young women begin producing estrogen in the ovaries sometime between the ages of 10 and 14. Most women reach their peak reproductive capability in their late twenties. As they age, diminishing levels of estrogen begin the process commonly referred to as "menopause," which actually consists of three different stages: perimenopause, menopause, and postmenopause.

The first stage, referred to as perimenopause or premenopause, starts for most women in their forties and can last five or more years. It is characterized by erratic periods, hot flashes, night sweats, moodiness, and insomnia, among other frustrating symptoms. The second stage, menopause, is considered to have occurred after one year without menstruation. It can be confirmed by a doctor testing for elevated levels of follicle-stimulating hormone (FSH). As estrogen levels fall, levels of FSH rise. Postmenopause, the third stage, refers to the time from that point on, although "menopause" is generally used instead. For about half of all women, menopause occurs between the ages of 45 and 50, with an average age of 51.

Signs and Symptoms

While the signs and symptoms of the three stages of menopause often overlap and vary from woman to woman, there does seem to be a progression of sorts. One of the most common early symptoms of perimenopause is hot flashes. They can begin with a sensation of pressure in your head, similar to a headache, along with a sudden feeling of heat flushing through the body. Skin temperature actually increases, and sweat may break out on the head, neck, upper chest, or back. Hot flashes can last anywhere from a few minutes to a half hour.

Several studies have looked at hormonal changes occurring during hot flashes. Although the levels of circulating estrogen have not been found to fluctuate before or after hot flashes, there does appear to be a correlation between a pulse in luteinizing hormone and the occurrence of hot flashes. Several studies (Freeman 2007; Smith-DiJulio 2007; and Zhao 2000) found a pulse in the FSH as well, while a second study by Randolf (2006) did not. Although estrogen does not seem to fluctuate during hot flashes, low levels of it may create the hormonal imbalance that results in hot flashes. Unfortunately, many hot flash episodes occur during the night, causing loss of sleep. Nocturnal hot flashes are significant contributors to sleep deprivation and fatigue, which can lead to mood swings, irritability, and depression.

Another symptom of perimenopause is irregular, unpredictable, and sometimes heavy bleeding. If you've charted your menstrual cycles from year to year (as discussed in Chapter 8), you'll have a record of your past history, which will be particularly helpful in tracking gradual changes as you begin menopause.

During menopause, vaginal tissues become dryer, thinner, and less flexible, which can cause painful intercourse. Products that can be used to lubricate the vagina include aloe vera gel, vitamin E capsules—puncture the capsule and use the gel—and commercial products such as Replens, Gynmoistrin, K-Y jelly, and Astroglide. For an inexpensive alternative, try Cornhusker's Lotion.

Because tissues begin to lose some elasticity, there can be sagging of the pelvic organs, which can contribute to incontinence. Fortunately, the Kegel exercises covered in Chapter 8 can strengthen the muscles of the pelvic floor and eliminate some, if not all, symptoms of incontinence.

Dropping estrogen levels can also cause new—and unwanted—hair growth. Reduced estrogen levels upset the balance between estrogen and testosterone in the female body, and the result can be dark, coarse hairs growing on the upper lip or chin.

As estrogen levels drop, so does women's natural protection from heart disease. Lower estrogen levels are associated with increased levels of LDL, lower levels of HDL, increased triglycerides, and rising blood pressure. With these changes, a woman's risk factors for heart disease become similar to a man's.

Osteoporosis Risks and Prevention

- A sedentary lifestyle can contribute to bone loss, so exercise! For best results, do weight-bearing exercises such as walking, running, hiking, soccer, step aerobics, racquet sports, gymnastics, stair-climbing, and dancing, among others.
- While men can get osteoporosis, women are more prone to it (in the United States, of those who have osteoporosis, 80 percent are women and 20 percent are men).
- Women who are thin and small-framed are at risk of getting osteoporosis, though being overweight does not protect you from getting it.
- Low levels of calcium are not adequate to build bone and prevent bone loss. According to the National Osteoporosis Foundation (NOF), adults under the age of 50 need 1,000 milligrams of calcium and 400-800 IU of vitamin D3 daily, while adults 50 and over need 1,200 milligrams of calcium and 800-1,000 IU of vitamin D3 daily. For those who do not get adequate amounts of calcium from their diet, they should be sure to take supplements.
- Smoking increases bone loss, so don't smoke. Some studies have indicated that tobacco use can increase bone loss by lessening the amount of estrogen a woman's body makes and interfering with calcium absorption in the intestines.
- Decreasing levels of estrogen are associated with an increased risk for osteoporosis because estrogen helps with the absorption of calcium. Supplemental estrogen can help alleviate some of this risk (for those who are able to take it).

CONTINUES

CONTINUED

- Caffeine and alcohol increase calcium excretion, so limit their use. Most current research says two to three cups of coffee a day and two alcoholic drinks a day are acceptable.
- Diets high in sodium and protein may contribute to osteoporosis. Sodium competes with calcium for reabsorption by your body, so if you're ingesting too much salt, calcium is likely to be excreted in your urine rather than reabsorbed into your blood. Likewise, excessive protein, especially animal protein, may cause calcium loss through your kidneys.
- Those who are confined indoors may be at risk for osteoporosis, because sunlight provides vitamin D, which increases calcium absorption from the intestines and reabsorption from the kidneys. Likewise, sunlight, in moderation (most studies suggest only 10 to 15 minutes of exposure per day), can help calcium absorption.
- Some drugs may inhibit the absorption of calcium and thus contribute to osteoporosis. These include anticonvulsants, antacids containing aluminum, corticosteroids, and diuretics (which increase the loss of calcium through urine). If you are on any medication, you should talk to your health care provider to see if it causes bone loss.
- Foods containing phytates (such as oatmeal and 100 percent wheat bran) and oxalates (such as cashews, almonds, rhubarb, beet greens, kale, and spinach) interfere with calcium absorption. If you are taking a calcium supplement, take it two hours before or after eating these foods.
- Other health conditions that may put you at risk for osteoporosis include amenorrhea, anorexia nervosa and bulimia, hyperthyroidism, rheumatoid arthritis, depression, and inflammatory bowel disease, among others. If you have a medical condition, be sure to talk with your health care provider so that you can maintain good bone health.

Preventing Osteoporosis

In women and men, bones continually undergo a process of remodeling—a process in which old bone is replaced by new bone. When we are young, old bone is lost, but because new bone is formed at a faster rate, total bone mass increases. The process of building new bone is called "formation," and in young adulthood, formation equals the pace of bone loss. Somewhere in our mid- to late thirties, bone loss exceeds formation, and we can begin to lose bone mass at a rate of approximately 1 percent per year.

Fully developed osteoporosis is considered to be when bone loss is 2 to 3 percent per year. According to the NOF, osteoporosis is a "major public health threat for an estimated 44 million Americans, or 55 percent of the people 50 years of age and older" (www.nof.org). Although some of the risks for osteoporosis are beyond our control (heredity and genetics, for instance), the NOF says that there are five steps we can take to help prevent osteoporosis:

1. Be sure to take the daily recommended amounts of calcium and vitamin D.
2. Participate in weight-bearing and muscle-strengthening exercises.
3. Do not smoke or drink excessive amounts of alcohol.
4. Discuss bone health with your health care provider.
5. Get a bone mineral density test, and take medication when appropriate.

While calcium supplementation and estrogen treatment may only slow calcium or bone loss, exercise is critically important because it has the ability to actually increase bone formation, even in older adults. Another way of decreasing the risk for osteoporosis is limiting sodium and protein intake.

Exercises that work best to increase bone formation are those that are weight-bearing, including strength training (free weights, resistance bands, weight machines, etc.), walking, running, hiking, stair-climbing, low-impact aerobics, dancing, racquet sports, and other activities that require your muscles to work against gravity. Gravity and muscular contraction apply force to bones, which influences the structure and integrity of the bone. The mechanical force of exercise is converted to electrical energy—a process that activates the bone-forming cells in the area of the stress and increases calcium levels.

Controversy exists as to whether cycling is an exercise that helps prevent osteoporosis. It's not clear why some scientists find cycling helpful and others do not, but it may have to do with how the cycling is done. If a woman simply sits on the bicycle and spins her legs, there is minimal stress to muscles and bones. If, however, she climbs hills, does intervals, or cycles out of the saddle, the exercise may better fit the bill of "weight-bearing."

In hill climbing, while seated, a woman can use forces that are similar to weight lifting by powering each pedal stroke to climb up a hill. Certainly, if she is out of the saddle climbing a hill, she supports her body weight with each push of the pedal. However, until more is known about cycling's ability to increase bone mass, it is probably best to augment cycling with a weight training program or other weight-bearing exercises.

Some women have found relief for menopausal symptoms by exercising and watching their diet. A diet with plenty of fruits, vegetables, low-fat dairy, and lean meats may be helpful. Exercise not only helps prevent osteoporosis, it can boost self-esteem; help maintain proper weight; tone muscles; and improve circulation, digestion, and elimination.

Hormone Therapy

Taking a dose of hormones in the form of a pill or a patch, known as hormone therapy, may offer some relief from menopausal symptoms. In the 1960s, when doctors began experimenting with estrogen supplementation, the results seemed very promising. Estrogen was being touted as a key to the fountain of youth that could prevent hot flashes, depression, vaginal drying, vaginal thinning, and even wrinkles. Women taking supplemental estrogen had high hopes of retaining their youthful appearance and sexual vigor.

But in the late 1970s, the picture for estrogen use changed. Researchers were finding that women who took estrogen alone—without progesterone—were six to fourteen times more likely to develop uterine cancer than women who did not use estrogen, due to uterine lining overgrowth. As more research was conducted and more women began using supplemental estrogen, doctors found that they could lower the doses to achieve positive effects and minimize the negative side effects. In addition, progestin—a synthetic version of progesterone—combined with estrogen could keep the uterine lining overgrowth problem in check.

The latest research has both good news and bad. First the bad news: In 2002, researchers abruptly ended the federal Women's Health Initiative study after it became clear that women on hormone therapy were developing invasive breast cancer and heart disease at a higher rate. Frightened women stopped filling their prescriptions, and breast cancer rates dropped by 7 percent in 2003, according to research released in 2007. The study also found that estrogen plus progestin increased heart disease, stroke, and pulmonary embolism, but there was good news too: It decreased the risk of colorectal cancer and hip fracture (see www.whi.org/findings/).

Researchers analyzing data from thirty studies of nearly 27,000 women found that age made a difference. In the younger group, with an average age of 54, hormone therapy was associated with a 39 percent reduction in risk of death from all causes. Their conclusion: Hormone therapy benefits might outweigh risks if treatment starts at a younger age, but the opposite may be true for first-time users over 60.

Hormone therapy is also a bad idea for women with severe liver disease, thrombotic disorders (blood clots), malignant melanoma, and estrogen-dependent tumors of the breast, uterus, or kidneys. Another reason for not utilizing estrogen therapy is a family history of uterine or breast cancer. A family history of uterine or breast cancer, where risks increase with estrogen supplementation, must be

TABLE 10.1 Benefits and Risks of Hormone Replacement Therapy

BENEFITS	RISKS
Reduces or eliminates hot flashes	Menstrual periods and/or cramping may begin again
Reduces the risks of osteoporosis	May increase the risk of breast cancer
Reduces the risk of developing heart disease	May increase the risk of uterine cancer
Reduces vaginal dryness	May increase the risk of gallbladder disease
May help with insomnia, depression, and memory problems	May cause nausea, vomiting, swelling of the extremities, and breast tenderness

weighed against a family history of heart disease and osteoporosis, where risks increase without estrogen supplementation.

Unexplained vaginal bleeding, a history of high blood pressure, or gallbladder disease are also reasons for caution. A summary of risks and benefits associated with hormone therapy is shown in Table 10.1. Women need to discuss all the options with their doctors.

Psychological and Emotional Symptoms

Some women breeze through the years of menopause, while others find it the most challenging time of their lives. While some women experience hot flashes as nuisances and major disruptions to their personal equilibrium, others welcome them as "power surges" that are harbingers of a joyfully anticipated next stage in life. Some women mourn the loss of their fertility, while others are empowered by not having to worry about birth control any longer, much less monthly periods. Regardless of how you approach your menopausal years, you will be much happier accepting the inevitable changes and being proactive in seeking help when you need it.

Herbal Remedies for Menopause

All women will, at some point, have to deal with menopause. While some women have few symptoms or problems, the majority of women will suffer at least some of the problems covered in this chapter. For the lucky ones, menopausal symptoms are mild and tolerable. A percentage of the others will choose synthetic estrogen replacement to minimize discomfort and prevent problems such as osteoporosis. Another percentage of women may spend years of their life in misery because they wanted to avoid synthetic estrogen replacement therapy. For them, the loss of quality of life can be costly.

For women wanting to relieve the symptoms of menopause yet not take synthetic estrogen, there may be another choice. Some plants have naturally occurring estrogens. Licorice, sage, saw palmetto, black cohosh, soybeans, tofu, miso, flaxseed, pomegranates, and dates contain phytoestrogens–all estrogen-like compounds, which when ingested mimic the chemistry of estrogen. Their chemical activity is slower and weaker than that of synthetic estrogens; however, they appear to be free of the side effects associated with those synthetics. Some of these substances are being combined in tonics, such as black-cohosh-licorice compound, available at some vitamin and supplement stores in a liquid-drop form.

While some plants contain estrogen, others, like chaste tree berries, are thought to restore a normal estrogen-progesterone balance by inhibiting the release of FSH and increasing LH. A tonic named Pulsatilla-Vitex Compound contains chaste tree berry, pulsatilla, motherwort, black cohosh, and licorice and some women use it for menopausal relief.

Certain natural remedies, such as those mentioned above, are thought to influence estrogen, progesterone, FSH, and LH; other remedies are thought to relieve symptoms. Those thought to help relieve hot flash symptoms include lecithin, an emulsifier for vitamin E; primrose oil or black currant seed oil; vitamin E; and vitamin C.

Although called "all-natural-herbal" when used for pharmaceutical purposes, these herbal options for relieving menopausal symptoms are still

CONTINUES

CONTINUED

considered drugs. Herbal remedies are not without problems. Some herbs can cause heart palpitations or interfere with the absorption of iron and other vitamins and minerals. If you choose to self-medicate, it is important to learn as much as possible about this topic and the specific doses of herbs that may be necessary to relieve symptoms.

AGING

As years pass, the process of aging affects everyone. How much aging affects each person and at what rate, however, are individual. Why is it that some people are frail, inactive, and highly dependent on others, while others are vigorous, athletic, and self-sufficient?

The rate of aging, or the change in function of organs and body systems per unit of time, is different for men and women. For example, women age at a slower rate from 45 to 60 than they do from 70 to 80. Men's aging rate, on the other hand, slows at a pace unvarying in time. In other words, the rate at which men age slows down as they age and doesn't vary during particular years, as does women's aging rate.

What can we expect as we age? That depends on genetics, sex, living environment, exposure to harmful chemicals, exercise history, and overall health maintenance, among other things. When asked their "secrets" to longevity and health, 85-year-old participants in one study listed hard work, exercise, and keeping active both physically and mentally. Other secrets were inheriting good genes; lifelong good health, including use of health care resources; strong religious beliefs; good nutrition; abstinence from alcohol, smoking, and drugs; adequate rest and sleep; a positive attitude toward themselves and others; and a good support system—parents, friends, spouses, or children.

There are changes we all face as we age, and the rate at which we experience them varies. Table 10.2 lists some of the changes that occur as we age and how athletes can compensate for or reduce the

TABLE 10.2 Changes That Come with Aging

CHANGE	ACTIONS TO MINIMIZE EFFECT OF CHANGE
Skin becomes thinner, dryer, less able to produce sweat.	Keep skin moisturized and, when exposed to the sun, protected with sunscreen. Wear light-colored clothing when in the sun and be cautious when exercising in extreme heat.
Basal metabolism decreases.	Exercise can increase metabolism.
Strength and flexibility decrease.	A strength training program, including a stretching plan, will help.
Aerobic capacity and anaerobic capacity decrease.	An aerobic cycling program, including some anaerobic work, will reduce the losses.
The body does not repair itself as quickly as it once did.	Older athletes may need to decrease the number of high-intensity or high-volume workouts per week. Another option is to increase the frequency of rest weeks throughout the training cycle.
Bone density decreases.	Participate in weight-bearing exercise and get an adequate calcium, reduce factors that increase calcium loss, and perhaps get hormone replacement therapy.
Decreased sight and hearing loss.	Keep vision prescriptions current and use a hearing aid if necessary.
Decreased sense of smell, taste, and thirst sensation.	Thirst is particularly important. Be adequately hydrated, drinking at least eight to ten glasses of water each day. When participating in athletic events, employ a hydration plan–do not wait to be thirsty in order to rehydrate.
Decreased ability to absorb and use vitamins, minerals and essential nutrients in foods.	Prepare foods that are nutrient-dense. Nutrient-dense foods tend to be the ones that are minimally processed: Fruits, vegetables, lean meats, nuts, and dairy products are some of the top contenders.
Digestion rate slows.	Increase the time between vigorous athletic events and heavy meals. Take easily digestible foods or liquid meals prior to athletic events.
Reaction time slows.	Adjust bicycle speed to accommodate corners and steep downhills.
Sleep patterns change.	Go to bed at a regular time each night. Avoid caffeine for at least two hours before bedtime. Exercise at least two hours before bedtime. Possibly eat a small snack.
Bladder capacity decreases.	Plan more frequent pit stops.

impact. Most studies of aging, however, have been conducted on nonathletes. Only recently have there been enough older athletes to study and evaluate established paradigms about the aging process.

Here's the beginning of lots of good news about aging: A study at the University of Florida had 10 sedentary senior men and women—average age 67—begin a training plan at the same time as 11 sedentary 30-year-old men and women. Both groups worked out three times per week for 16 weeks. Over that period, they all doubled their exercise duration to 40 minutes each time and increased intensity from 60 to 80 percent of maximal heart rate. At the end of the 16-week training plan, the younger group had increased their aerobic capacity by 12 percent, while the seniors had increased their aerobic capacity by 14 percent. The difference between the two groups was not statistically significant.

Researchers found that similar training yielded similar results, regardless of age. San Diego State University conducted a study of 13 women, with an average age of 47, who were highly competitive members of the U.S. Cycling (USAC). The women were field-tested in 13.5 km and 20 km time trials for aerobic capacity and lactate threshold. The USCF women's aerobic capacity tested approximately 10 percent higher than that reported for other age-matched women athletes. Researchers found the women's maximal heart rate was unrelated to age.

The women's laboratory lactate threshold heart rates tested at 88 percent of their maximal heart rates. During the time trials, the women were able to average 92 to 94 percent of their maximal heart rates. The study showed that traditional methods of estimating maximal heart rate and lactate threshold training intensities would be incorrect for masters women cyclists.

Other studies in other sports have also found the traditional method of "220 − age = maximum heart rate" to be incorrect. This is why it is important to base training intensities on individual lactate threshold heart rates and perceived exertions and not to use estimates from age-graded charts. A method for doing this is discussed in Chapter 2.

One of the theories on aging is that it is a result of the accumulation of mitochondrial DNA mutations. These mutations interfere with respiratory ATP production, which impairs cell function. When the cell is unable to go about its business of utilizing oxygen and producing energy, tissue dysfunction becomes a problem, leading to decline and eventually death.

One study by Bierley (1996) looked at the muscle mitochondria of test subjects who were matched for levels of physical activity. Interestingly, the study found that exercise improved and may mask mitochondrial "aging" in muscle. Exercise appears to have multiple benefits for both younger and older women.

• • •

IF YOU FEAR GROWING OLDER, MAYBE A CHANGE IN PERSPECTIVE would help. Women can age beautifully and minimize some discomforts if they are armed with knowledge. Older women have freedom from menstrual cycles, and usually from the time and expense of child rearing as well, allowing them to be more active and carefree.

Research shows that people who remain active as they age tend to lead overall healthier lives. Exercise has helped people lose weight, increase strength, quit smoking, and eat better. Exercise can also significantly help with the symptoms of menopause and osteoporosis.

It seems that the synergistic effects of wellness are changing how we age and our paradigm of the typical aging process. Perhaps you can find a role model like the 74-year-old German woman swimmer introduced at the beginning of this chapter.

chapter eleven

Comfort and Safety

We should not only use all the brains we have, but all that we can borrow. —WOODROW WILSON

This chapter is a collection of tips I've found useful over the years. Hopefully they can help you prevent uncomfortable situations or remedy a problem once it has occurred. As the saying goes, "An ounce of prevention is worth a pound of cure," but even when we start out well prepared, factors beyond our control may occur. Therefore, I have included treatment options as well as tips on prevention. Nothing in this chapter is intended as a substitute for a physician's advice or treatment. You need to determine whether the situation is just discomfort—something you can handle—or something that needs professional treatment.

RIDING IN ALL KINDS OF WEATHER
Cycling and Heat Stress
Although you're careful about hydration and conditioning, there might be times when the weather suddenly becomes very hot, or

you travel from a cool to a hot climate to do an event. For those reasons, it's important to know the stages of heat stress.

In **Stage 1**, heat cramps often occur in the form of muscle pain and involuntary spasms, but body temperature is not necessarily elevated. Heat exhaustion, **Stage 2** of heat stress, is caused by ineffective circulatory adjustments compounded by a depletion of extracellular fluid, especially blood volume, due to excess sweating. Symptoms of heat exhaustion include a weak and rapid pulse, low blood pressure in the upright position, headache, dizziness, and general weakness.

The most serious and complex of heat-stress maladies, heatstroke, occurs during **Stage 3** and requires immediate medical attention. It is the failure of heat-regulating mechanisms in the body brought on by excessive body temperatures. Sweating usually ceases, skin becomes hot and dry, body temperature rises to at least 104°F, and excessive strain is put on the circulatory system. Some people will sweat, but heat gain by the body outstrips the avenues for heat loss. Untreated, it can result in circulatory collapse, central nervous system damage, and death. Heatstroke is a medical emergency.

TREATMENT

If you're having heat cramps, stop whatever physical activity you're participating in; find a cool place to rest; and drink a sports drink, clear juice, or water. Don't resume any physical activity for at least a few hours, since this could bring on heat exhaustion or heatstroke. If you're experiencing heat exhaustion, you should stop physical activity, move to a cooler environment, and drink fluids, but if you're experiencing more severe symptoms (blood pressure changes, weakness, a rapid pulse, etc.), you should see a physician. In extreme cases, intravenous therapy may be needed. As mentioned previously, full-blown heatstroke is a medical emergency and requires a physician's care.

PREVENTION

Heat acclimatization generally takes ten to fourteen days, so give yourself some time to adjust if you know you'll be riding in hot weather. If you don't have problems with sodium, try adding a small amount of salt to food and drinking extra water. This helps because with prolonged exercise in the heat, sweat loss may deplete the body of sodium. Since dehydration is a problem with excessive sweating, avoid diuretics such as alcohol and caffeine. Drink before you become thirsty, and keep in mind that cold fluids are absorbed faster than warm fluids. Drink diluted, 4 to 8 percent glucose solutions immediately before, during, and after exercise in the heat. During prolonged exercise, 60 to 90 minutes or longer, drink 4 to 8 ounces every 15 to 20 minutes.

When you're riding in hot weather, it may be necessary to take frequent rests to avoid the onset of heat-related problems. Wear loose-fitting, light-colored clothing or fabrics that wick moisture away from your body. Finally, be aware that some prescription drugs may increase heat sensitivity. Ask your doctor if you have questions about the side effects of medications.

It is possible to artificially acclimatize to heat. For example, if you live in a cool location and plan to travel to a hot location for training or racing, it is desirable to be acclimatized prior to arriving at your destination. One option is to wear extra clothing during workouts. A second option is to sit in a sauna two or three times per week for 20 to 30 minutes per session, beginning four to six weeks prior to your event. These strategies are not exact substitutes for actual environmental acclimatization, but they can help you minimize the impact of heat when you arrive at your destination.

Cycling and Cold Stress

Cold stress on the body has multiple stages. It's important to recognize the early signs of hypothermia so exposure to the cold doesn't become dangerous. During **Stage 1**, the body shivers to exercise muscles and produce heat as core temperature drops from around 98.6° to 96°F. As you will recall from Chapter 8, women's body temperatures often run lower than men's, so a two-degree drop from what is normal will probably produce shivering. In **Stage 2**, body temperature drops to between 91° and 95°F, shivering becomes violent, speech is difficult, thinking is slow, and amnesia may occur.

During **Stage 3**, when body temperature drops to between 86° and 90°F, muscles may become rigid and skin will become blue and puffy. It is a critical sign when shivering stops. The person may have poor coordination, muddled thinking, and muscle spasms that appear as jerking, but may still be able to sit or stand unassisted.

In **Stage 4**, a body temperature between 78° and 85°F will usually result in unconsciousness, with reflexes depressed. In **Stage 5**, when body temperature dips below 78°F, the person usually experiences ventricular fibrillation and cardiac arrest.

TREATMENT

The first step in the treatment of hypothermia is to remove the affected person from the cold environment. If possible, get her out of any wet clothing and into dry gear. Heat can be added to the body with hot drinks high in carbohydrates and by bringing the person near electric heat or a fire. Blankets or spare clothing can be used to trap air and heat close to the person's body.

In cases of extreme hypothermia, the person can be immersed in a tub of water heated to 105° to 110°F. Submerge only her torso, leaving her arms and legs out of the hot water. This allows warming of the body core and a gentle warming of the limbs. A condition called "after drop" can be avoided by submerging only the torso: If the entire body is submerged, large volumes of cold blood will circulate from the extremities to the heart. This can be a shock to the system and send the person into cardiac arrest.

It's unlikely you'll ever experience the later stages of hypothermia on a bicycle unless you're riding in extreme conditions.

Hyperthermia is also a risk when you are participating in winter sports for crosstraining.

PREVENTION

Papa Bear Whitmore, a noted authority on wilderness survival, has observed that when the weather is cold, say 20° or 30°F, people know it's cold and they prepare for it. Often, however, problems occur when the temperature is in the 40° or 50° range, and people are unprepared for a sudden weather change. Or an accident may occur that keeps them out longer than expected.

In addition to unexpected weather changes and accidents, people who travel to new places for cycling events may simply be unaware of the dangers associated with cool- and cold-weather riding. In one possible scenario, two riders set out for a two-hour ride, beginning the ride in 40° temperatures. The riders expect the weather to warm up as they ride, and they each take one bottle of energy drink and one bottle of water.

Halfway through a two-hour ride, one rider gets a flat, and they realize the temperature is not warming up as they expected. It looks like it may rain. One of the riders realizes that she has only one bottle filled with water—the other is empty. They were distracted and forgot to fill the second bottle with energy drink.

The story has two endings, one not so good and the second very good. In one, mechanical problems force them off the bikes again to make repairs. It begins to rain, and the wind starts to blow. They end up being out an hour longer than intended in weather they didn't expect. They shared only 150 calories of energy drink between them—after racing each other for the first hour. On the way home, they both experience hypothermia.

In the second ending, the cyclists were prepared for potential problems by carrying plenty of fluids and fuel. They each carried a cell phone in case of trouble. They did take one last look at the weather forecast before leaving the house. They know weather forecasters are not 100 percent accurate, so they took appropriate clothing to take care of themselves in case the afternoon storm moved in early. Because they had a cell phone and adequate clothing, they had options if the weather turned on them—and little to no risk of hypothermia.

Dressing in layers when the weather gets cold is important, but cold is relative. An acceptable riding temperature for one person may be blue-lip weather for another. It helps to understand how our bodies lose heat. Heat is lost through four primary methods: radiation, convection, conduction, and evaporation. Radiation occurs when our exposed skin loses heat to the atmosphere via electromagnetic waves. For example, radiated heat is lost when standing in cool weather, with no wind, waiting for a riding partner to arrive.

Convection heat loss is associated with air moving across the body. The body warms air molecules that come into contact with the skin; then the air molecules move away, taking precious body heat with them. This is why the air temperature can be one numerical value, and wind—such as what occurs when riding—can create a chill factor.

The windchill factor can make bearable air temperatures downright dangerous. For example, a 40°F ambient temperature changes to 28° on your skin with a 10 mph wind. Add a cycling speed of 20 mph to that headwind and the windchill takes the temperature to a chilling 13°F.

Conduction is similar to convection, except that body heat is lost through a cold object instead of the air, such as sitting on a cold surface or holding a cold handlebar with your hands. Heat is sucked from the body to warm the cold object.

Finally, evaporation is the heat loss that occurs when moisture changes to vapor. Wet skin or wet clothing loses heat several times faster than the same surface when it is dry. Many materials, such as cotton, lose their insulating properties when they become wet.

To stay warm in cold-weather riding, it's important to dress properly. The layer next to the skin of the upper body should be a material such as propylene, CoolMax, or one of the other many materials on the market that wick moisture away. This includes sports bra material. Fibers such as cotton retain moisture, keeping you feeling chilled. If your neck gets cold, use a moisture-wicking turtleneck as a base layer.

The second layer on the upper body can be a cycling jersey with arm warmers or a long-sleeved jersey made of fleece, depending on the temperature. If you'll be peeling layers off down to short sleeves, go for the cycling jersey and arm warmers. If the temperatures don't allow bare-arm exposure, stick with a long-sleeved jersey or a fleece jersey.

Finally, make the outer layer a breathable wind and moisture barrier made of a fabric such as Gore-Tex. If the weather is extremely wet, go with a totally waterproof shell.

For the lower torso and legs, there are cycling tights and pants made specifically for cold and wet weather. In cool, dry weather, cycling shorts and a pair of regular tights or leg warmers do the trick. For colder weather, a pair of propylene thermal underwear between your cycling shorts and tights may help. Very wet, cold-weather riding may require waterproof pants to cover the tights.

Head, ears, nose, fingers, and toes seem to be the areas that get cold first. Helmet wind covers are available to protect the head. Covered helmet and ear warmers will help keep the wind off sensitive areas. A balaclava can be worn under the helmet and pulled over the nose when necessary. If your ears get particularly cold, ear warmers can be worn under the balaclava.

There are a wide variety of gloves on the market with varying thicknesses of insulation for warmth. The outer coverings vary to protect from simple chill to cold and wet conditions. Layering can work for the hands as well. An inner liner of propylene next to your hands and fingers wicks moisture away, while a second glove insulates and protects from the elements.

For the feet, there are several booties on the market. Some are simply wind covers, while others insulate toes from cold and water.

There are booties that just cover your toes and others that cover your foot and some portion of your lower leg. Be careful not to wear socks that are so thick they cramp your feet. Cramped feet don't have adequate circulation, resulting in cold toes.

For those whose toes get cold, even with a bootie, chemical heat packets can be used. These packets are often used in the skiing industry and can be found at sporting goods stores and some bike shops. These small packets of self-generating warmth can be slipped into the bottom of your cycling shoe and help keep your toes toasty. The cloth-covered chemical packs generate heat when the outer plastic pack is opened. They can also be very helpful in warming cold fingers after changing a flat tire.

For overall body warmth, another trick is to fill a Camelbak with a warm sports nutrition drink. The warm bladder against your body will help you stay warm, and depending on the sports drink, the fluid can taste like hot lemon tea or hot apple cider.

OWIES, GI DISTRESS, AND ISSUES DOWN UNDER
Road Rash

When flesh meets earth in a sliding-type accident, the result is a burnlike injury known as road rash. After damage assessment, the question becomes how to heal as quickly as possible and minimize time off the bike. You'll notice that no "prevention" section is included below, as for other tips in the chapter. Anyone who bikes eventually takes a fall, no matter how many safety precautions are in place. Fortunately, you can minimize the damage done by knowing what to do when it happens.

Third-degree road rash, in which the skin is stripped away and underlying layers of fat and other tissues are exposed, requires immediate medical attention and might require skin grafts. First-degree road rash, in which only the surface of the skin is reddened, usually doesn't require treatment beyond keeping the wound clean. Second-degree road rash occurs when the surface layer of the skin is broken but a deep layer remains that will allow the skin to heal and repair itself.

> ## What If I Crash and Hit My Head?
> If you hit your head in a bike crash, you should seriously consider a trip to the emergency room. Symptoms of a concussion include headache, dizziness, confusion, nausea, vision changes, and ringing in the ears. See a doctor if you experience any of these symptoms and they don't subside after 15 minutes, or if you lost consciousness, even briefly. Know that concussions won't show up on CT scans or MRIs and that internal bleeding can develop a week or more after the trauma. If you've had a head injury, avoid straining on the toilet or holding your breath when lifting anything. Avoid sharp changes in pulse rate or blood pressure, such as suddenly standing on the pedals of your bike to climb hard. Give your head a rest for a few days.

TREATMENT

Past healing recommendations included keeping the wound covered with bandages and plenty of antibiotic ointment. The treatment cycle included hot bath soaks to soften scabs and scrubbing to remove them. But I've learned a better way, thanks to athletic trainer Diana Palmer, who introduced me to moist wound care. Wound care is one of Diana's specialties in her job as the head athletic trainer and sports medicine program director for Westmont College in Santa Barbara. She has extensive experience patching up cyclists and various other outdoor athletes. Her suggestions and strategies helped me quickly heal from a mountain bike crash.

Unfortunately, I had a chance to retest Diana's protocol this season when I went down on my road bike for the first time in twenty years of training and racing. Her method healed a good case of road rash in four to seven days. (The deeper wounds took a few days longer than the surface wounds.)

The wound care process includes a thin, clear dressing with adhesive on one side. It keeps water, dirt, and germs away from the wound while allowing the skin to breathe. This property keeps the wound healthy and does not allow deep, scarring scabs to form. Because it is clear, you can constantly monitor the wound-healing process, which is a real advantage. These kinds of dressings are available over the counter at some drugstores and pharmacies.

For serious wounds, you need to be checked out by a medical professional. If your wounds are the self-care type, perhaps the tips below will help you heal quickly:

- Clean the wound with clean water (not stagnant stream water), a soft child's toothbrush (or a sponge), and soap. Sterile saline wash can be used in place of water and is often included in athletic trainer kits because it puts out a stream that helps flush wounds. Baby shampoo works well as the soap because it is mild. The biggest issue in this part of the process is cleaning the wound thoroughly. Most people won't clean their own wounds well enough because it is really painful. If you or someone you know cannot do a good job of thoroughly cleansing the wound, go to an urgent care office to get cleaned up. The last thing you want to deal with is a nasty infection.
- If the wound is an abrasion and not free-bleeding, use hydrogen peroxide for the first day only.
- Get a tetanus shot if you haven't had one within the past ten years.
- Put an antibiotic salve on the wound and cover it with a thin dressing.

Gastrointestinal (GI) Problems

During racing or training, there should be no fluids exiting the body uncontrollably from either end. In short, there should be no vomiting and no diarrhea. Unfortunately, most cyclists will experience GI problems at one time or another.

Using Antibiotic Ointments

Always remember that antibiotic ointments may cause skin reactions and allergic responses in some people, and their overuse may also result in new strains of bacteria that are antibiotic-resistant. If you do prefer the use of an ointment on your minor wounds, follow these suggestions:

- Apply any antibacterial ointment to a well-cleansed wound to avoid "sealing in" bacteria.

- Apply a very thin layer of ointment. This will coat and protect the wound.

- Use a clean swab or sterile gauze to apply the ointment. Do not apply ointments directly from the tube, to avoid contaminating the tube and any future wound. You can apply ointments up to two times daily; however, always clean the wound before each new application of ointment.

- Unless there are signs of infection, you can stop using antibacterial ointments after twenty-four to forty-eight hours, but continue to keep the wound dressed.

- Check the wound daily. Change the dressing as needed, peeling it from top to bottom, particularly if excessive pus develops. Some fluid buildup under the dressing is normal, but watch for a dark yellow, green, or brown discharge; excessive redness; increasing pain; fever; or red streaks moving up the extremity.

- Keep the wound covered until the redness, wound, or both are gone. Protect the newly healed wound from the sun by using sunscreen with a sun protection factor of 30+. New skin is very sun-sensitive.

In Chapter 7, you learned there are different digestion rates between men and women and that individual stomach empty rates vary substantially. In an article written by Dr. Robyn G. Karlstadt for the American College of Gastroenterology (www.gi.org), she notes that in addition to women having slower stomach empty times, women have slower large intestine and gallbladder empty times. The primary function of the large intestine is to absorb water and electrolytes. The gallbladder stores bile, which is a digestive liquid that emulsifies fats and neutralizes acids of partially digested food.

Women also have different enzyme systems in the liver and small intestine. The liver has many functions, including breaking down fats, converting glucose to glycogen, and maintaining proper levels of glucose in the blood. Most food products are absorbed in the small intestine.

Dr. Karlstadt notes that women are two to six times more likely to have irritable bowel syndrome, where the gut is functioning either at a superlevel (diarrhea) or at a suboptimal level (constipation). If you have chronic problems with either issue, go see your doctor.

If your problems are not chronic but intermittent, it may take some trial and error to figure out what is causing your specific quandary. While diarrhea and constipation are both undesirable, diarrhea tends to be more of an issue for race day. If you do have intermittent problems with diarrhea, you may have issues with pre-race nerves, fuels that do not work well for your body for one reason or another, fluid solutions that are too concentrated, and perhaps dehydration. If you have one loose bowel movement, don't panic. If diarrhea continues, do something about it. Continued loose stools contribute to dehydration and loss of valuable nutrients.

While some problems may be related to gender and our differing physiologies, some of the problems may be related to fluid or fueling choices. This is true for diarrhea as well as vomiting, as either issue might have the same root cause. Unfortunately, you will likely need to endure some amount of individual trial and error to find the fueling combination that is right for you.

TREATMENT

For immediate treatment of diarrhea, many over-the-counter remedies are available at the pharmacy to treat short-term problems. Diarrhea that doesn't respond to over-the-counter remedies or is recurring needs the attention of a physician.

On the other end, after one round of vomiting, you often feel better and can continue racing once the stomach is emptied. You will have to pay close attention to your fluid and fueling rates. Multiple episodes of vomiting usually require ending your race on that day to rehydrate and recover.

PREVENTION

If pre-race nerves are the cause of your diarrhea, check with your doctor about using antidiarrheal medication as a preventive medicine. If you are consuming fuels and fluids at the concentration and rates recommended in Chapter 5 but still have problems, you may have to adjust those rates to meet your own digestive needs. Or you may need to use different fuels.

Saddle Sores

Sores in the groin, upper leg, and butt area can be a nuisance—or worse, force you to take time off the bike. The most common sores are blocked or infected glands that show up as lumps, pain in the pelvic bone area where your weight may be resting, and chafing problems.

TREATMENT

Soaking in comfortably hot bathwater one to three times per day will help boils to surface and drain. Antibiotic ointments such as Neosporin aid healing. Moleskin with an area cut out around the sore may help keep pressure off the sore itself.

PREVENTION

Be certain your bike is set up correctly by referring to Chapter 1. A saddle that is too high can lead you to reach too far for the pedals, causing either pressure or chafing. A saddle that is too low doesn't allow the legs to support the body and puts excess pressure directly on your crotch—ouch!

Here are some other preventive measures:

- Liberally apply a good emollient such as petroleum jelly to your genital area and upper thigh to avoid chafing. If you prefer a product made specifically for sports or cycling, you can use Body Glide, chamois cream, or chamois butter. Some of the sports specialty products come with added features such as aloe cream or antibiotics. Select the product that best suits your needs.
- Wear padded cycling shorts without underwear. Cycling shorts are designed to reduce friction from seams and give you some padding to help reduce pressure on sensitive areas.
- After the ride, get out of those dirty shorts. Good hygiene is essential. Wash your crotch and don't wear those shorts again until they have been washed.
- Don't suddenly increase weekly or daily mileage on the bike.
- If you shave the upper legs and lower torso, a light application of antibiotic ointment after shaving may help prevent red spots and infected bumps.
- Be certain the bike seat isn't tilted too far up or down, causing pressure or making you constantly push back in the saddle.

If problems persist, a different saddle may help, especially one with a soft or cutout ("relieved") area near the nose.

Vaginal Problems

Vaginal irritations can put a woman off the bike in a flash. Several disorders related to the vaginal area are lumped under the term "vaginitis." Three of the most common problems women experience are vaginitis (sometimes referred to as "crotchitis"), bacterial infections, and yeast infections. Some causes of these problems are warmth, moisture, poor hygiene, overzealous hygiene, chafing of the inner labia, oral medications such as antibiotics, and allergies.

Crotchitis is irritation or inflammation of the inner labia, urethra, clitoris, and skin around the vagina. Figure 11.1 shows the anatomy of this area. Redness, itching, and pain are trademark symptoms.

FIGURE 11.1 Female Genital Anatomy

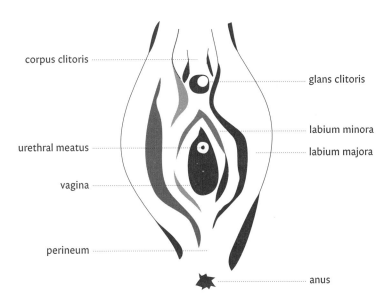

corpus clitoris

glans clitoris

labium minora

urethral meatus

labium majora

vagina

perineum

anus

Crotchitis is different from saddle sores. Both conditions, however, share some of the same causes, such as friction, pressure, warmth, and moisture. A second type of vaginal problem is *bacterial vaginosis*. Its primary symptom is foul-smelling, profuse, and watery vaginal discharge. *Yeast infections*, the third type of vaginal problem, often produce a vaginal discharge that is thick, cheesy, and foul-smelling, along with intense itching.

TREATMENT

If you are experiencing vaginal symptoms for the first time, you should consult your doctor because treatment will differ depending on what type of infection you have. If you're suffering from crotchitis, a nonprescription cream may relieve itching and help make your bike ride more comfortable. Many different brands are available in the feminine-hygiene aisle at drugstores. This can be particularly helpful if crotchitis occurs during a multiday bike tour.

Typical treatment for bacterial vaginosis includes a prescription antibiotic, as these infections do not usually respond to over-the-counter treatments. If you are experiencing a yeast infection for the first time, you should see your doctor, who will help you decide which medication to use to treat it. Recurring yeast infections, once recognized, may be self-treated with one of the many over-the-counter medications available at pharmacies.

PREVENTION

The preventive measures for saddle sores will also help prevent crotchitis. Further tips for preventing vaginal infections include keeping your crotch dry and ventilated when you're off the bike (there are nontalc powders in the feminine-hygiene section that may help), wearing cotton underwear and loose-fitting shorts or dresses to allow air into this area (thus making it less inviting for

Hygiene Tips for Travel

Traveling can present problems for your vaginal health. After all, sitting in a car or an airplane seat for hours with a sweaty crotch is the perfect environment for unwelcome bacterial growth that can cause problems. Wear cotton underwear and cotton pants, a skirt, or shorts that allow the crotch to breathe. You can also wear sports underwear made of materials designed to wick moisture and breathe. Nylon underwear and tight-fitting pants or shorts trap heat and moisture, making the perfect breeding ground for bacteria.

For extralong flights, such as those overseas, take along baby wipes and perhaps a change of underwear. Freshening up in the rest room midway through a flight can prevent problems later. If you are prone to bacterial or yeast infections and are traveling overseas, take along the meds you might need to avoid having to explain your vaginal problems to a pharmacist in a foreign country.

germ growth), and remembering to wipe from front to back to reduce the chances of contaminating the vaginal area with stool.

Flushable, fragrance-free baby wipes, particularly those formu-
lated for sensitive skin, can help keep the area clean. Aggressive
wiping and rough toilet paper can be irritants. Patting the area dry,
rather than swiping, is another option. Many women who have recurring yeast infections are also encouraged to eat one cup of yogurt
a day to help replenish "friendly" bacteria in their systems.

The vaginal environment is a delicate balance of organisms, including normal bacteria and lubricating secretions. See your doctor
if normal secretions become thick and smelly or the vaginal area
becomes inflamed or itchy. Keep a small problem from becoming
a big one.

• • •

TAKE CARE OF YOURSELF AND YOUR RIDING BUDDIES. PREVENTION
of problems is always better than trying to remedy a bad situation.
Hopefully, you'll be able to use all the preventive tips in this chapter,
and not the treatment tips.

Two very useful resources for cycling-related injuries are *Bicycling Medicine* by Arnie Baker and *Andy Pruitt's Complete Medical
Guide for Cyclists* by Andy Pruitt. Both are must-buys for the serious cyclist.

appendix A
Tests for Estimating Lactate Threshold Heart Rate

10-MINUTE TIME TRIAL FOR BEGINNERS

If you are using one of the beginner plans in this book and have limited fitness, start with this 10-minute test. After gaining some base fitness, conduct a short time trial to estimate your lactate threshold heart rate (LTHR). Warm up for 10 to 15 minutes at rate of perceived exertion (RPE) Zones 1 and 2. After the warm-up, ride for about 10 minutes, increasing your pace each minute. If you expect to go beyond the first minute, it's obvious you can't start out at a sprint. As you increase pace, notice your heart rate at the end of each minute. How do you feel? What is your breathing rate?

When your breathing becomes noticeably labored, and soon after that a burning sensation creeps into your legs, take note of your heart rate. Use this heart rate as your lactate threshold for now. Also take note of when you felt the burning sensation, since that sensation is often several minutes after your change in breathing. If you use the burning sensation to estimate LTHR, you might be overestimating your threshold. Overestimating threshold will lead to overestimating all the training zones, which means you might be working anaerobically when you intended to work aerobically. The result could be overtraining and underdevelopment of your aerobic system.

As you gain more sport experience and fitness, your estimated lactate threshold number can be further refined.

**RACE OR INDIVIDUAL TIME TRIAL
FOR EXPERIENCED CYCLISTS**

If you are an experienced cyclist, you can use the average heart rate you achieve during a race of 20 to 30 minutes to estimate lactate threshold heart rate. This is best accomplished by using a heart rate monitor that calculates average heart rate over a selected interval or period. The average heart rate you achieve in an all-out 20- or 30-minute race is going to be higher than in a 60- to 90-minute all-out race, which is often lactate threshold heart rate. So divide your 20- to 30-minute average race heart rate by 1.04. In other words, this value is about 104 percent of your lactate threshold heart rate.

For example, assume you ride the local time trial in 25 minutes. Let's say your average heart rate during the race, excluding warm-up and cool-down heart rates, was 170 beats per minute. Your estimated lactate threshold heart rate is 170 divided by 1.04, or a value of 163.

To conduct your own time trial, find a flat course with no stop-lights and minimal distractions. After a good warm-up, start your monitor and time trial as fast as possible for 20 minutes. This means metering your speed so you can produce the highest average, best effort for the full 20 minutes. (Note: Avoid a fast 5-minute effort followed by a slow fade.) Collect your heart rate average for the time trial, and divide this value by 1.02. For example, if your average heart rate for the 20-minute time trial was 160, dividing that by 1.02 gives you a value of 157.

INDOOR TEST ON COMPUTRAINER

One way to estimate LTHR involves a CompuTrainer. The newer models of CompuTrainers have a calibration feature, so the instrument can be calibrated for each test, and accurate retesting can be done at a later date. The use of the CompuTrainer method makes it easy for a coach or assistant to note athletes' ventilatory threshold (VT) and perceived exertion by standing next to them. Exertion and noticeable change in ventilation are best recorded while the test is in progress, instead of trying to recall the information later.

Equipment, Setup, and Assistance

1. Recruit an assistant with clipboard, paper, pencil, a heart rate monitor, and a CompuTrainer. It is best to position the heart rate monitor readout where both the athlete and the assistant can see it. You can create your own data sheet using the piece of paper, or make a copy of the LTHR Data Sheet in this appendix (see Figures A.1 and A.2).

FIGURE A.1 Sample LTHR Test Data Sheet

NAME *Betsy Guist*

DATE *September 6*

BIKE AND RIDER WEIGHT *128 + 23 = 151*

WATTS	HEART RATE	RATE OF PERCEIVED EXERTION
50	*106*	*6*
70	*109*	*7*
90	*118*	*7*
110	*125*	*9*
130	*130*	*10*
150	*134*	*10*
170	*142*	*12*
190	*147*	*12*
210	*154*	*13*
230	*157*	*14*
250	*159*	*15*
270	*164*	*16*
290	*165*	*16 * Noted VT*
310	*166*	*17*
330	*169*	*19*
350	*170*	*19*
370		
390		
410		
430		
450		
470		
490		
510		
530		
550		
570		

Zone	RPE	Breathing
1	6-9	Hardly noticeable
2	10-12	Slight
3	13-14	Aware of breathing a little harder
4	15-16	Starting to breathe hard
5a	17	Breathing hard
5b	18-19	Heavy labored breathing
5c	20	Maximal exertion noted in breathing

Notes about bike setup, current training status, how you feel:

1) BG felt good and well rested

2) VT seemed to occur at 290 watts

FIGURE A.2 LTHR Test Data Sheet

NAME

DATE

BIKE AND RIDER WEIGHT

WATTS	HEART RATE	RATE OF PERCEIVED EXERTION
50		
70		
90		
110		
130		
150		
170		
190		
210		
230		
250		
270		
290		
310		
330		
350		
370		
390		
410		
430		
450		
470		
490		
510		
530		
550		
570		

Zone	RPE	Breathing
1	6–9	Hardly noticeable
2	10–12	Slight
3	13–14	Aware of breathing a little harder
4	15–16	Starting to breathe hard
5a	17	Breathing hard
5b	18–19	Heavy labored breathing
5c	20	Maximal exertion noted in breathing

Notes about bike setup, current training status, how you feel:

2. Warm up on the CompuTrainer for around 10 minutes and calibrate according to the instructions in the manual.
3. Set "Program" to "Road Races/Courses," program 70.
4. Program the course to 10 miles, although you will not use the entire distance.
5. Input your body weight plus the bike weight and record these data on the log sheet for later reference.
6. Turn "Drafting" off.

Procedure

1. During the test, hold a predetermined power level (plus or minus 5 watts) as displayed on the screen. Begin the test at 50 watts and increase by 20 watts every minute, until you can no longer continue—meaning you cannot sustain the power plus or minus 5 watts or the rating of perceived exertion is too high. Stay seated throughout the test. You can change gears at any time. Highly fit or professional athletes may need to begin the test at more than 50 watts, around 110 watts may be more appropriate.
2. At the end of each minute, tell the assistant how your RPE is for the particular wattage just completed. Use the Borg Scale in Table A.1; in other words, on a scale of 6 to 20, 6 being very easy and 20 being very, very hard, how difficult is it for you to hold a particular wattage? Keep the scale easily visible so you can grade your exertion.
3. The assistant will record your exertion rating and your heart rate at the end of the minute and instruct you to increase power to the next level. She or he can also encourage you to keep your power at the designated intensity. If you have no assistant but do have a heart rate monitor that records data, store your heart rate at each "lap" minute. Mentally note perceived exertion or, better yet, jot it down on a copy of the data sheet.
4. The assistant will listen closely to your breathing to detect when it becomes labored and shallow. She or he will note the

TABLE A.1 Borg Rate of Perceived Exertion (RPE)
Scale and Training Zones

ZONE		RPE	DESCRIPTION
1	Recovery	6	
1	Recovery	7	Very, very light
1	Recovery	8	
2	Extensive endurance	9	Very light
2	Extensive endurance	10	
2	Extensive endurance	11	Fairly light
3	Intensive endurance	12	
3	Intensive endurance	13	Somewhat hard
3	Intensive endurance	14	
4	Threshold	15	Hard
5a	Threshold	16	
5b	Anaerobic endurance	17	Very hard
5b	Anaerobic endurance	18	
5c	Power	19	Very, very hard
5c	Power	20	

associated heart rate with the beginning of labored breathing and note VT.

5. Continue until you can no longer hold the power level (for at least 15 seconds) or feel you can't go on.

6. The data should look similar to those shown in Figure A.1. VT heart rate and power is usually comparable to an RPE in the range of 15 to 17, and is usually a close estimate of LTHR; athletes are seldom able to go more than three to five minutes beyond their lactate threshold on this test.

7. Create an XY graph with the vertical coordinate representing heart rate and the horizontal coordinate representing wattage. Plot the data points from the test onto a chart and connect them, as shown in Figure A.3. Lactate threshold can be estimated by using three references:

a. Note the heart rate at which breathing becomes labored (ventilatory threshold), which can be subjective.

b. Lactate threshold is usually from 15 to 17 on the RPE scale.

c. Lactate threshold is usually no more than three to five data points from the end of the test—that is, when the test subject wishes to stop.

If the ventilatory threshold found in (a) does not agree with (b) and (c), disregard it.

8. Now that you have an estimate for your LTHR, use Table A.2 to calculate your training zones. Find your LTHR in the "Zone 5a" column (in bold). Read across, left and right, for training

FIGURE A.3 Heart Rate Data Plot for Betsy Guist

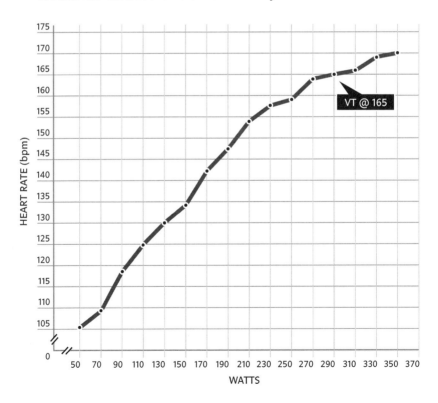

TABLE A.2 Cycling Heart Rate Zones

ZONE 1 Recovery	ZONE 2 Aerobic	ZONE 3 Tempo	ZONE 4 Sub-Threshold	ZONE 5a Super-Threshold	ZONE 5b Aerobic Capacity	ZONE 5c Anaerobic Capacity
90–108	109–122	123–128	129–136	**137–140**	141–145	146–150
91–109	110–123	124–129	130–137	**138–141**	142–146	147–151
91–109	110–124	125–130	131–138	**139–142**	143–147	148–152
92–110	111–125	126–130	131–139	**140–143**	144–147	148–153
92–111	112–125	126–131	132–140	**141–144**	145–148	149–154
93–112	113–126	127–132	133–141	**142–145**	146–149	150–155
93–112	113–127	128–133	134–142	**143–145**	146–150	151–156
94–113	114–128	129–134	135–143	**144–147**	148–151	152–157
95–114	115–129	130–135	136–144	**145–148**	149–152	153–158
95–115	116–130	131–136	137–145	**146–149**	150–154	155–159
97–116	117–131	132–137	138–146	**147–150**	151–155	156–161
97–117	118–132	133–138	139–147	**148–151**	152–156	157–162
98–118	119–133	134–139	140–148	**149–152**	153–157	158–163
98–119	120–134	135–140	141–149	**150–153**	154–158	159–164
99–120	121–134	135–141	142–150	**151–154**	155–159	160–165
100–121	122–135	136–142	143–151	**152–155**	156–160	161–166
100–122	132–136	137–142	143–152	**153–156**	157–161	162–167
101–123	124–137	138–143	144–153	**154–157**	158–162	163–168
101–124	125–138	139–144	145–154	**155–158**	159–163	164–169
102–125	126–138	139–145	146–155	**156–159**	160–164	165–170
103–126	127–140	141–146	147–156	**157–160**	161–165	166–171
104–127	128–141	142–147	148–157	**158–161**	162–167	168–173
104–128	128–142	143–148	148–158	**159–162**	163–168	169–174
105–129	130–143	144–148	149–159	**160–163**	164–169	170–175
106–129	130–143	144–150	151–160	**161–164**	165–170	171–176
106–130	131–144	145–151	152–161	**162–165**	166–171	172–177
107–131	132–145	146–152	153–162	**163–166**	167–172	173–178
107–132	133–146	147–153	154–163	**164–167**	168–173	174–179
108–133	134–147	148–154	155–164	**165–168**	169–174	175–180
109–134	135–148	149–154	155–165	**166–169**	170–175	176–181

CONTINUES

TABLE A.2 Cycling Heart Rate Zones (continued)

ZONE 1 Recovery	ZONE 2 Aerobic	ZONE 3 Tempo	ZONE 4 Sub-Threshold	ZONE 5a Super-Threshold	ZONE 5b Aerobic Capacity	ZONE 5c Anaerobic Capacity
109–135	136–149	150–155	156–166	**167–170**	171–176	177–182
110–136	137–150	151–156	157–167	**168–171**	172–177	178–183
111–137	138–151	152–157	158–168	**169–172**	173–178	179–185
112–138	139–151	152–158	159–169	**170–173**	174–179	180–186
112–139	140–152	153–160	161–170	**171–174**	175–180	181–187
113–140	141–153	154–160	161–171	**172–175**	176–181	182–188
113–141	142–154	155–161	162–172	**173–176**	177–182	183–189
114–142	143–155	156–162	163–173	**174–177**	178–183	184–190
115–143	144–156	157–163	164–174	**175–178**	179–184	185–191
115–144	145–157	158–164	165–175	**176–179**	180–185	186–192
116–145	146–158	159–165	166–176	**177–180**	181–186	187–193
116–146	147–159	160–166	167–177	**178–181**	182–187	188–194
117–147	148–160	161–166	167–178	**179–182**	183–188	189–195
118–148	149–160	161–167	168–179	**180–183**	184–190	191–197
119–149	150–161	162–168	169–180	**181–184**	185–191	192–198
119–150	151–162	163–170	171–181	**182–185**	186–192	193–199
120–151	152–163	164–171	172–182	**183–186**	187–193	194–200
121–152	153–164	165–172	173–183	**184–187**	188–194	195–201
121–153	154–165	166–172	173–184	**185–188**	191–195	196–202
122–154	155–166	167–173	174–185	**186–189**	190–196	197–203
122–155	156–167	168–174	175–186	**187–190**	191–197	198–204
123–156	157–168	169–175	176–187	**188–191**	192–198	199–205
124–157	158–169	170–176	177–188	**189–192**	193–199	200–206
124–158	159–170	171–177	178–189	**190–193**	194–200	201–207
125–159	160–170	171–178	179–190	**191–194**	195–201	202–208
125–160	161–171	172–178	179–191	**192–195**	196–202	203–209
126–161	162–172	173–179	180–192	**193–196**	197–203	204–210
127–162	163–173	174–180	181–193	**194–197**	198–204	205–211
127–163	164–174	175–181	182–194	**195–198**	199–205	206–212

zones. The training zones will need to be confirmed: Compare the heart rates and perceived exertion you achieved during the test with the exertion levels and heart rates you experience during workouts and races. Based on training and racing information, the zones may need slight modification. Be aware that LTHR can change with improved fitness, particularly for beginners.

OUTDOOR TEST FOR FIT ATHLETES

Find an 8-mile course you can ride where there are no stop signs and there is limited traffic. After a good warm-up, do a time trial on the course. This means all out, as fast as you can go for 8 miles. You will need to either mentally notice the average heart rate during the time trial or use a heart rate monitor with an averaging function. It is best to have the averaging function. Do not use the maximum heart rate you saw during the test as the average. After the test, recall your average heart rate for the 8 miles. This average heart rate is approximately 101 percent of LTHR. For example, if your average heart rate for the test was 165, 165 divided by 1.01 equals 163 for LTHR.

If you happen to do an 8-mile time trial during a race, use 105 percent as your multiplier. In the example mentioned in the last paragraph, you would calculate your LTHR as follows:

$$165 \div 1.05 = 157$$

Why use a different multiplier if the time trial was an actual race compared with a workout? Because we are typically able to push ourselves much harder in a race than in a workout.

If your optimal course is shorter than 8 miles, can that be used? Yes. Time trial distances and their various multipliers are listed in Table A.3. If you are in the beginning stages of improving your cycling, you might be better off using one of the shorter time trial distances, such as a 5K (3.1 miles). As you improve season after season, increase the time trial distance or continue to use a distance in the 3.1- to 4-mile range.

TABLE A.3 Predicting Lactate Threshold Pulse Rate from Average Heart Rate in an Individual Time Trial

DISTANCE OF TT	AS RACE	AS WORKOUT
5K	110% of LT	104% of LT
10K	107% of LT	102% of LT
8-10 miles	105% of LT	101% of LT
40K	100% of LT	97% of LT

appendix B
Strength Training Data Sheet

Exercises		Weight	Sets	Reps	Weight	Sets	Reps	Weight	Sets	Reps
	Date: Name:									
	1. Hip extension (pick 1)									
	Squat									
	Leg press									
	Step-up									
	2. Chest press									
	3. Seated row									
	4. Abdominals									
	5. Back extension									
	6. Hip extension (another from #1)									
	7. Lat pull									
	8. Personal weakness/ choice									

AA: 3–5 sets, 15–20 reps, RI = 60–90 sec, slow speed, exercises 1,2,3,4,5,6,7,8
MS: 3–6 sets, 3–6 reps, RI = 2–4 min, slow to moderate speed, exercises [1,2][3,4]5
PE: 3–5 sets, 8–15 reps, RI = 3–5 moderately fast speed, exercises [1,2][3,4]5
SM: 2–6 sets, 40–60 reps, RI = 1–2 min, moderate speed, exercises 1 [2,7][6,3]

Note: Exercises 4, 5, and Personal weakness are always done at AA load, sets, and reps.
This chart can be enlarged for more room to fill in the boxes.

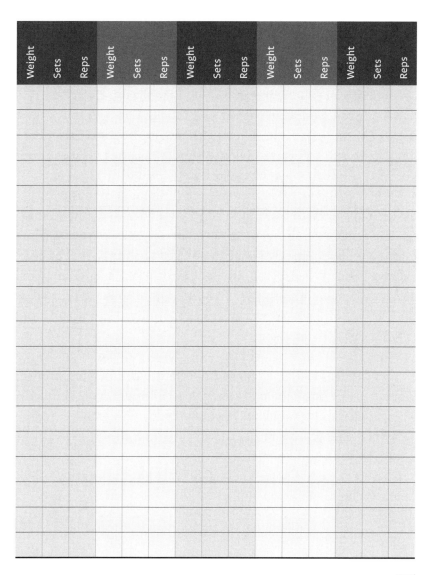

appendix C
Health Questionnaire

The Health Questionnaire is intended to help you record health risks related to heredity and current health condition. This information will need to be updated as more information becomes available about family members, and as your personal health changes.

Sometimes, women unwittingly put the goal to be thin ahead of the goal to be healthy. Severely restricting calories will affect current health and will certainly affect future health if wellness does not become the number-one priority.

Each question was designed to prompt thoughts about personal health and genetic risks, and to convey the idea that nutrition affects several areas of overall health. These areas can be used as markers to determine if change in nutrition habits should be considered. Physical well-being, athletic performance, mental attitude, and nutrition are synergistic. They each need to be optimized in order for the athlete to perform at peak capability. Here is a bit more detail about each question:

1. Your family health history is important when making decisions about nutrition and estrogen supplementation. Record any major health problems of your grandparents, parents, and siblings in this section.
2. Record any health problems you've had in past years.
3. Do you currently have any health problems? Is your overall health improving or declining?
4. Describe your current diet. It is best to have a food log, giving details, but you can also describe how you eat. Do you eat

highly processed foods? Do you eat out? If so, how many times each week? How many times each day do you eat? Do you eat because you are hungry or nervous? Do you eat a wide variety of foods, or do you tend to eat the same things each day?

5. Has your diet always been similar to how it is now, or have you made recent changes? Why did you change? Have the changes improved how you feel?

6. What does your blood-chemistry work say? Are there any items that are outside the recommended ranges? If so, can the answers to questions one through five yield any help in correcting the problem?

Questions one through six are intended to stimulate thoughts about overall health as a function of time. The answer to any one of the questions may not yield valuable information, but the answers to all the questions together may help you and your health care providers flesh out solutions to problems.

Questions seven through fourteen are subtle matters that may point to something wrong with your health. These small details, again, when examined in total, may tell a tale of good health or pending trouble. When seeking the help of a physician, take the answers from this questionnaire along, as they can give a small snapshot of your health.

Questions one through six give you a health snapshot, including hereditary health.

1. What is my family history of health disorders?

2. What is my personal health history? What problems have I had in past years?

3. What health problems do I currently have?

4. What is my diet currently like? (Give a verbal description. A food log can provide more detail.)

5. Have I made recent changes to my diet?

6. What does my most recent blood-chemistry work say about my health?

If you answer yes to several of the following questions, your diet may not be serving your needs. Chapter 5 may help you modify your diet, or you might consider seeking the help of a registered dietitian specializing in sports nutrition.

7. Are my periods irregular, often skipping months?

8. Am I frequently awake throughout the night?

9. Is my hair dry and brittle?

10. Do I have acne or wounds that won't heal?

11. Are my nails weak and brittle?

12. Am I frequently ill or injured?

13. Am I often tired or have low energy?

14. Do I often have to skip training or reduce the intensity because I have "no legs"?

appendix D
Charts

TABLE D.1 Menstrual Cycle Chart   Month:

DATE	1	2	3	4	5	6	7	8	9	10	11	12	13	
Days since last period														
Basal body temp.														
Menstruation														
Cervical mucus														
PMS SYMPTOMS														
MENSTRUAL SYMPTOMS														
TREATMENTS														

Menses: S = Spotting   L = Light flow   M = Medium flow   H = Heavy flow

PMS or menstrual symptoms: S = Slight, hardly noticeable   L = Light, but noticeable
M = Moderate, aware of problem   H = Problem, high aggravation, affecting
activities/lifestyle

Cervical mucus: C = Clear, stringy   Y = Yellow, tacky   L = Limited mucus
M = Moderate mucus   H = Heavy flow, copious mucus

TABLE D.2 Basal Body Temperature Chart   Month:

DATE	1	2	3	4	5	6	7	8	9	10	11	12	13	
Days of menstrual cycle														
Temp. > 100°F record here														
100														
99.9														
99.8														
99.7														
99.6														
99.5														
99.4														
99.3														
99.2														
99.1														
99.0														
98.9														
98.8														
98.7														
98.6														
98.5														
98.4														
98.3														
98.2														
98.1														
98.0														
97.9														
97.8														
97.7														
97.6														
97.5														
97.4														
97.3														
97.2														
97.1														
97.0														

General Instructions

Before writing on the chart, make copies as needed. » Record the month at the top of the chart. » Record the day of your cycle in the row below the date box. » Record basal body temperature each day, before getting out of bed and before activity causes your body

	14	15	16	17	18	19	20	21	22	23	24	25	26	27	28	29	30	31

temperature to rise. **»** Put an "X" in the date box, across from the correct temperature reading. **»** If you are tracking an illness and your body temperature rises above 100°F, record your temperature in the second row of the chart.

Glossary

Aerobic, aerobic metabolism. Requiring oxygen for energy transfer.

Aerobic capacity. A term used in reference to VO$_2$max. Aerobic capacity training is in the range of 90–100 percent of VO$_2$max pace, or 95–98 percent of maximal heart rate in women (90–95 percent in men.)

Anaerobic, anaerobic metabolism. Describes energy transfers that do not require oxygen.

Atherosclerosis. The accumulation of fat inside the arteries.

ATP. Adenosine triphosphate, molecules whose potential energy is stored for use at the cellular level.

Concentric contraction. Process during which a muscle contracts, exerts force, shortens, and overcomes resistance. For example, concentric contraction occurs in the quadriceps muscles when lifting the weight in a knee extension exercise.

DNA. Deoxyribonucleic acid, the molecules that determine heredity. The units of heredity are the genes on chromosomes. Each gene is a portion of the DNA molecule.

Eccentric contraction. Process during which a muscle contracts, exerts force, lengthens, and is overcome by resistance. For example, eccentric contraction occurs in the quadriceps muscles when lowering the weight in a knee extension exercise.

Economy. When used in reference to exercise, this term usually means the highest level of exercise achievable at the lowest energy cost.

Extension. Movement of a joint that increases the angle between the bones on either side of the joint.

Fartlek. Swedish for "speed play." Intervals at a fast pace, inserted into a workout at the athlete's will or desire. Full recovery follows each fast bout.

Flexion. Movement of a joint that brings the bones on either side of the joint closer together.

HDL. High-density lipoprotein, the "good" cholesterol that helps prevent atherosclerosis.

Hemoglobin. The oxygen-transporting component of red blood cells.

Interval. A specified amount of time between events. Workouts that contain intervals typically have a series of work bouts (work intervals) in which the athlete attempts to achieve a specific exercise intensity. The work intervals are separated by specified rest periods (rest intervals).

Isometric contraction. A muscular contraction in which the muscle exerts force but does not change in length.

Lactate. A salt of lactic acid formed when lactic acid from within the cells enters the bloodstream and lactate ions separate from hydrogen ions.

Lactate threshold. The point during exercise where increasing intensity causes blood lactate levels to accumulate.

Lactic acid. An organic acid produced within the cell from anaerobic carbohydrate metabolism.

LDL. Low-density lipoprotein, the "bad" cholesterol that contributes to athero-sclerosis.

Measures:
  Metric to English conversion factors: 1 kilometer (km) = 0.62 miles (mi); 1 mi = 1.61 km; 1 meter (m) = 1.09 yards (yd); 1 yd = 0.914 m; 1 centimeter (cm) = 0.934 inches (in); 1 in = 2.54cm; 1 millimeter (mm) = 0.039 in; 1in = 25.4 mm; 1 kilogram (kg) = 2.205 pounds (lb); 1 lb = 0.4536 kg; 1 liter (l or L) = 0.264 gallons (gal); 1 gal = 3.785 L; 1L = 1.057 quarts (qt); 1 qt = 0.946L

  Metric conversions: 1 cm = 0.01 m; 1 m = 100 cm; 1 mm = 0.001 m; 1 m = 1,000 mm.

Mitochondria. Organelles within the cells responsible for ATP generation for cellular activities.

Myoglobin. Oxygen-binding matter in muscle.

Negative split. A workout or interval that is split in half, with the second half executed faster than the first half.

Torque. A measure of a force that rotates the body upon which it acts around an axis. It is commonly expressed in pound-feet, pound-inches, kilogram-meters, or similar units of measure.

Triglycerides. Often called "neutral fats," these are the most plentiful fats in the body—more than 95 percent of body fat is in the form of triglycerides—are the body's most concentrated source of energy fuel.

Ventilation. The circulation of air through—in this context—the lungs. Ventilatory threshold is the rate of exercise in which the relationship between ventilation and oxygen consumption deviates from a linear function. Breathing rate at ventilatory threshold becomes noticeably labored.

VO_2max. A quantitative measure of an individual's ability to transfer energy aerobically. The value is typically expressed in terms of milliliters of oxygen consumed per kilogram of body weight per minute. The maximum value can be measured in a laboratory, where resistance is incrementally increased on a bicycle ergometer and the test subject's oxygen consumption is constantly measured. As the workload increases, there is a point at which the test subject's oxygen consumption no longer increases to meet the increasing demand of the workload. The maximum oxygen consumption value achieved is considered VO_2max.

Work-to-rest ratio. The ratio of fast swimming, running, or cycling to easy recovery in the same sport. For example, a 4:1 work-to-rest ratio could be 4 minutes of fast running followed by 1 minute of easy jogging.

References

Chapter 1: Anatomy and Bike Fit

Allen , P., MD. Interview with author, February 24, 1998.

Bernhardt, Gale. *Triathlon Training Basics*. Boulder, CO: VeloPress, 2004.

Bradley, J. Product manager for Trek road bike division, telephone interview with author, February 19, 1998.

Burke, Edmund R., PhD. *High-Tech Cycling*, 94–96, 159–85. Champaign, IL: Human Kinetics, 1996.

———. *Serious Cycling*, 79–99. Champaign, IL: Human Kinetics, 1996.

Colorado Cyclist. "Bike Fit." http://www.coloradocyclist.com, March 1997.

Eastman Kodak Company. *Ergonomic Design for People at Work*. Vol. 1: 284–97. New York: Van Nostrand Reinhold, 1983.

———. *Ergonomic Design for People at Work*. Vol. 2: 448–53. New York: Van Nostrand Reinhold, 1986.

Henry Dreyfuss Associates. *The Measure of Man and Woman: Human Factors in Design*. Rev. ed. Hoboken, NJ: Wiley, 2002.

Henry, S. J. "Do You Need a Women's Bike?" *Bicycling*, April 1997, 46–48.

Krogman, W. M., PhD, LLD. *The Human Skeleton in Forensic Medicine*, 149–50, 188. Springfield, IL: Charles C. Thomas, 1978.

Petrie, T. Velimpex Marketing, telephone interview with author, March 19, 1998.

Pruitt, Andy, EdD. Facsimile communication with author, March 3, 1998.

———. *Andy Pruitt's Complete Medical Guide for Cyclists*, 3–5. Boulder, CO: VeloPress, 2006.

Puhl, J., et al. *Sport Science Perspectives for Women*, 6. Champaign, IL: Human Kinetics, 1988.

Radford, K. *USA Cycling Elite Coaching Clinic Manual*, February 17–19, 1997.

———. Professional bicycle mechanic, personal interview with author, May 1998.

USA Cycling International Coaching Symposium. The Integration of Science, Technology, and Coaching in the Sport of Cycling, 1997, personal notes.

Zinn, Lennard. Custom frame builder, e-mail interview with author, March 16, 1998.

———. Custom frame builder, chapter review, January 1999.

———. Custom frame builder. "Crank Length for Women's Bikes." *VeloNews*, March 1, 1999.

———. E-mail correspondence, January 2–5, 2004.

———. *Zinn's Cycling Primer*. VeloPress, 2004.

Chapter 2: Training and Fitness

Bernhardt, G. "Reflections and Goals." *Triathlete*, November 1997.

———. *Training Plans for Multisport Athletes*. Boulder, CO: VeloPress, 2007.

———. *Triathlon Training Basics*. Boulder, CO: VeloPress, 2004.

Burke, E. R., PhD. *Serious Cycling*. Champaign, IL: Human Kinetics, 1995.

Coogan, A. "Training with Power Levels." http://www.twowheelblogs.com/training-with-power/power-levels-0, 2006.

Daniels, A. C. *Performance Management*. Atlanta, GA: Performance Management Publications, 1989.

Edwards, S. *The Heart Rate Monitor Book*. Finland: Polar Electro Oy, 1992.

Friel, J. *The Cyclist's Training Bible*. Boulder, CO: VeloPress, 1996.

———. *The Triathlete's Training Bible*. Boulder, CO: VeloPress, 1998.

Janssen, P. G. J. M. *Training Lactate Pulse-Rate*. Finland: Polar Electro Oy, 1987.

Martin, D. E., PhD, and P. N. Coe. *Better Training for Distance Runners*. 2nd ed. Champaign, IL: Human Kinetics, 1997.

McArdle, W. D., et al. *Exercise Physiology, Energy, Nutrition, and Human Performance*. 3rd ed. Malvern, PA: Lea & Febiger, 1991.

Chapter 3: Training Plans

Friel, J. *The Cyclist's Training Bible*. Boulder, CO: VeloPress, 1996.

Numerous athletes I've worked with over the years (thanks for your help).

Chapter 4: Strength Training and Stretching

Alter, Michael, J. *Sport Stretch*. Champaign, IL: Human Kinetics, 1998.

Anderson, B. *Stretching*. 20th anniversary ed. Bolinas, CA: Shelter Publications, 2000.

Anderson, J. C. "Stretching Before and After Exercise: Effect on Muscle Soreness and Injury Risk." *Journal of Athletic Trainers* 40, no. 3 (2005): 218–20.

Bishop, D., et al. "The Effects of Strength Training on Endurance Performance and Muscle Characteristics." *Medicine and Science in Sports and Exercise* 31, no. 6 (1999): 886–91.

Friedlander, A. L., et al. "A Two-Year Program of Aerobics and Weight Training Enhances Bone Mineral Density of Young Women." *Journal of Bone and Mineral Research* 10 (1995): 574–85.

Friel, J. *The Triathlete's Training Bible.* Boulder, CO: VeloPress, 1999.

Gremion, G. "Is Stretching for Sports Performance Still Useful? A Review of the Literature." *Review of Medicine Suisse* 1, no. 28 (2005): 1830–34.

Hickson, R. C. "Potential for Strength and Endurance Training to Amplify Endurance Performance." *Journal of Applied Physiology* 65, no. 5 (November 1988): 2285–90.

Ingraham, S. J. "The Role of Flexibility in Injury Prevention and Athletic Performance: Have We Stretched the Truth?" *Minnesota Medicine* 86, no. 5 (2003): 58–61.

Jackson, N. P., et al. "High Resistance/Low Repetition vs. Low Resistance/High Repetition Training: Effects on Performance of Trained Cyclists." *Journal of Strength and Conditioning* 21, no. 1 (2007): 289–95.

Kerr, D., et al. "Exercise Effects on Bone Mass in Postmenopausal Women Are Site-Specific and Load-Dependent." *Journal of Bone and Mineral Research* 11, no. 2 (February 1996): 218–25.

Kraemer, W. J., and S. J. Fleck. "Exercise Technique: Seated Cable Row." *Strength and Health Report* 1, no. 3 (June 1997).

———. "Exercise Technique: Classic Lat Pull-Down." *Strength and Health Report* 1, no. 6 (June 1997).

———. "Exercise Technique: Machine Standing Calf Raise." *Strength and Health Report* 2, no. 1 (March 1998).

LaRoche, D. P., et al. "Effects of Stretching on Passive Muscle Tension and Response to Eccentric Exercise." *American Journal of Sports Medicine* 34, no. 6 (2006): 1000–1007.

Marcinik, E. J., et al. "Effects of Strength Training on Lactate Threshold and Endurance Performance." *Medicine and Science in Sports and Exercise* 23, no. 6 (June 1991): 739–43.

McArdle, William D., et al. *Exercise Physiology, Energy, Nutrition, and Human Performance.* 3rd ed. Malvern, PA: Lea & Febiger, 1991.

McCarthy, J. P., et al. "Compatibility of Adaptive Responses with Combining Strength and Endurance Training." *Medicine and Science in Sports and Exercise* 27, no. 3 (March 1995): 429–36.

Nelson, A. G. "Acute Muscle Stretching Inhibits Muscle Strength Endurance Performance." *Journal of Strength and Conditioning Research* 19, no. 2 (2005): 338–43.

Nelson, A. G., et al. "Chronic Stretching and Running Economy." *Scandinavian Journal of Medicine and Science in Sports* 11, no. 5 (2001): 260–65.

Newton, R. U., et al. "Kinematics, Kinetics, and Muscle Activation During Explosive Upper Body Movements: Implications for Power Development." *Journal of Applied Biomechanics* 12, no. 1 (1996): 31–43.

O'Connor, D. M., et al. "Effects of Static Stretching on Leg Power During Cycling." *Journal of Sports Medicine and Physical Fitness* 46, no. 1 (2006): 52–56.

Paavolainen L., et al. "Explosive-Training Improves 5-Km Running Time by Improving Running Economy and Muscle Power." *Journal of Applied Physiology* 5, no. 86 (May 1999): 1527–33.

Shrier, I. "Does Stretching Improve Performance? A Systematic and Critical Review of the Literature." *Clinical Journal of Sports Medicine* 14, no. 5 (2004): 267–73.

Tanaka, H., and T. Swensen. "Impact of Resistance Training on Endurance Performance: A New Form of Crosstraining?" *Sports Medicine* 25, no. 3 (March 1998): 191–200.

Thacker, S. B. "The Impact of Stretching on Sports Injury Risk: A Systematic Review of the Literature." *Medicine and Science in Sports and Exercise* 36, no. 3 (2004): 371–78.

Witvrouw, E., et al. "Stretching and Injury Prevention: An Obscure Relationship." *Sports Medicine* 34, no. 7 (2004): 443–49.

Chapter 5: Nutrition

Armstrong, L. E. *Performing in Extreme Environments*. Champaign, IL: Human Kinetics, 2000.

———. "Caffeine, Body Fluid–Electrolyte Balance, and Exercise Performance." *International Journal of Sport Nutrition and Exercise Metabolism* 12 (2002): 189–206.

Balch, J. F., and P. A. Balch. *Prescription for Nutritional Healing*. Garden City Park, NY: Avery, 1997.

Barr, S. "Women, Nutrition and Exercise: A Review of Athletes' Intakes and a Discussion of Energy Balance in Active Women." *Progress in Food and Nutrition Science* 11, nos. 3–4 (1987): 307–61.

Book, C. Interview by Gale Bernhardt, July 7, 1998, McKee Medical Center, Loveland, Colorado.

Burke, L. *The Complete Guide to Food for Sports Performance*. New York: Allen & Unwin, 1995.

Coleman, E. *Eating for Endurance*. Palo Alto, CA: Bull, 1997.

Colgan, M. *Optimum Sports Nutrition*. Ronkonkoma, NY: Advanced Research Press, 1993.

Correll, D. "Young Girls Attempt to Mimic Model Bodies." *Loveland Reporter-Herald*, June 21, 1998 (Sunday ed.).

Cox, G. R., et al. "Effect of Different Protocols of Caffeine Intake on Metabolism and Endurance Performance." *Journal of Applied Physiology* 93, no. 3 (September 2002): 990–99.

Coyle, E. F. "Substrate Utilization During Exercise in Active People." *American Journal of Clinical Nutrition* supplement b1 (1995): 968S–79S.

Davis, J. M., et al. "Central Nervous System Effects of Caffeine and Adenosine on Fatigue." *American Journal of Physiology* 284, no. 2 (February 2003): R399–R404.

Eades, M. R., and M. Eades. *Protein Power.* New York: Bantam Books, 1996.

Frentsos, J. A., and J. T. Baer. "Increased Energy and Nutrient Intake During Training and Competition Improves Elite Triathletes' Endurance Performance." *International Journal of Sports Nutrition* 1 (March 1997): 61–71.

Friel, J. *The Cyclist's Training Bible.* Boulder, CO: VeloPress, 1996.

Graham, T. E. "Caffeine and Exercise: Metabolism, Endurance and Performance." *Sports Medicine* 31, no. 11 (2001): 785–807.

Janssen, G. M., et al. "Marathon Running: Functional Changes in Male and Female Subjects During Training and Contests." *International Journal of Sports Medicine* supplement (October 10, 1989): 118–23.

Klesges, R. C. "Changes in Bone Mineral Content in Male Athletes: Mechanisms of Action and Intervention Effects." *Journal of the American Medical Association* 276, no. 3 (July 1996): 226–30.

Lampert, E. V., et al. "Enhanced Endurance in Trained Cyclists During Moderate Intensity Exercise Following 2 Weeks of Adaptation to a High Fat Diet." *European Journal of Applied Physiology* 69, no. 4 (1994): 287–93.

Liebman, B. "3 Vitamins and a Mineral: What to Take." *Nutrition Action,* May 1998.

———. "Avoiding the Fracture Zone: Calcium; Why Get More?" *Nutrition Action,* April 1998.

Lutter, J. M., and L. Jaffee. *The Bodywise Woman.* 2nd ed. Champaign, IL: Human Kinetics, 1996.

McArdle, W. D., et al. *Exercise Physiology, Energy, Nutrition, and Human Performance.* 3rd ed. Malvern, PA: Lea & Febiger, 1991.

———. "The Big Jolt: Mountain Biking's Love Affair with Coffee." *Mountain Biker,* February 1998. [Gale: McArdle and others?]

NOHA News. "The Downside of Soybean Consumption." Vol. 26, no. 4 (Fall 2001): 3.

Norager, C. B., et al. "Caffeine Improves Endurance in 75-Year-Old Citizens: A Randomized, Double-Blind, Placebo-Controlled, Crossover Study." *Journal of Applied Physiology* 99, no. 6 (December 2005): 2302–6.

Paluska, S. A. "Caffeine and Exercise." *Current Sports Medicine Reports* 2, no. 4 (August 2003): 213–19.

Roberts, A. T., et al. "The Effect of an Herbal Supplement Containing Black Tea and Caffeine on Metabolic Parameters in Humans." *Alternative Medicine Review* 10, no. 4 (December 2005): 321–25.

Ryan, M. "Less Is More: Taking the Sensible Approach to Shedding Weight." *Inside Triathlon*, July 1998.

———. *Sports Nutrition for Endurance Athletes.* Boulder, CO: VeloPress, 2002.

Sabo, D., et al. "Modification of Bone Quality by Extreme Physical Stress: Bone Density Measurements in High-Performance Athletes Using Dual-Energy X-Ray Absorptiometry." *Zeitschrift Orthopädie und Ihre Grenzgebiete* 143, no. 1 (January–February 1996): 1–6.

Sears, B. *The Zone.* New York: HarperCollins, 1995.

Sharkey, B. J. *Fitness and Health.* Champaign, IL: Human Kinetics, 1997.

Shulman, D. Exercise physiologist. Interviews by Gale Bernhardt, July 1998.

Ulene, A. *The NutriBase Nutrition Facts Desk Reference.* 2nd ed. Garden City Park, NY: Avery, 2001.

USA Cycling Elite Coaching Clinic Manual. Colorado Springs, CO: USA Cycling, February 17–19, 1997.

Yeo, S. E., et al. "Caffeine Increases Exogenous Carbohydrate Oxidation During Exercise." *Journal of Applied Physiology* 99, no. 3 (September 2005): 844–50.

Chapter 6: Mental Tools

Bean, A. "Runner's Guide to Pain." *Runner's World*, November 1997.

Callanan, T. *Playing to Win: Playbook and Study Guide.* Minneapolis, MN: Pecos River Learning Centers, 1992.

Loehr, J. E., EdD. *Mental Toughness Training for Sports.* Harrisburg, VA: R. R. Donnelley & Sons, 1987.

Loehr, J. E., EdD, and P. J. McLaughlin. *Mentally Tough.* New York: M. Evans, 1986.

Chapter 7: The Physiology of a Cyclist

Adachi, N., et al. "Relationship of the Menstrual Cycle Phase to Anterior Cruciate Ligament Injuries in Teenaged Female Athletes." *Archives of Orthopaedic Trauma Surgery*, October 2, 2007.

Anderson, O. "Are Women Better Than Men in the Long Run?" *Running Research News* 10, no. 6 (November/December 1994).

———. "Question and Answer Section." *Running Research News* 11, no. 4 (May 1995).

———. "Getting High: Part Seven." *Running Research News* 11, no. 5 (July 1995).

———. "The Best Place in the World to Train Is in . . . Finland!" *Running Research News* 11, no. 6 (August 1995).

———. "Dad, Mom, and You: Do Your Genes Determine Your Performances?" *Running Research News* 11, no. 8 (October 1995).

Belanger, M. J., et al. "Knee Laxity Does Not Vary with the Menstrual Cycle, Before or After Exercise." *American Journal of Sports Medicine* 32, no. 5 (July–August 2004): 1150–57.

Bernhardt, G. "The Hi-Life." *Triathlete*, February 1997.

———. "Acclimatizing to Altitude Before a Race: Parts I and II." http://www.active.com/cycling/Articles/Acclimating-to-Altitude-Before-a-Race_-Part-Two.htm. *Active Cyclist Newsletter*, August and September 2007.

Beynnon, B. D., et al. "The Relationship Between Menstrual Cycle Phase and Anterior Cruciate Ligament Injury: A Case-Control Study of Recreational Alpine Skiers." *American Journal of Sports Medicine* 34, no. 5 (May 2006): 757–64.

Datz, F. L., et al. "Gender-Related Differences in Gastric Emptying." *Journal of Nuclear Medicine* 28, no. 7 (July 1987): 1204–7.

Degen, L. P. "Variability of Gastrointestinal Transit in Healthy Women and Men." *Gut* 39, no. 2 (August 1996): 299–305.

Downing, S. "The Body Shop: The Latest Wisdom About Sports Medicine from the Best Minds in the Business." *Women's Sports and Fitness*, October 1997.

Eiling, E., et al. "Effects of Menstrual-Cycle Hormone Fluctuations on Musculotendinous Stiffness and Knee Joint Laxity." *Knee Surgery Sports Traumatology Arthroscopy* 15, no. 2 (February 2007): 126–32.

Grybäck, P., et al. "Gastric Emptying of Solids in Humans: Improved Evaluation by Kaplan-Meier Plots, with Special Reference to Obesity and Gender." *European Journal of Nuclear Medicine* 23, no. 12 (December 1996): 1562–67.

Hermansson, G., and R. Sivertsson. "Gender-Related Differences in Gastric Emptying Rate of Solid Meals." *Digestive Diseases and Sciences* 41, no. 10 (October 1996).

Hewett, T. E., et al. "Effects of the Menstrual Cycle on Anterior Cruciate Ligament Injury Risk: A Systematic Review." *American Journal of Sports Medicine* 35, no. 4 (April 2007): 659–68.

Hicks-Little, C. A. "Menstrual Cycle Stage and Oral Contraceptive Effects on Anterior Tibial Displacement in Collegiate Female Athletes." *Journal of Sports Medicine and Physical Fitness* 47, no. 2 (June 2007): 255–60.

IDEA Personal Trainer. "Knee Injuries in Female Athletes," 12 October 1997.

———. "Evaluating Research," 13 January 1998.

Karageanes, S. J., et al. "The Association of the Menstrual Cycle with the Laxity of the Anterior Cruciate Ligament in Adolescent Female Athletes." *Clinical Journal of Sport Medicine* 10, no. 3 (July 2000): 162–68.

Levine, B. D. "Living High–Training Low: Effect of Moderate-Altitude Acclimatization with Low-Altitude Training on Performance." *Journal of Applied Physiology* 83, no. 1 (July 1997): 102–12.

McArdle, William D., Frank I. Katch, and Victor L. Katch. *Exercise Physiology, Energy, Nutrition, and Human Performance.* 3rd ed. Malvern, PA: Lea & Febiger, 1991.

National Osteoporosis Foundation website. http://www.nof.org. "Research Matters." *U.S. Council on Exercise*, vol. 1, no. 1 (May 1995).

Reider, M., PhD. Professor at the Department of Molecular Biotechnology, University of Washington. Personal correspondence with author via e-mail, May 1998.

Roepstorff, C., et al. "Gender Differences in Substrate Utilization During Submaximal Exercise in Endurance-Trained Subjects." *American Journal of Physiology, Endocrinology, and Metabolism* 282, no. 2 (February 2002): 435—47.

Sadik, R., et al. "Gender Differences in Gut Transit Shown with a Newly Developed Radiological Procedure." *Scandinavian Journal of Gastroenterology* 38, no. 1 (January 2003): 36—42.

Seiler, S. "Gender Differences in Endurance Performance Training." Exercise Physiology website for MAPP, March 1998.

Speechly, D. P., et al. "Differences in Ultra-Endurance Exercise in Performance-Matched Male and Female Runners." *Medicine and Science in Sports and Exercise* 28, no. 3 (March 1996): 359—65.

Tarnopolsky, L. J., et al. "Gender Differences in Substrate for Endurance Exercise." *Journal of Applied Physiology* 68, no. 1 (1990): 302—8.

———. "Gender Differences in Carbohydrate Loading Are Related to Energy Intake." *Journal of Applied Physiology* 91, no. 1 (July 2001): 225—30.

Tarnopolsky, M. A., et al. "Carbohydrate Loading and Metabolism During Exercise in Men and Women." *Journal of Applied Physiology* 78, no. 4 (April 1995): 1360—68.

———. "Sex Differences in Carbohydrate Metabolism." *Journal of Applied Physiology* 78, no. 4 (April 1995): 1360—68.

U.S. Medical Women's Association. *The Women's Complete Handbook*, 498, 557. New York: Delacorte Press, 1995.

Verrengia, Joseph B. "Peak Condition." *Rocky Mountain News*, November 10, 1996.

Viclocky, L. M., et al. "Gender Impacts the Post-Exercise Substrate and Endocrine Response in Trained Runners." *Journal of the International Society of Sports Nutrition* 5, no. 1 (February 2008): 7.

Wojtys, E. M., et al. "Gender Differences in Muscular Protection of the Knee in Torsion in Size-Matched Athletes." *Journal of Bone and Joint Surgery* 85-A, no. 5 (May 2003): 782—89.

Chapter 8: Menstrual Cycles

Anderson, O. "Female Athletes Fire Up Fat Burning After Ovulation, but Does It Make a Difference for Weight Loss and Competitive Performances?" *Running Research News* 10, no. 5 (October 1995).

Baker, A., MD. *Bicycling Medicine*, 209. San Diego, CA: Argo, 1995.

Barr, S., PhD. "Women, Nutrition, and Exercise: A Review of Athletes' Intakes and a Discussion of Energy Balance in Active Women." *Progress in Food and Nutrition Science* 11 (1997): 307–61.

Drinkwater, B. L., et al. "Bone Mineral Content of Amenorrheic and Eumenorrheic Athletes." *New England Journal of Medicine* 311, no. 5 (August 1984): 277–81.

Dueck, C. A., et al. "Treatment of Athletic Amenorrhea with a Diet and Training Intervention Program." *International Journal of Sport Nutrition* 6, no. 1 (March 1996): 24–40.

Fruth, S. J., and T. W. Worrell. "Factors Associated with Menstrual Irregularities and Decreased Bone Mineral Density in Female Athletes." *Journal of Orthopaedic and Sports Physical Therapy* 22, no. 1 (July 1995): 26–38.

Ganong, W. F. *Medical Physiology,* 174–75, 184–85, 344–50. Los Altos, CA: Lange Medical Publications, 1979.

Lutter, J. M., and L. Jaffee. *The Bodywise Woman,* 139–79. 2nd ed. Champaign, IL: Human Kinetics, 1996.

Myerson, M., et al. "Resting Metabolic Rate and Energy Balance in Amenorrheic and Eumenorrheic Runners." *Medical Science and Sports Exercise* 23, no. 1 (January 1991): 15–22.

Puhl, J., et al. *Sport Science Perspectives for Women,* 111–26. Champaign, IL: Human Kinetics, 1988.

Scialli, A. R., and M. J. Zinaman. *Reproductive Toxicology and Infertility,* 133–86. New York: McGraw Hill, 1993.

U.S. Food and Drug Administration. "FDA Approves Contraceptive for Continuous Use." May 22, 2007.

U.S. Medical Women's Association. *The Women's Complete Handbook,* 210–13. New York: Delacorte Press, 1995.

Yen, Jaffee. *Reproductive Endocrinology,* 275–79. 3rd ed. Orlando, FL: W. B. Saunders, 1991.

Chapter 9: Pregnancy and Exercise

American Academy of Pediatrics Work Group on Breastfeeding. "Breastfeeding and the Use of Human Milk." *Pediatrics* (February 2005): 496–506.

American College of Obstetricians and Gynecologists. "Episiotomy." *Obstetrics and Gynecology,* April 2006.

Baker, A., MD. *Bicycling Medicine,* 209. San Diego, CA: Argo, 1995.

Bean, A. "Running Mom = Smart Kid." *Runner's World,* June 1997, 28.

Carey, G. B., and T. J. Quinn. "Exercise and Lactation: Are They Compatible?" *Canadian Journal of Applied Physiology* (2001): 55–74.

Carey, G. B., T. J. Quinn, and S. E. Goodwin. "Breast Milk Composition After Exercise of Different Intensities." *Journal of Human Lactation* (1997): 115–20.

Carey, G. B., T. J. Quinn, and K. S. Wright. "Infant Acceptance of Breast Milk After Maternal Exercise." *Pediatrics* (April 2002): 585–89.

Clapp, J. F., III. "Effect of Recreational Exercise on Pregnancy Weight Gain and Subcutaneous Fat Deposition." *Medicine and Science in Sports and Exercise* 27, no. 2 (February 1995): 170–77.

———. "Morphometric and Neurodevelopmental Outcome at Age Five Years of the Offspring of Women Who Continued to Exercise Regularly Throughout Pregnancy." *Journal of Pediatrics* 129, no. 6 (December 1996): 856–63.

———. "The One-Year Morphometric and Neurodevelopmental Outcome of the Offspring of Women Who Continued to Exercise Regularly Throughout Pregnancy." *American Journal of Obstetrics and Gynecology* 178, no. 3 (March 1998): 594–99.

Davies, G. A. L., L. A. Wolfe, M. F. Mottola, and C. MacKinnon. "Joint SOGC/CSEP Clinical Practice Guideline: Exercise in Pregnancy and the Postpartum Period." *Canadian Journal of Applied Physiology* 28, no. 3 (2003): 329–41.

Dumas, G. A., and J. G. Reid. "Laxity of Knee Cruciate Ligaments During Pregnancy." *Journal of Orthopaedic and Sports Physical Therapy* 26, no. 1 (July 1997): 2–6.

Dye, T. D., et al. "Physical Activity, Obesity, and Diabetes in Pregnancy." *American Journal of Epidemiology* 146, no. 11 (December 1997): 961–65.

Entin, P., and K. M. Munhall. "Recommendations Regarding Exercise During Pregnancy Made by Private/Small Group Practice Obstetricians in the USA." *Journal of Sports Science & Medicine* 5 (2006): 449–58.

Foley, N. "The Mommy Track." *Women's Sports and Fitness*, April 1998, 48–51.

Huch, R. "Physical Activity at Altitude in Pregnancy." *Seminars in Perinatology* 20, no. 4 (August 1996): 303–14.

IDEA Today. Highlights from the 1996 World Research Forum, October 1996, 31.

Kakuma, R., and M. S. Kramer. "The Optimal Duration of Exclusive Breastfeeding: A Systematic Review." World Health Organization, 2002, 1.

Kardel, K. R., and T. Kase. "Training in Pregnant Women: Effects on Fetal Development and Birth." *American Journal of Obstetrics and Gynecology* 178, no. 2 (February 1998): 280–86.

Koltyn, K. F., and S. S. Schultes. "Psychological Effects of an Aerobic Exercise Session and a Rest Session Following Pregnancy." *Journal of Sports Medicine and Physical Fitness* 37, no. 4 (December 1997): 287–91.

Lutter, J. M., and L. Jaffee. *The Bodywise Woman*, 181–217. 2nd ed. Champaign, IL: Human Kinetics, 1996.

Mottola, M. F., M.H. Davenport, C. R. Brun, S. D. Inglis, S. Charlesworth, M. M. Sopper. "VO2peak Prediction and Exercise Prescription for Pregnant Women." *Medicine & Science in Sports & Exercise* 38, no. 8 (2006): 1389–95.

Norton, C. "Pre/Postnatal Water Exercise." *IDEA Health and Fitness Source*, April 1998, 55–59.

Ohtake, P. J., and L. A. Wolfe. "Physical Conditioning Attenuates Respiratory Responses to Steady-State Exercise in Late Gestation." *Medicine and Science in Sports and Exercise* 30, no. 1 (January 1998): 17–27.

Penttinen J., and R. Erkkola. "Pregnancy in Endurance Athletes." *Scandinavian Journal of Medicine in Science and Sports* 7, no. 4 (August 1997): 226–28.

Puhl, J., et al. *Sport Science Perspectives for Women,* 151–60. Champaign, IL: Human Kinetics, 1988.

Quinn, T. J., and G. B. Carey. "Does Exercise Intensity or Diet Influence Lactic Acid Accumulation in Breast Milk?" *Medicine and Science in Sports and Exercise* 31, no. 1 (1999): 105–10.

Sampselle, C. M., et al. "Effect of Pelvic Muscle Exercise on Transient Incontinence During Pregnancy and After Birth." *Obstetrics and Gynecology* 91, no. 3 (March 1998): 406–12.

Schramm, W. F., et al. "Exercise, Employment, Other Daily Activities and Adverse Pregnancy Outcomes." *American Journal of Epidemiology* 143, no. 3 (February 1996): 211–18.

Thompson, D. L. "Exercise During Pregnancy." *ACSM's Health & Fitness Journal* 11, no. 2 (2007): 4

U.S. Medical Women's Association. *The Women's Complete Handbook,* 210–13. New York: Delacorte Press, 1995.

Weaver, S. *A Woman's Guide to Cycling.* Berkeley, CA: Ten Speed Press, 1991.

Chapter 10: The Masters Cyclist

Anderson, O. "Young Versus Old." *Running Research News* 11, no. 1 (January– February 1995).

Balch, J. F., MD, and P. A. Balch, CNC. *Prescription for Nutritional Healing.* Garden City Park, NY: Avery, 1997.

Bierley, E. J., et al. "Effects of Physical Activity and Age on Mitochondrial Function." *QJM, Monthly Journal of the Association of Physicians* 89, no. 4 (April 1996): 251–58.

Bortz, W. M., IV, and W. M. Bortz II. "How Fast Do We Age? Exercise Performance over Time as a Biomarker." *Journal Gerontology: Biological Sciences* 51, no. 5 (September 1996): 223–25.

Cairo, B., PhD. Personal interviews with author, CryoGam Colorado, May–July 1998.

Friel, J. *Cycling Past 50.* Champaign, IL: Human Kinetics, 1998.

Ganong, W. F. *Medical Physiology.* Los Altos, CA: Lange Medical Publications, 1979.

Kujala, U. M., et al. "Hospital Care in Later Life Among Former World-Class Finnish Athletes." *Journal of the U.S. Medical Association* 276, no. 3 (July 1996): 216–20.

Lutter, J. M., and L. Jaffee. *The Bodywise Woman*. 2nd ed. Champaign, IL: Human Kinetics, 1996.

Marieb, E. N. *Human Anatomy and Physiology*. 3rd ed. San Francisco, CA: Benjamin/ Cummings, 1995.

National Osteoporosis Foundation. www.nof.org.

Nichols, J. F., et al. "Relationship Between Blood Lactate Response to Exercise and Endurance Performance in Competitive Female Athletes." *International Journal of Sports Medicine* 18, no. 6 (August 1997): 458–63.

Pollock, M. L., et al. "Twenty-Year Follow-up of Aerobic Power and Body Composition of Older Track Athletes." *Journal of Applied Physiology* 82, no. 5 (May 1997): 1508–16.

Scialli, A. R., and M. J. Zinaman. *Reproductive Toxicology and Infertility*, 133–86. New York: McGraw Hill, 1993.

Smith, E. *Therapeutic Herb Manual*. Published by author, 1997.

Spirduso, W. W. *Physical Dimensions of Aging*. Champaign, IL: Human Kinetics, 1995.

U.S. Heritage Dictionary. 2nd college ed. New York: Dell, 1983.

U.S. Medical Women's Association. *Women's Complete Handbook*. New York: Delacorte Press, 1995.

Vickery, D. M., MD, and J. F. Fries, MD. *Take Care of Yourself*. Upper Saddle River, NJ: Addison-Wesley, 1994.

Writing Group for the Women's Health Initiative Investigators. "Risks and Benefits of Estrogen Plus Progestin in Healthy Postmenopausal Women." *JAMA* (2002): 321–33.

Yen, Jaffee. *Reproductive Endocrinology*. 3rd ed. Philadelphia: W. B. Saunders, 1991.

Chapter 11: Comfort and Safety

Baker, A., MD. *Bicycling Medicine*. San Diego, CA: Argo, 1995.

McArdle, William D., Frank I. Katch, and Victor L. Katch. *Exercise Physiology, Energy, Nutrition, and Human Performance*. 3rd ed. Malvern, PA: Lea & Febiger, 1991.

Vickery, D. M., MD, and J. F. Fries, MD. *Take Care of Yourself*. 5th ed. Upper Saddle River, NJ: Addison-Wesley, 1994.

Whitmore, Papa Bear, and J. Bunstock. *The W.I.S.E. Guide to Wilderness Survival*. Lincoln, NE: Astonisher Press, 1992.

Index

About the Author

Gale Bernhardt has been an athlete and coach for more than thirty-four years. With a Level 1 coaching certification from USA Cycling and a Level III coaching certification from USA Triathlon, Gale is among the nation's premier endurance coaches. She coached the 2004 USA men's and women's triathlon teams at the Olympics in Athens, Greece, the triathlon teams at the 2003 Pan American Games, and serves as a World Cup Coach for the International Triathlon Union (ITU) Sport Development squad. Her athletes are Olympic and professional cyclists; top national-level masters road cyclists, ultraendurance cyclists, runners, triathletes, and multisport athletes with podium finishes at Olympic trials, national championships, and world championship events. Thousands of amateur athletes have used a training plan from Gale Bernhardt to prepare for a big race or event, whether they find it in a book, magazine, or website.

Gale is the author of several VeloPress books including *Training Plans for Cyclists, Training Plans for Multisport Athletes,* and *Triathlon Training Basics,* and series editor of the popular Workouts in a Binder® series: *Swim Workouts for Triathletes* (coauthor); *Workouts for Swimmers, Triathletes, and Coaches; Indoor Cycling;* and *Run Workouts for Runners and Triathletes.* She lives and trains in Loveland, Colorado.